CH00659910

THE GOOD WORSHIP GUIDE

THE GOOD WORSHIP GUIDE

GUIDE

Leading liturgy well

Robert Atwell

CANTERBURY
PRESS
Norwich

© Robert Atwell 2013

Illustrations on pp. xvi, 36, 56, 132 and 186 are by Frank Kacmarcik,
OblSB, St John's Abbey, Collegeville, Minnesota. Used with permission.

First published in 2013 by the Canterbury Press Norwich
Editorial office
3rd Floor, Invicta House,
108–114 Golden Lane,
London EC1Y 0TG.

Canterbury Press is an imprint of Hymns Ancient & Modern Ltd
(a registered charity)
13A Hellesdon Park Road, Norwich,
Norfolk, NR6 5DR, UK

www.canterburypress.co.uk

All rights reserved. No part of this publication may be reproduced,
stored in a retrieval system, or transmitted,
in any form or by any means, electronic, mechanical,
photocopying or otherwise, without the prior permission of
the publisher, Canterbury Press.

The Author has asserted his right under the Copyright, Designs and
Patents Act, 1988, to be identified as the Author of this Work

Scripture quotations are from the New Revised Standard Version of
the Bible, copyright 1989 by the Division of Christian Education of
the National Council of the Churches of Christ in the USA. Used by
permission. All rights reserved.

The words of the hymn, 'Advent candles tell their story', may be reproduced
for use in worship by churches which have a CCLI copyright licence. The use
of the song should be recorded in the annual report to CCLI.

British Library Cataloguing in Publication data

A catalogue record for this book is available
from the British Library

978 1 85311 719 0

Typeset by Regent Typesetting, London
Printed and bound in Great Britain by
CPI Group (UK) Ltd, Croydon

Contents

List of Illustrations

The publisher and author acknowledge with thanks permission to use copyright owners' photographs. Every effort has been made to contact the sources of photographs and we would be grateful to be informed of any omissions. Wikimedia Commons images are used by a Creative Commons Attribution-ShareAlike 3.0 licence.

About this Book

This book is designed to be a practical guide to 'leading worship'. Sunday is the shop window of the church and there are few things more important for our mission than getting our worship right. The last forty years have seen huge changes both in society and in the church. In response there has been considerable liturgical experimentation with an explosion of new services, but how do we bring these texts to life? How do we help congregations encounter God through them? If we can improve the quality of worship in our parishes, in our church schools, colleges and universities, then much else will follow.

Drawing upon the treasury of Anglican tradition and experience, this *Guide* identifies good practice. Its opening Sections 1 and 2 offer an overview of the changing landscape of worship, together with a critique of the current unhelpful detachment of 'spirituality' from doctrine and worship. If the worship of a Christian community is to come alive, it is vital that a minister bridge this gap. It is also important that a minister read the culture of a parish accurately and think about how the context we set for worship can be improved. To this end, each chapter ends with a series of questions. These can be a stimulus to further reflection by the reader or be adapted as a tool for corporate reflection by a ministry team or PCC. A worship audit can also be a useful tool in reflecting on a parish's worship, enabling a congregation to take stock and renew its spiritual life. This *Guide* explains how to go about one.

Section 3 focuses on the most common liturgical services in the Church of England. A step-by-step guide is offered to Holy Communion, celebrated according to the *Book of Common Prayer*; Holy Communion, celebrated according to *Common Worship*; All-Age worship; and Prayer

Book Evensong. Many clergy and Readers these days, unlike our forebears, have not been brought up on the Prayer Book and have consciously to learn 'how to do it'. Curates are increasingly moving directly into first incumbencies with just three or so years' ministerial experience under their belt. Eager to serve their congregations, they can find themselves operating outside their comfort-zone and root around for help. This section also includes guidance on the occasional offices: baptisms, confirmations, weddings and funerals. There is also a beginner's guide to public worship for lay people who can sometimes find themselves leading a service at short notice in the absence of the vicar, particularly in rural parishes. Finally, there is a note on liturgical processions and the protocols to be observed in civic services or when the bishop comes.

Section 4 explores how worship can be enriched by observing the feasts and fasts, and the rhythm of the seasons of the Christian Year to better effect. To some, the church's festivals and fast-days are anachronisms, echoes of an antique drumbeat we no longer follow. But if celebrated imaginatively these ancient and trusted landmarks can be powerful signposts in an otherwise barren spiritual landscape. There is no attempt to duplicate liturgical material that is freely available elsewhere. Instead a variety of ideas and commentary is included, interspersed with a range of information, from what an Advent Wreath is to how to mark a Paschal Candle during the Easter Liturgy. Throughout the *Guide* are checklists to help clergy, Readers, servers and other lay ministers prepare for services.

Section 5 'Behind the Scenes' provides a catalogue of basic information on everything from liturgical colours and icons, to tips for getting wax off the altar linen. Parish administrators, Readers and churchwardens can find themselves doing all sorts of jobs which in earlier generations would have been done by the clergy. The *Guide* assumes no prior knowledge, and offers a wealth of practical advice, assisted by the occasional illustration or diagram.

Finally, just as every kitchen boasts an extraordinary collection of utensils with names corresponding (in theory) to their function, so churches can accumulate a host of furnishings and liturgical objects, the purpose of which can be mysterious even to the clergy. Many people are happy to help out, but then hesitate to volunteer, held back by their lack of 'specialist' knowledge. They feel awkward, often intimidated by the technical terms that the initiated bandy about. What is a purificator? What is a burse? What are they for? Therefore, at the end of the book is a comprehensive Glossary of terms used in liturgy and worship to help both the seasoned sacristan and the new server alike. This is followed by a Resources section of publications for further reference.

Robert Atwell

1

WORSHIP MATTERS

Worship is the submission of all our nature to God. It is the quickening of conscience by his holiness; the nourishment of mind with his truth; the purifying of imagination by his beauty; the opening of the heart to his love; the surrender of will to his purpose – and all of this gathered up in adoration, the most selfless emotion of which our nature is capable, and therefore the chief remedy for that self-centredness which is our original sin and the source of all actual sin.

William Temple (1881–1944)

Worship Today

If you will, you can become all flame.

The Sayings of the Desert Fathers, 4th century

Alan Bennett, that shrewd observer of the eccentricities of the clergy, describes attending a friend's memorial service and becoming increasingly irritated by the priest. He apologized to the congregation for being in church; and then announced that, although there would have to be a prayer during the proceedings, people should treat it 'more as an opportunity for personal reflection'. Whenever the word 'worship' pops up in conversation, it is often embarrassing moments such as these that people rehearse. Why have so many clergy lost confidence in their core business?

Talk of 'church' and most people instinctively think of a building, whether an imposing red-brick Victorian pile on a street corner or a little medieval church tucked down a quiet country lane. In the New Testament the word refers not to a building at all, but to people. *Ecclesia* literally means 'called out'. God calls men and women into a community of faith to be witnesses to Christ's resurrection. The church is to be a sacrament of God's unconditional love: an outward and visible sign of his presence among us.

God wants us to make a difference in the world, but first he needs to make a difference to us. When we gather for worship it is more than a meeting of volunteers who are working together for a worthy cause. As Jesus reminds us, it is not we who have chosen him, but he who has chosen us (John 15.16). In worship, as in the rest of our lives, we are responding to God's call. In words of the First Letter of Peter, 'Like living stones, let yourselves be built into a spiritual house, to be a holy priesthood, to offer spiritual sacrifices acceptable to God through Jesus Christ' (1 Peter 2.5). We are invited to co-operate with God in the construction of a living edifice which is nothing less than the Body of Christ in the world. And Sunday, the Christian Sabbath commemorating Christ's resurrection, is the supreme time for being shaped by God's Spirit to this end.

In his monastic *Rule* St Benedict gives priority to prayer because in worship we encounter God for ourselves and are transformed. He urges his monks 'to prefer nothing to the love of Christ'. He calls prayer the *opus dei,* the work of God. Prayer is not about persuading God to do what we want. We are making ourselves available to God. Prayer is God's forgiving, healing, reconciling work in us through which we become alert to the Holy Spirit's leading. Which is why we need to give to it our best energy and for that, says Benedict, 'heart and mind need to be in harmony'. God wants us to be alive with his life, burning with the transformative power of the Holy Spirit. In the words of one of the early Desert Fathers, 'If you will, you can become all flame.' When our worship is centred on Christ a contemplative quality emerges which is profound. Like a stone thrown into a pond, which goes deep before its ripples disturb the surface, the grace of God reaches deep places and we are changed.

Sadly, the experience of worship can be in sharp contrast to this ideal. If the readings from scripture are inaudible, the sermon banal, intercessions poorly prepared, and the music group or organist embarrassing, we should not be surprised when people undervalue church. Without warmth or welcome the liturgy soon feels tired and routine. Without an opportunity for reflection or silence there is little chance of a contemplative dimension emerging. Matters are made worse if those leading worship lose their way in the service or lard the liturgy with inappropriate matiness. None of us can get it right all the time, but we will be justly criticized if we fail to prepare properly or if we lead a service in a slovenly manner. Whatever our churchmanship, whether the style of a congregation's worship is traditional or contemporary, whether we are leading Choral Evensong or praising God in Hillsong Music, we should aspire to excellence. Nothing else will do.

Caffè latte religion

A major high street coffee shop chain commissioned research into its customer base. Researchers came up with four things, each characterized by a 'C', which their customers valued. Predictably people wanted decent coffee. But they also wanted to drink it in surroundings that were clean, comfortable and contemporary. The trouble with some of our churches is that they are dirty, uncomfortable and old-fashioned. Many of our buildings are not fit for purpose. They are poorly lit and ill-equipped, with facilities that are badly in need of updating. Many young parents are happy to take their toddlers to the supermarket or to the library, but don't want their babies crawling around under a dark pew. If they migrate to the crèche with their toddlers, too often what they encounter is a dank ill-lit room with few facilities, cut off from the rest of the church. The home team do not always see this, confusing the smell of damp hassocks with the odour of sanctity. They are puzzled why many young professionals, armed with their Sunday papers, prefer sipping a latte in comfort to drinking lukewarm brown liquid from a cracked cup at the back of a draughty church.

Admittedly, this is a suburban middle-class take on church. Inner city parishes and rural churches have their own challenges to negotiate. But whether we worship in the town or country, all of us are influenced by our surroundings. The decoration and feel of a church matter. It is sacred space and it should speak of the beauty and holiness of God. Gloomy and uncared for churches do not advance the kingdom of heaven. With imagination and style, however, they can be brought to life and become signs of the enduring power of the Gospel. Good lighting, sensitive liturgical re-ordering, improved seating, toilets and a decent sound system may not convert the world, but they do put out a strong signal that a church is cared for and (most important of all) that the worship of God matters. Clergy often fall into the trap of speaking negatively about their buildings, but they can be an asset in the mission of God.

Church statistics reveal the aging profile of many congregations and the worrying absence of children and young families in some parishes. But there is huge pressure on families today. Time is at a premium in households with two hard-working parents, and church can find itself in competition with sport, weekend shopping, and visits to grandma. Securing the interest of boys is a particular challenge. That said, even busy young families can find time to do the things that really matter to them, and there are plenty of churches that are bucking the trend and doing imaginative work with children and young people.

What militates against attracting young families is often a mismatch of style and expectations. Ask parents what 'works' for them in terms of church and the majority will state a preference for a worship style that is warm and engaging, informal but organized. Too often what they encounter is not organized informality, but disorganized formality. However, being informal and being casual are different things. If the worship of God doesn't matter to the minister, why should it matter to his or her congregation? Worship that is lack-lustre is unlikely to deepen anyone's spirituality.

Patterns of church-going

'Remember the Sabbath day, and keep it holy' (Exodus 20.8). The deregulation of shopping on Sunday has also had a profound impact on patterns of church-going and has broken down, probably irretrievably, the traditional association of religion and the rhythm of daily life. The fact that our shopping malls have arcades resembling the nave and transepts of cathedrals, and that supermarkets have aisles and sometimes even a crèche, has not escaped the attention of the sociologists. Unconsciously, many people import the expectations of consumers into their worship, shopping around local churches until they find what suits, sometimes more interested in what they can get out of a service than in what they can contribute to the life of the church. Personal choice has moved centre stage. The sociologist, Grace Davie, has observed that nowadays many people go to church to fulfil a particular rather than a general need in their life, and carry on going as long as it meets that need, but that's where their commitment ends. She says that as a generation we have moved 'from an understanding of religion as a form of obligation and towards an increasing emphasis on consumption'.[1]

Fifty years ago most committed Anglicans went to church twice on a Sunday. Depending on a person's churchmanship, that might mean attending variously 8 o'clock Holy Communion, Matins, Parish Communion or High Mass; and Evensong (with or without a twenty-minute sermon) in the evening. It is often said that evening worship in the Church of England was killed off in the 1960s by the BBC costume drama, 'The Forsyte Saga', which was broadcast on Sunday evenings. Whether or not that is true, by the end of the Swinging Sixties in most parishes the pattern of church-going had become focused on Sunday mornings.

Today Sunday observance has been eroded to such a point that many now feel it sufficient to tip up at church once a fortnight or even once every three weeks. Many Anglicans would be offended if their commitment were questioned. For a younger generation duty and obligation do not exercise the pull they did for our grandparents. Robert Wuthnow says, 'Young adults are no longer born into faith communities that embrace them fully and command their allegiance over a lifetime. It becomes necessary to shop for a place of worship, rather than simply inheriting the congregation in which a person was raised.'[2] Religion has become something we do in our spare time, a leisure activity that competes for our attention. Worship has evolved into an optional extra. The majority of the population still claim to believe in God, but fewer exhibit a desire to belong to the church.

Economists tell us that we are richer per head of the population than we have ever been in the West. Affluence has opened up a wealth of possibilities, with cheap flights to exotic destinations and weekends chilling out in the countryside. Increasing mobility means that many middle-class families regularly decamp for school term breaks. Some even go abroad at Christmas, which was unheard of a generation ago. Poorer parishes in industrial heartlands have also been affected by changing patterns of church-going. Whit Walks, with Sunday Schools and brass bands parading through the parishes, were once a highlight of the year. Today Sunday Schools are a shadow of their former selves. Whitsun has not been on the radar for decades and Advent disappeared under a coating of tinsel long ago. The current worry is that the changing pattern of school terms, exams and holidays will further undermine the observance of Holy Week and Easter. We do not realize just how much the rhythm of the church's year helps communicate the Christian story until we discover that half of the congregation is missing at a major festival.

How should we respond to this fast-evolving situation? To our increasingly not just de-churched but un-churched society, Sunday is special but only as a day for family and friends, a day for catching up on chores or doing the shopping. Its religious character has been eroded beyond all recognition. To expect people who have never been to church suddenly to wake up one Sunday morning and choose to start attending worship is a pipe dream. It can happen, but rarely. Instead we need to find ways to lay down stepping stones to faith which will connect with people and families where they are, rather than where we feel they ought to be.

Some parishes have shifted their children's work to Sunday afternoons or to a midweek slot after school, often with great success, rather than compete with the junior football academy in the park on Sunday mornings. Others have gone further and made a policy decision not to run children's or youth work during term time at all, and instead pile energy into holiday clubs, activity weeks and workshops out of term. Experience shows that stopping activities during school holidays, particularly during the long summer break, can be a tactical mistake, not least because parents may be desperate to find things for their children to do.

One initiative that seems to fit the bill is Messy Church. There is a growing body of evidence that shows just how effective Messy Church is in connecting with families who have little or no previous experience of church or for whom Sunday worship is rendered impossible by their lifestyle choices. Many parishes are finding that Messy Church provides them with the right setting and materials to engage with those who would never darken the door of a conventional service. It seems the learning-through-doing approach, where families worship, eat, make and play all together, rather than hiving children off for separate activities, is proving a rich seam to mine. The challenge is how best to guide attendees, both children and adults, along the journey into discipleship because it is unlikely that they will make the transition to traditional church which many church-goers hope for.

There is no easy solution. But before we throw in the towel and abandon Sunday mornings to Mammon, we should perhaps pause lest we unwittingly accelerate decline rather than arrest it. There is a time to go with the flow and accept cultural changes. But there is also a time to be counter-cultural and robust about commitment. Bonhoeffer's cry in the 1930s about the perils of 'cheap grace' may have fresh resonance. We should also be alert to a change in tone and vocabulary coming from the Government, and respond to the mood change. We hear less about GNP – Gross National Product – and more about GWB – General Well-Being. The Government is rightly worried about the levels of depression and breakdown, particularly among young people, which are running at an all-time high. The psychologist, Oliver James, says we are suffering from the virus 'affluenza'.[3]

There is a seam of cultural restlessness in western society, a desire to find a more holistic way of living that we need to be alert to and capitalize upon. We should stop talking about worship as a life-enhancing activity and have the confidence to proclaim it as foundational and life-transforming. Above all, we should stop apologizing about going to church. A raft of research over the last twenty years shows that church-going changes lives.[4] Those who attend church regularly are more likely to give to charity, trust strangers, vote in elections, become school governors, participate in community schemes, do an elderly neighbour's shopping or visit the housebound. These are tangible things which can be measured and assessed. They generate the 'social capital' that glues together a society, and the Christian church is at its vanguard.

The changing liturgical landscape

One of the hallmarks of the Church of England as it emerged from the Reformation, and which it bequeathed to worldwide Anglicanism, was its retention of a set liturgy for the Eucharist and for the offices of Morning and Evening Prayer. An authorized translation of the Bible in combination with Coverdale's liturgical psalter and a set lectionary meant that a minister was not at liberty to pick and choose edited highlights of scripture. The requirement for the minister to robe for Divine Service emphasized function rather than personality. With the passing of the years this spawned a tradition of preaching that was biblically based and scholarly. Charles Simeon, the great Evangelical Divine, spoke often of the 'excellence' of the liturgy, but still expected preaching to breathe life into it. As he said at one of his 'conversation parties':

> It is true that the Word of God is in the liturgy, and constantly read; and when it is properly read, it may communicate much good, even when the pulpit is poorly filled. But, in point of fact, when the pulpit is poorly filled, the reading-desk is generally so also.[5]

For Simeon, the happiest combination was for a parish to be served by a minister who loved both scripture and the Prayer Book. But even if the priest was a poor preacher, lacking in pastoral sensitivity, at least the congregation heard the undiluted Word of God and received the grace of the sacrament. As the Articles of Religion state, 'the unworthiness of the minister hinders not the effect of the sacrament' (Article XXVI).

Today all authorized ministers, whether ordained or lay, make a solemn declaration when they are licensed by the bishop that in public prayer  [and in the administration of the sacraments] they 'will use only the forms of service which are authorized or allowed by Canon'. The word 'canon' comes from the Greek *kanon,* meaning a rule or measuring rod, and evolved into a technical term for the rules governing the ordering of worship. A liturgical 'free for all' is not permitted because in Anglican understanding liturgy expresses doctrine. This is neatly summed up in a Latin adage from the early centuries: *lex orandi, lex credendi.* Roughly translated, 'the law of prayer is the law of belief'. If you want to know what people believe, study how they pray. Conversely, what people believe will determine how they pray. As we worship, so we live; and as we pray so by God's grace we will become.

In spite of this historic commitment to regulation and liturgical coherence, the Church of England finds itself in unchartered territory today. For generations its clergy said the Daily Office from the *Book of Common Prayer.* It formed the bedrock of ministerial formation and sustained their spiritual life. Today in large sections of the church this discipline has disappeared. Swathes of ordinands no longer presume that they will say the office as part of their devotions. Alongside this change of culture has been the loss of an agreed translation of the psalms. Which of the contemporary translations will endure? The jury is out. The King James Bible and the uniformity imposed by the Prayer Book have been replaced by a plethora of translations and a liturgical permissiveness which, at its best, enriches worship.[6] However, with so many alternatives and seasonal variations to choose from it is equally easy for a service to lose its way. In fact *Common Worship* sometimes offers so much flexibility it is difficult to know what value to put on the word 'common'.

A 'Service of the Word' is now an authorized service in the Church of England. *Common Worship* supplies a structure for such a service, but that is all. In theory it is designed to 'allow for considerable local variation and choice within a common structure', but in practice it militates against liturgical coherence. What is most worrying is that the meagre biblical content of such services can belie their name. Matins and Evensong in the Prayer Book require the saying of psalms, the reading of two lessons, one from the Old Testament and one from the New Testament, and the singing of Gospel canticles. A Service of the Word typically has no psalm and may have only one scriptural reading, usually from the New Testament. There is an irony that the Church of England, once passionate about ensuring the scriptures were at the heart of its worship, should think this state of play satisfactory.

The loss of a common language in worship has had the unforeseen effect of further fragmenting religious observance. The most serious casualty has been the loss of an agreed version of the Lord's Prayer. For generations this was a key spiritual resource uniting regular worshippers of all denominations and those on the fringes of the church in prayer to God. Many schools have ceased to teach children the Lord's Prayer with the result that a whole generation has grown up not knowing any Christian prayer by heart. Of course, just as there are educationalists who baulk against learning by rote, claiming that it crushes creativity, so there have always been clergy who rebel against 'vain repetition', preferring extempore and spontaneous prayer to set liturgy. Wherever we stand in that argument what is clear is that our current obsession with variety is not facilitating the vital spiritual practising through which words of scripture take root in our memory.

The saying 'practice makes perfect' applies as much to prayer as it does to sport or playing the violin or driving a car. Champions and musicians are not simply born: they put in hundreds of hours of practice to reach the top of their field. After years of driving a car you change gear automatically. The more you pray the less you need to think about it. What distinguishes church-goers is not simply that they believe different things, but that they *do* certain things like praying, over and over again. Worship creates new habits of heart and mind that change the way a person looks at life. This is why the repetitive nature of liturgy should never be undervalued. Sameness is important: it enables us to go deeper.

Hymnody came late on to the scene in Anglicanism, mainly from the Methodism that it rejected. However, in contradistinction to Methodism and Lutheranism, where much of their doctrine is communicated through hymns, the Church of England has never had any hymnody in common. In the nineteenth century there was an explosion of interest in hymns, as a result of which *Hymns Ancient & Modern* became the nearest thing to being mainstream, with Anglo-Catholics favouring its rival, *The English Hymnal.* Along with the King James Bible and the *Book of Common Prayer* these hymnals were exported to the British Empire and the English-speaking world in general. What distinguished the hymnals and contributed to the distinctive nature of Anglican worship was the commitment of their editors to translate hymns from the ancient and medieval church, and make them available as spiritual resources to a new generation of worshippers.

Asked what sustained him during years of captivity and solitary con-finement in Beirut, Terry Waite, the Archbishop of Canterbury's Special Emissary, answered the liturgy and hymns. Cut off from normal human intercourse, his childhood years as a choirboy served him well because in his memory were stored a library of hymns, prayers and music to keep alive his hope. During worship in a residential care home for people with dementia, residents who could not tell me their name, what day it was or sustain any meaningful conversation would join in singing familiar hymns. Some could even recite the Lord's Prayer with me – or at least most of it. Most extra-ordinary of all, a few in response to the words, 'O Lord, open thou our lips', would answer, 'And our mouth shall show forth thy praise.'

Sadly, the Christian corporate memory is diminishing fast. Traditional hymnody is in decline and some commentators gloomily predict even the loss of Christmas carols, with the triumph of 'Jingle Bells' and 'I'm Dreaming of a White Christmas' over 'O Little Town of Bethlehem'. We seem to have abandoned any attempt (not least in our schools) to give people a sense of mental furniture. Unless we wake up to the challenge, the next generation will have fewer spiritual resources to sustain them in the autumn of their lives.[7] In Alan Bennett's play, *The History Boys,* the boys moan at their eccentric history teacher about having to learn poetry by heart. 'Please sir,' complains one pupil, 'I don't understand it.' To which Hector replies, 'I know, but one day you will.' Scripture, the liturgy, singing hymns, poetry, all give us inner signposts when we have lost our way, concepts and a vocabulary with which to interpret the raw material of our lives and give them meaning.

Given the scale and pace of change in both society and church, it is small wonder that some clergy feel themselves liturgical whales washed up on Dover Beach, overwhelmed by their new role of worship entrepreneurs. Leading worship is a wonderful privilege, but in the current climate it can be exhausting. Not all clergy are expert liturgists, and bringing texts to life is a challenge. Some have lost confidence in the power of liturgy to sustain the spiritual lives of their parishioners, and in desperation have substituted novelty. The cult of celebrity sweeping western society is placing additional expectations on clergy and Readers, many of whom feel burdened by a pressure to entertain. Media-saturated congregations bring to worship high expectations of performance, of clergy and musicians alike. That may not be a bad thing, but it is yet one more pressure. Thankfully the vast majority of clergy, Readers and worship leaders are rising to all these challenges admirably, but some flounder in this brave new Anglican world.

Reading the culture

Professional broadcasters are well-tuned to their public. Different radio and television channels serve different audiences with different tastes. Clergy need to exhibit the same sensitivity, tuning their preaching and conduct of worship to the culture of their parish. It is sometimes said that the culture of the Church of England is too high-brow for most people's taste which is why we no longer relate to the vast swathe of the population. Like all generalizations there is truth as well as fiction in the observation, and we need to be alert to it.

In response to a 'dress-down culture' and a perceived preference for organized informality, some churches are fostering a more relaxed and contemporary style of worship. Traditional liturgy, if it happens at all, is relegated either to early morning slots or to an occasional Evensong. Traditional hymnody is replaced by worship songs and choruses. In some evangelical parishes the clergy sit light to the authorized lectionary and have abandoned robes. In some cases this is succeeding in stimulating growth and attracting a younger clientele all of which is to be welcomed. The desire to have worship that is more culturally appropriate, however, should never constitute a *carte blanche* for imposing anything and everything on an unsuspecting congregation.

In discerning the culture of a parish and what is appropriate, the contrast between transcendence and immanence in worship can be a useful model. In a church where worship is transcendent, where reverence is important and the mystery of God is valued, matiness will not work. But neither will formality and ceremonial be welcome in a charismatic evangelical congregation where the fostering of intimacy and togetherness through song is important. We should be cautious about labels too. A congregation may describe itself as 'conservative'. But is this a statement about its preferred style of worship or doctrine or morality, or all three? It could be code simply for preferring the Authorised Version of the Bible or the services of the *Book of Common Prayer*.

We should be similarly cautious about lumping rural parishes under one umbrella. They are much more diverse than many imagine. Some congregations describe themselves as rural, but in fact are suburban in outlook. Parishioners may claim to live in a village, except the majority of them are newcomers and in reality the 'village' is a dormitory of commuters who moan about the local farmer dropping manure outside their driveway. Ironically, such 'suburban' congregations may be more open to change and experimentation than a conventional rural parish where the same families have tilled the land for generations. Even if they do not attend church regularly, most traditional villagers presume that they belong to the church. 'Back to Church Sunday' puzzles them because they didn't know they had left it in the first place. Home groups and Alpha Courses may founder and fail because the villagers don't like going into one another's houses. They know one another's business only too well and value privacy. A minister must find other ways of enabling relating. Inviting everyone to sit in the front three rows of his otherwise empty village church could constitute the end of a promising incumbency.[8]

Whether a parish is rural, inner city or suburban, reading and understanding its culture is vital if the mission of the church is to go forward. We will not commend the Gospel by being po-faced or telling the congregation off at Midnight Mass for not having come for the rest of the year. We get nowhere if we oppose the so-called secularism of our age with pious moralizing or with a version of sober sadness. What is needed is not plaintive sermonizing, but worship that aspires to excellence, quiet confidence in the truth of the Gospel, and above all a renewed vision of God.

Thomas Merton, a Trappist monk writing of Bernard of Clairvaux and the impact of the Cistercian monks on Europe in the twelfth century, says: 'One of the signs of a spiritual revival that is really spiritual is the way it affects every kind of life and activity around it, inspires new kinds of art, awakens a new poetry and a new music, even makes lovers speak to one another in a new language and think about one another with a new kind of respect.'[9] If we can raise the standard of worship in our churches, we can expect a similar transformation of our national life and culture because we will be opening up a new generation to the transforming power of God.

Questions for reflection

1 How can you maximize your church building as an asset in the mission of God?

2 What initiatives can you make to reach those on the fringe (such as young families, the elderly or the marginalized) who may be interested but for whom Sunday worship is simply not on their radar?

3 How can you get a better balance between 'sameness' and variety in your worship so that people can go deeper in their relationship with God?

4 How can you nourish people with scripture and hymns so that our great Christian spiritual heritage lives in the hearts of a new generation?

5 How would you describe the culture or cultures of your parish? In what ways can your worship reflect this better?

Notes

1 Grace Davie, 'From Obligation to Consumption: Understanding the patterns of religion in Northern Europe', *The Future of the Parish System*, ed. Steven Croft, London: Church House Publishing, 2006, pp. 41–4.

2 Robert Wuthnow, *After the Baby Boomers*, Princeton NJ: Princeton University Press, 2010, p. 124; quoted by Bryan Spinks, *The Worship Mall*, London: SPCK, 2010, p. xxiii.

3 Oliver James, *Affluenza: How to be successful and stay sane*, London: Vermillion, 2007.

4 Robin Gill of the University of Kent examined a mass of research and concluded that 'churchgoers are indeed distinctive in their attitudes and behaviour. Some of their attitudes do change over time, especially on issues such as sexuality, and there are obvious moral disagreements between different groups of churchgoers in a number of areas. Nevertheless, there are broad patterns of Christian beliefs, teleology and altruism which distinguish churchgoers as a whole from non-churchgoers. It has been seen that churchgoers have, in addition to their distinctive theistic and christocentric beliefs, a strong sense of moral order and concern for other people. They are, for example, more likely than others to be

involved in voluntary service and to see overseas charitable giving as important. They are more hesitant about euthanasia and capital punishment and more concerned about the family and civic order than other people. None of these differences is absolute. The values, virtues, moral attitudes and behaviour of churchgoers are shared by other people as well. The distinctiveness of church-goers is real but relative.' Robin Gill, *Churchgoing and Christian Ethics*, Cambridge: Cambridge University Press, 1999, p. 197.

5 Quoted by Andrew Atherstone, *Charles Simeon on 'The Excellency of the Liturgy'*, Norwich: Alcuin Club, Joint Liturgical Studies 72, 2011, p. 9.

6 With the exception of the psalms, all Bible references in *Common Worship* are to the *New Revised Standard Version* (New York: Division of Christian Educa-tion of the National Council of the Churches of Christ in the USA, 1989), but that is the nearest the Church of England comes to designating a preferred or 'author-ized' translation of scripture.

7 See the study by Anne Harrison, *Recovering the Lord's Song: Getting sung scripture back into worship*, Cambridge: Grove Worship Series 198, 2009.

8 See Alan Smith, *God-Shaped Mission: Theological and practical perspectives from the rural church*, Norwich: Canterbury Press, 2008.

9 Thomas Merton, *The Last of the Fathers*, London: Burns & Oates, 1954, p. 29.

Mission-Shaped Worship

Tell all the truth, but tell it slant.

Emily Dickinson (1830–86)

The report *Mission-Shaped Church* urges us to listen to our culture and to shape worship in culturally appropriate ways. For many of our contemporaries, however, it is not the shape of the church or its worship that matters, but whether it has anything relevant to say. Preoccupied with work, with earning enough money and raising a family, many people discount Christianity. They do not bother to come to church or to read the Bible because they do not expect it to have anything meaningful to say to them.

Negative attitudes are not universal, but they are fashionable. Antagonism is fuelled by an underlying assumption that religion is the partner of arrogance and intolerance. Faith and fanaticism are seen by some as inextricably linked. The facts do not support the stigmatization, but there is no escaping the way Christianity is regularly pilloried and contrasted with the so-called enlightened forces of science and egalitarianism. As a result a whole generation is is danger of growing up blind to the way Christianity has shaped for good our laws and culture.

When I was a vicar in north London I received an invitation from my local council, along with other faith leaders in the borough, to a special reception at the British Museum. The reception was entitled: 'Multi-cultural, multi-faith, multi-truth'. Great that the council should have wanted to bring us together in the wake of the London bombings, but it was the last epithet in the civic trinity that needled me: multi-truth. Not everything is true, and yet this is where many people are today. Society has lost confidence in the very notion of truth. 'You tell me your truth, and I'll tell you mine' is today's mantra. My truth is valid for me: your truth may be different, but equally valid. Even to question this neo-orthodoxy makes you open to ridicule. Pilate's question to Jesus at his trial, 'What is truth?' is as pertinent as ever.

All perceptions of truth are partial and to an extent provisional, including those of Christians, but this does not mean that we should not evaluate competing claims to truth. The idea that everything is true or that everything in life is equally worthwhile is illusory. We need to reflect on the ordinary, sad and funny events of our lives and identify wholesome values by which to live. We owe it to our congregations to share our discoveries and our convictions, as well as our questions, if we are to flourish as individuals and as a society. As Jesus says, 'the truth will make you free' (John 8.32). Lies imprison.

Believing and belonging

Society today is increasingly diverse, mobile and informal. Claims to truth are treated with suspicion. Some people are more interested in how something feels than whether or not it is true. Does it feel right? Does it work for you? Bono, the lead vocalist of the rock band U2, epitomized an attitude widespread in Northern Europe when he remarked: 'I'm not into religion. I am completely anti-religious. Religion is a term for a collection, a denomination. I am interested in personal experience of God.'[1] People frequently identify themselves as 'spiritual but not religious'. They dislike the perceived constraints of religion and are often contemptuous of tradition and ritual. Religious adherence can be perceived as compromising a person's liberty or integrity.[2] But there is evidence that attitudes are shifting or at any rate are fluid. The way Remembrance Sunday has re-ignited the national imagination contradicts the claim that *all* ritual is out. Poppies have made a come-back. There is also a widespread search for identity, and in this search religion and ritual have a part to play.

In our fast-moving anonymous society people long to belong. Who am I? Where do I belong? Who will look after me when I'm old? How am I connected with those who came before me? The explosion of interest in tracing family trees via the national database witnesses to people's need to be rooted, to be connected. Religion is about God, but it is also about identity. Paradoxically, the New Testament is ambivalent about belonging, insisting that our identity is rooted in God, not in this passing age. 'Here we have no lasting city,' says the writer of the Epistle to the Hebrews (Hebrews 13.14). Faith challenges our belonging and earthly ties, and gives us a new identity in the Body of Christ. It is why the Eucharist is uniquely formative of the Christian community. In the Eucharist we both receive and are made into what we are: Jesus' body. As Paul says, 'Your life is hidden with Christ in God' (Colossians 3.3).

There is nostalgia for the rootedness that religion fosters and which the church embodies. The rituals and traditions that the church preserves, particularly in its rites of passage, are still valued by many as the means of honouring the most precious things in life, from the birth of a child to the death of a parent. In the paradox of our age ridicule and respect seem to go hand-in-hand. A younger generation is reluctant to use religious language and mistrusts dogma, but craves the ether of spirituality.

It is tempting to latch on to nostalgia or signs of spiritual awakening and load them with exaggerated significance, but just because someone turns up to a carol service doesn't mean they believe in the Incarnation. Of course, turning up at church is significant, but it is more likely to represent a mission opportunity than a statement of nascent belief or affiliation. The question is how can we maximize our contacts with this silent penumbra of well-wishers, the anonymous semi-Christians who lurk in the shadows? Their presence on Mothering Sunday or Harvest Festival may not constitute the heart of belief, but it might be its prelude.

Of course, being helped by belief is no reason to believe. You believe because you are convinced that God exists and that belief in God is true. You are a Christian because you believe that the love of God has been uniquely revealed in Jesus Christ and that changes the way you look at life. But faith is also a journey and we need to give more energy to helping those who find themselves wandering across a moral and spiritual landscape that has been largely denuded of signposts. 'Stand at the crossroads, and look,' advised the prophet Jeremiah, 'and ask for the ancient paths, where the good way lies; and walk in it, and you will find rest for your souls' (Jeremiah 6.16). We need to re-visit the ancient spiritual maps and explore their contours because they can help us in our search for lasting happiness.

A priest told me about reading the Bible with a young man who was finding his way in the Christian faith. After a couple of minutes he interrupted the priest and said, 'Stop a moment. What are all these numbers for?' He had never opened a Bible and was puzzled by the chapter and verse numbers. We have to face the fact that young people's knowledge of Christianity is falling off a cliff. Most young people have no inherited map to guide them in their spiritual exploration and virtually no religious vocabulary with which to express their aspirations. We keep making the mistake of assuming that there is something approaching dormant Christianity waiting to be awakened. We're wrong – most of the time there's nothing there, just spiritual fog.

What parish priests know intuitively, and research bears out, is that most people today are neither Christian nor anti-Christian. They are indifferent. They see little that organized religion can add to their lives and are put off not only by its strident advocates but also by its strident detractors. In Alan Billings' assessment, our contemporaries tend to be 'open agnostics rather than hostile atheists'.[3] So what is to be done?

Whatever the context in which we minister, we need to express our beliefs without rancour, quietly and confidently in the strength that only God can supply. We need to communicate a passion about God and an excitement about the landscape of faith. And what the truth of God gives is more than nostalgia or a feeling of 'rootedness', more than a fabric of ritual and traditions, and more than bulwarks against which to lean through bad times. The truth of God opens up a whole unimaginable life to us. There is love, the certainty of God's love, and there may even be courage and strength and goodness to discover in ourselves. Above all, the truth of God opens up the reality of grace in a world that can seem sterile.

Conversion as process rather than event

Conversion is not simply about acquiring a new set of beliefs; it is about becoming a new person, a person in communion with God and others through Jesus Christ. Research suggests that just as faith is a journey, so conversion is a process rather than an event. We are familiar with the dramatic conversion of the apostle Paul, but ignore the possibility that the seeds of his conversion, as the Acts of the Apostles hints, may have been laid earlier in his life when he witnessed the stoning of Stephen. Reading the *Confessions of St Augustine* one cannot but be moved by the story of his conversion. Sitting in the back garden of a villa outside Milan, Augustine hears children playing tag in the garden next door when up goes the cry, *'Tolle lege, tolle lege'*, meaning 'pick it up and read it, pick it up and read it'. In the children's laughter Augustine hears the voice of God telling him to pick up the Bible and read it. He describes going into the house and reading Paul's Letter to the Romans and being profoundly moved. In these words Augustine describes his conversion, but its roots can be traced much earlier in his life to his disenchantment with the philosophy of Manichaeism and its inability to explain the problem of evil to his satisfaction.

That there is a time lag between a person first dipping their toe in the water of faith and coming to mature Christian commitment is proven. Research by John Finney[4] reveals that on average the gap with women is two years; with men it can be as long as five or six years. We need to frame expectations and strategies that reflect this reality. It may be years, not months, before we see the fruit of initiatives such as Back to Church Sunday or Alpha Courses. It may also be that with some people belonging to a church comes first, and belief comes later. To repeat an old cliché, 'faith is caught, not taught'. Evangelization likes to plot a tidy route from belonging

THE ALPHA COURSE

alphacourse.org

an **opportunity** to explore
the **meaning** of life

starting soon at a church near you   *Alpha*

to believing, and from believing to behaving. But the process may be more complicated and with men it is usually far from straightforward.

The Gospels record the incident when the young man comes questioning Jesus saying, 'Teacher, what good deed must I do to have eternal life?' (Matthew 19.16). It is a forthright question to which Jesus gives a direct answer: 'Go, sell what you possess and give your money to the poor; and come, follow me.' Some men like to do things, and often the process of conversion begins with them getting involved in a project or task, such as helping run a night shelter for the homeless. This leads them to explore faith, which in turn leads them to throw in their lot with a parish and eventually to make a commitment to Christ. They want to be part of a church that is serving people and making a difference. Action comes first. Other men come to faith as a result of the baptism of their baby or because they are invited by a friend to an Alpha or Emmaus group or to a men's breakfast. In contrast to others they may not want to be enlisted on the rota for mowing the churchyard, especially if they have a demanding job and a young family, but they may be looking for a place to talk with other like-minded men.

Doing apologetics today

We are in the throes of an intellectual battle about what it is to be human. We have been telling people for years that they don't have to go to church to be good, and now we are puzzled that they don't want to be good. How do we share our convictions about life, human worth and responsibility in today's bracing climate? How do we frame the claims of the Gospel in a world whose mind is complex, often rebellious and unreceptive? 'Always be ready to make your defence (*apologian*) to anyone who demands from you an account of the hope that is in you' (1 Peter 3.15). Now, as in the early decades of the church, we need to give a coherent account of our faith. As we do so, it is vital not to confuse defence with defensiveness, or apologetics with apologizing. The ghetto, whether religious or intellectual, spells death.

The ancient Greek philosopher Aristotle famously identified three aspects of arguments that convince the hearer: *logos*, *pathos* and *ethos*. *Logos* is focused on coherent logical reasoning. *Pathos* works by emotional appeal, getting alongside the hearer and evoking sympathy. *Ethos* relates to the ethical dimension of an argument. Words without moral commitment fail to make an impact. Preachers, like politicians, are judged by their integrity, the way their lives match their oratory. Personal testimony remains a powerful tool in the church's armoury. Nothing anonymous will communicate, let alone convert, as the highly personalized style of modern media shows. Preaching, detached from spirituality and the moral life, becomes remote and abstract. Ethical exhortation detached from doctrine or prayer becomes moralistic, and spirituality divorced from discipleship descends into gimmicks. If Christianity is to flourish in the twenty-first century, we need to recover the unity of the Christian life in terms of intelligent, moral, prayerful and imaginative discipleship. 'Tell all the truth,' wrote Emily Dickinson, 'but tell it slant.' Her words deserve to be erected into a strategy.

Scripture sees the heart as the core of a human person, the place of willing and choosing. If we are to reach the hearts of a new generation it is unlikely to be through reason alone – important though that is – but through feelings and through the imagination. Alister McGrath, one of the best Christian apologists of our day, argues that atheism captured the human imagination in the nineteenth century. The atheistic regimes of Stalin, Hitler and Mao Tse Tung in the twentieth century reveal the bankruptcy of atheistic totalitarianism. Their regimes led to unbelievable mass exterminations. In the history of the world Christians may not have a blameless record, but there is scope for countering the blustering of Richard Dawkins, Sam Harris and Christopher Hitchens. We need 'to give an account for the hope that is in us'. Indeed our worship, preaching and teaching will gain energy as it is shaped through engagement with our secular contemporaries.

Listening to be heard

There are many competing voices in today's market-place and Christians have to earn the right to be heard. We open up dialogue by first listening, and being known to listen. If we are to re-capture the imagination of a younger generation, we have to be prepared to allow their imagination to capture ours.[5] We need to identify their concerns and attend to their questions. In spite of current antagonism and disinterest in religion, the church can still act as an honest broker.

During elections it is often the local churches that hold the ring and invite parliamentary candidates to debate before constituents. Many of our contemporaries, including some who have had little or no contact with the church, are eager to explore controversial issues such as assisted dying, and are willing to come into a church to do it. When Christians grapple seriously with issues, others are more willing to take Christians seriously. Furthermore, with the decline in 'social capital' in society widely lamented by politicians, we should be proud of hospitality that builds trust between and across divided communities.

In the opinion of Jeremy Morris, 'there needs to be a renewed conviction that Christian faith has public resonance, and a renewed determination not to concede ground to arguments that have little or nothing to contribute to the Christian vision of human well-being. As a matter of historical justice, the weight of the Christian tradition in our national culture needs to be recognised once more.'[6] I share his conviction. Christianity has the power to inform our choices for good and invigorate our national life. Christianity challenges the relentless pursuit of money and pleasure, and promotes values that strengthen family life and build community. If we can share with our contemporaries a vision of life and of human flourishing that is more than just having a great time, then we can expect the transformation of our culture.

Questions for reflection

1 How can you maintain and build on your contacts with the anonymous semi-Christians who turn up only on special occasions?
2 How can you shape a ministry to and among men, given that some men may like to be asked to do something practical while others may be looking for something else?
3 'Be ready to make your defence to anyone who demands from you an account of the hope that is in you' (1 Peter 3.15). How do we share our convictions about life, human worth and God in today's market-place? How do we do apologetics without apologizing? How do we 'tell it slant'?

Notes

1 Bono as quoted by N. McCormick, *I Was Bono's Doppleganger*, London: Penguin, 2004, p. 114.

2 See Rowan Williams, 'The spiritual and the religious: Is the territory changing?', *Faith in the Public Square*, London, Delhi and New York: Bloomsbury, 2012, pp. 85–96.

3 Alan Billings, *Making God Possible: The task of ordained ministry present and future*, London: SPCK, 2010.

4 John Finney, *Finding Faith Today: How Does It Happen?* Stonehill Green: British and Foreign Bible Society, 1992.

5 See 'Changing World: Changing Church?' – address by Timothy Radcliffe OP to the Forum of Churches Together in England, 2009.

6 Jeremy Morris, *Faith and Freedom: Exploring Radical Orthodoxy*, London: Affirming Catholicism, 2003, p. 3.

Reclaiming Spirituality for God

If we had a keen vision and feeling of all ordinary human life, it would be like hearing the grass grow and the squirrel's heartbeat, and we should die of that roar which lies on the other side of silence.

George Eliot (1819–80), *Middlemarch*

For most of the last century aspects of institutional religion have been in decline, at least in the West. Life has been privatized. Choice has become a dominant feature of twenty-first-century living, impacting church-going as well as the type of jeans we buy. People are accustomed 'to doing their own thing' and are eclectic in their tastes. Membership of societies and political parties has declined. Pubs and clubs have closed in their thousands. Even attendance at football matches has gone down. Church attendance has also waned, though in comparison with many other organizations it is actually holding up relatively well. Although people increasingly prefer to stay at home and watch the television, the search for meaning remains strong. Interest in the soul and the geography of the mind is alive and kicking. In our fast-moving and apparently secular culture spirituality has become cool. But what exactly is it?

A glance along the shelves of any bookshop reveals the extent of our confusion. The term 'Religion' is giving way to the more all-embracing term, 'Mind, Body, Spirit'. Shelves may display the occasional Bible or prayer book, but the focus of the titles on sale is now on 'spiritual experience' conceived in highly personal and somewhat esoteric terms. Spirituality designates something less organized than institutional religion. It is about exploration and quest. Spirituality has become synonymous with any way of making us feel better about ourselves. Relaxation techniques, astrology, the occult, popular psychology, harmony with nature, magic now all find their home under spirituality's generous umbrella. Turn on the television and we discover a free channel called 'Psychic Today' devoted to reading people's fortunes. These days you can even have spirituality without God. I am reminded of G. K. Chesterton's alleged remark, 'When a man ceases to believe in God, he doesn't believe in nothing: he believes in anything.'

At one level, 'the proof of the pudding is in the eating'. As a former parishioner once said to me, 'If it works, does it matter?' Hugging trees, crystals, candles, drugs, angels, incense, yoga, aromatherapy, organic food, tai chi are now equally valid paths to enlightenment. People are interested in talking about prayer, but not necessarily in actually praying. Alternative types of spirituality, some of which may be labelled 'New Age', tend to be unashamedly escapist, turning away not only from organized religion but from the complexity of the modern world. In this safer, privatized world of the 'spirit' the individual is not subject to any external authority, be it the church or the Bible. An individual is his or her own arbiter. The spiritual realm is attained not by looking outwards to God, but by turning inwards to the self. It's not just truth and morality that have been privatized; so has worship. Prayer and meditation are marketed as the means to growth in self-awareness. The God of grace has been replaced by a scheme for self-nurture. God has been annexed to the drive for self-improvement, a tool in the quest for self-realization.

Sadly much contemporary spiritual writing treats symptoms without addressing underlying causes, and as a consequence fails to deliver what it promises – happiness. There is naiveté as well as generosity in accommodating voguish philosophies and spiritual fads, and a lack of discrimination can be self-defeating. This sort of 'spirituality' does little to promote personal maturity. It fails lamentably to nourish in times of crisis, hardship or failure. Typically, people experience relief, but not the lasting contentment that is God's will for us and his supreme gift.

As a generation we burn ourselves out on shallow religion. We hanker after new experiences, but we are less good in countering what is self-indulgent. As T. S. Eliot lamented more than a generation ago in his poem,

'The Dry Salvages': 'we had the experience, but missed the meaning'.[1] With our supermarket mentality we are vulnerable to becoming spiritual butterflies, skipping from one exotic flower to the next in search of spiritual nectar, but never settling or staying long enough to see what happens when the sun goes in. Few of us can claim to be immune to the temptation. In the current spiritual and moral fog we need to rediscover the virtue of the old monastic prayer: 'God give me grace to persevere with joy'. We need to encourage one another to persevere, to distil the meaning in our experiences, not notch them up like trophies. Life needs to be directed to something more than having a great time.

The Judaeo-Christian tradition protests against escapism. It insists that faith must be reflected in how a person acts in the world. 'Religion that is pure and undefiled before God, the Father, is this: to care for orphans and widows in their distress, and to keep oneself unstained by the world' (James 1.27). The injustices and inequalities of the world are not something from which we should be remote. Just as spirituality cannot afford to become divorced from public worship, so it also needs to generate a passion for the better ordering of the world.

Spiritual alchemy

In the Christian tradition the quest for personal enlightenment is rooted in our relationship with Jesus Christ. Spirituality, discipleship and the pursuit of truth go hand-in-hand, and we need to recover this coherence. Discipleship oscillates between two spiritual polarities: the need for acknowledgement of sin, repentance and self-denial; and Jesus' invitation to live abundantly. The great theologians of the early centuries had a special Greek word for self-discipline: *ascesis*. We discipline ourselves in order to follow Jesus who bids us deny ourselves, take up our cross and follow him. But the same Lord also invites us to live abundantly. 'I have come that you may have life and have it abundantly' (John 10.10); or as some translations have it, 'that you may have life in all its fullness'. We know from the Gospels that Jesus was regularly castigated for being a wine-bibber. 'Look, a glutton and a drunkard!' (Matthew 11.19). The challenge is to plot a middle way between these polarities.

The New Testament operates with two words for 'life'. *Bios*, from which we derive the word 'biology', meaning life or existence. And *zoe*, meaning energy, animation, vibrant living. In John 10.10 Jesus uses the second word. God wants us to make the transition from *bios* to *zoe*. He does not want us to vegetate. He wants us to be vibrant, energized men and women, realizing our full potential. And of this, Jesus Christ is both the Way and the role model, and the Holy Spirit our enabler. In words from Charles Causely's poem, 'Ballad of the Bread Man', Jesus came 'to bring the living to life'. Jesus comes to transform our *bios* into *zoe*. The question is, where are we on that journey of personal transformation? Where are we on the *bios–zoe* spectrum?

Paradoxically, our answer will be shaped by our response to other words of Jesus: 'If any want to become my followers, let them deny themselves and take up their cross and follow me. For those who want to save their life will lose it, and those who lose their life for my sake will find it. For what will it profit them if they gain the whole world but forfeit their life? Or what will they give in return for their life?' (Matthew 16.24–26). Familiarity with Jesus' words can mean that we no longer hear their force. But as Dietrich Bonhoeffer reminds us in *The Cost of Discipleship*, 'When Jesus Christ calls a man, he bids him come and die.'[2] In marketing terms, it is not an attractive sales-pitch.

Because being a Christian is about following Jesus Christ, it is of necessity about the cross, death and resurrection. It is about abundant living, but it is a quality of life discovered through repentance, service, forgiveness, and costly, sacrificial, self-giving love. This unusual spiritual cocktail contrasts with many of the more simplistic notions of what it means to be happy being promulgated today. And here we encounter a missional problem: communication.

Talk of restraint or self-denial immediately reinforces parodies of the church as repressive. The word *ascesis*, from which we derive our word asceticism, instantly conjures up images of hair-shirts or eccentric monks like St Simon Stylites, perched on his pillar in Turkey, hurling down abuse at adulterers and fornicators. Christians are regularly stereotyped as anti-sex, anti-drink and anti-fun. Self-discipline rarely enjoys a good press even among Christians. Lent, the great season of abstinence and fasting, has degenerated into an annual diet between Christmas and the summer holidays lest we look foolish on the beach in our latest designer swimwear.

With obesity a root cause of many diseases in the developed world, it comes as no surprise that the number of fitness centres and gyms has mushroomed. The young are desperate to be seen as fit and sexually attractive, and the middle-aged are terrified of looking old. Death is not the only taboo in western society: so is old age. In the quest to look healthy and fit, far from being ridiculed self-discipline has become a virtue. And here is an irony. Much of the New Testament's language of self-discipline is rooted in the Greek gymnasium. Paul uses the image of an athlete preparing for a competition and of a boxer training his body for a contest (1 Corinthians 9.24–27) to talk about the merit of personal discipline. It might help a younger generation to re-connect with this ancient wisdom if, instead of retreating with embarrassment from the challenge of spiritual discipline, it were promoted like a physical fitness programme set by a personal trainer. Young people are up for a challenge and we sell the Gospel short by making so few demands.

Getting a good work–life balance, including a right attitude to our bodies, is important for all of us, whatever our age. Contrary to popular misconceptions, Paul recognized the danger of treating the body harshly. There were plenty in his day, as in our own, who beat themselves up, sometimes in the name of God. 'Such regulations', he wrote to the Colossians, 'have an appearance of wisdom in promoting self-imposed piety, humility, and the severe treatment of the body, but they are of no value in checking self-indulgence' (Colossians 2.23). We now know, thanks to modern psychology, that dieting can become obsessive and lead to anorexia. Self-hatred can masquerade as self-discipline. When self-discipline becomes an end in itself and loses sight of Jesus' call to abundant living it is usually about self-punishment.

Self-knowledge and the knowledge of God

So far we have identified three strands in Christian spirituality: a passion for the better ordering of the world, Jesus' invitation to abundant living, and his call to self-transcendence. To these should be added a fourth: self-knowledge. Gregory of Nyssa, a fourth-century bishop and theologian living in what we now call Turkey, claims that self-knowledge is our greatest protection in life. He says: 'How can you protect a person you do not know? Each of us must know ourselves as we are, and learn to distinguish ourselves from what we are not. Otherwise we may end up unconsciously protecting somebody who does not exist, and leave our true selves unguarded.'[3]

Gregory's advice should be set alongside Jesus' statement that 'when the Spirit of truth comes, he will guide you into all the truth' (John 16.13). All lies enslave, and the worst lies are the ones we tell ourselves. The quest for self-knowledge is universal and life-long. Even the apostle Paul observed, 'I do not understand my own actions. For I do not do what I want, and I do the very thing that I hate' (Romans 7.15). Frustration, lack of self-control, power-lessness and a longing for self-understanding are things we all experience.

In the Christian tradition, however, self-exploration is subsumed and shaped by a more profound quest: the search for God. It is not who we are, but who God is that is all important. Augustine believed that the search for God and the search for self are two sides of the same coin because we are made in the image of God. 'If I knew myself,' he argued, 'I would know God.'[4] He says that the deepest truth about our nature is that in God we discover who we really are.

Alongside 'spirituality', counselling and therapy have mushroomed in the vacuum created by the retreat of organized religion. In some quarters a therapeutic culture has grown up that has spawned a fantasy that we can find inner healing in isolation from others. This is illusory. The Gospel maintains the unpalatable truth that there is no perfect healing, at least not in this life, and that (to borrow a phrase of Augustine) 'our hearts are restless till they find their rest in God'.

The true purpose of therapy is to enable people to face themselves and their inner restlessness. Each of us carries a ragbag of memories, aspirations, failings, hopes and fears. True therapy helps us understand these things and take responsibility for our lives. At its best the therapeutic process deepens a person's spiritual life and enables them to be more alive. For some, however, therapy degenerates into evasive and self-justifying talk about the past which feeds self-centredness. Growth in self-awareness is good, but only in ways that include awareness of others and which lead to healthy and fruitful relationships. As the teaching of Jesus makes clear, the goal of human striving must be self-transcendence, not self-obsession.

Reconnecting spirituality and worship

We should resist, therefore, all attempts to dumb down Christianity or reduce spirituality to the quest for self-fulfilment. Authentic Christian spirituality is not about self-fulfilment: it is about seeking the face of God. It is about being in the company of Jesus. It is about the way of the cross. It is about the struggle to make sense of why sometimes bad things happen to good people. It is about trying to make sense of our lives and relationships under God. Ultimately, as Jacob discovered at the Ford of Jabbok (Genesis 32.22), it is about wrestling with God.

Christianity does not claim to have all the answers. Being a Christian is about walking by faith, living in the provisional, and that may mean living with unanswerable questions. But this does not permit us to abdicate responsibility for translating our private experiences into the public realm we share and create. As the origin of the word 'religion' in the Latin verb to bind reminds us, religion is that which binds us to God and to one another. Worship, spirituality, doctrine and loving our neighbour form the spiritual cord that unites us to God and enables the transfusion of grace.

In the Bible the word for spirit (both in Hebrew and Greek) is linked to the word for wind and breath. 'The wind blows where it chooses,' says Jesus, 'and you hear the sound of it, but you do not know where it comes from or where it goes. So it is with everyone who is born of the Spirit' (John 3.8). Following his resurrection Jesus breathes on the disciples his life-giving breath, his Spirit. He shares the energy of his being in an act of new creation. In Christian understanding, therefore, authentic spirituality is about the life of God within us, about the personal transformation that comes from being radically open to God's Spirit. The challenge today is to help people to discover this reality for themselves.

Questions for reflection

1 In a society where people want everything instantly, how can we help them learn to pray in the midst of a busy life?
2 How can we help people recalibrate their lives so that they have a better work–life balance?
3 When the idea that 'you are worth it' dominates our self-understanding today, how can we help people explore the need for self-denial as an important aspect of the Christian tradition?
4 How can the Christian tradition of offering *spiritual direction* respond to the widespread desire for therapists and counsellors?

Notes

1 T. S. Eliot, 'The Dry Salvages', *Four Quartets*, London: Faber and Faber, 2001.
2 Dietrich Bonhoeffer, *The Cost of Discipleship*, London: SCM Press, 2001.
3 Gregory of Nyssa, *Homily 2 'On the Song of Songs'.*
4 *Noverim te, Domine, noverim me*, Augustine, *On the Trinity*, IX, 18.

2

THE CONTEXT WE SET

It is madness to wear ladies' straw hats to church; we should all be wearing crash helmets. Ushers should issue life preservers and signal flare; they should lash us to our pews. For the sleeping God may wake someday and take offence, or the waking God may draw us out to where we can never return.

Annie Dillard, *Teaching a Stone to Talk*

Coming to Worship

Don't let worry kill you off – let the church help.

Church noticeboard

This is proof to me, that the deadness and formality experienced in the worship of the church arise far more from the low state of our graces, than from any defect in our liturgy; if only we had our hearts deeply penitent and contrite, I know from my experience at this hour, that no prayers in the world could be better suited to our wants, or more delightful to our souls.

Charles Simeon (1759–1836)

'O worship the Lord in the beauty of holiness' is a phrase familiar to most Anglicans. But worship has to strike a balance. It needs to blend the holy with the homely. If people do not feel at home in church, the chances of them being sufficiently at ease to encounter the holiness of God or to be receptive to his Word and the grace of the sacraments are slim. The poet Philip Larkin was ambivalent about organized religion, but still recognized the church as 'a serious house on serious earth'. If those conducting worship fail to recognize its seriousness or to communicate a sense of God's presence, then we should not be surprised when a congregation feels uninspired and votes with its feet. We may succeed in getting new folk through the door for a special occasion, but they are unlikely to come back.

The context we set for worship begins with the welcome we extend at the church door. The meeting and greeting of people sets the tone for what follows, as does the quality of personal preparation a minister brings to the worship. The way we lead worship, speak, sing, preach, move and hold ourselves can all enhance or wreck a service. How visitors are treated at the end of a service will also affect how they remember the occasion. In fact sometimes this can count more than the sermon! It all contributes to the experience of church and it affects the credibility of our mission.

Communication

Over the last fifteen years the installation of disabled access has been systematically rolled out across the ecclesiastical landscape. When it comes to signage, however, the church lags behind other public buildings. The decrepit state of many church noticeboards bearing a clutch of out-of-date or irrelevant notices signals a dying institution, devoid of self-confidence. Locked churches, where no information is given about when the services are held or who has the key, compounds a sense of exclusion. It projects an image of the church not as the Body of Christ but as a private club. Churches should be open, accessible and used. Paradoxically, the churches that are vandalized most are the locked ones. Thieves and vandals can do what they like because they know that no one is likely to disturb them.

A church on a street corner or in a busy road could do worse than invest in one huge noticeboard simply saying 'Welcome' and advertising the

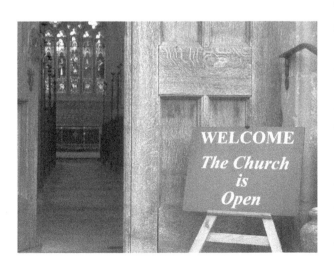

time of their main service in lettering big enough to read as you drive past. A noticeboard on the church door or porch can supply further details or at least give a web address where information can be accessed. A smart banner advertising Easter services or white lights slung around the trees along a path through the churchyard at Christmas will raise the profile of a church and at least communicate life. Such things don't have to look tacky. Sometimes the Church of England would prefer to die of good taste rather than take risks.

The message on the vicarage or parish office answerphone is also significant. It needs to be warm as well as informative. When a stranger phones up with an inquiry and gets the vicar's answerphone, we forget that at that moment the voice they are listening to will be (for them) the voice of the church. Parishes that have their own websites (and maintain them) are at a huge advantage in an age when most people instinctively turn to the internet for information. And really there is no excuse. Even parishes that have no website can still direct visitors to the website 'A church near you' which will happily store a wide range of helpful information at no cost.

How we present ourselves and the language we use in modern media is important in presenting a contemporary image of the church, particularly to a younger clientele. Festivals represent special opportunities to reach out to those on the fringe of the church. We should make it easy for parents hunting for somewhere to take their children to a carol service on Christmas Eve to access the relevant information. Communication, communication, communication.

Timing

Getting the timing right for a service is as important as getting the welcome right. For the majority of parishes, Sunday morning will be the main focus of worship, and it is crucial to pitch the time of a service to maximize its appeal. With so much competition from the gamut of leisure activities, we need to be alert to the needs of families if we want to attract them. Most will prefer a time in the middle of the morning around 10am or 10.30am. By and large, 11am is too late and 9am too early. Ideally a service should not last longer than an hour and ten minutes. An hour is even better.

The timing of services in multi-parish benefices in rural areas is more challenging. Changing service times on different Sundays in the month militates against building consistent attendance across a benefice. The in-crowd will know the subtleties of the system and who is where and when, but those on the fringe will fall by the wayside defeated by the complexity. It is a recipe for decline. It is much better (though admittedly tiring) for the priest to dash between services of Holy Communion, and to invest in training lay people to lead non-eucharistic services at the same time each Sunday when the priest is elsewhere in the benefice.

Getting the welcome right

Every congregation thinks of itself as warm, welcoming and friendly, but this is not always the experience of visitors. Regular church-goers soon forget how scary it can be for someone unfamiliar with the rituals and customs of worship to cross the threshold of a church. Vast numbers of the population have had little or no contact with the church for generations. Coming to Sunday worship, attending a funeral or the christening of a friend's baby can be an intimidating experience, as well as a puzzling one.

First impressions count. Research undertaken by the national Wedding Project has discovered that what matters most to couples investigating getting married in church is the quality of the welcome in their initial contact and their relationship with the priest conducting the service. Similar expectations, whether or not articulated, will be lodged in the mind of the occasional visitor on a Sunday morning. Research indicates that the most significant strategic action a church can take towards growth is to improve its welcome. Theologically, the principle of welcome goes right to the heart of the mission of the Trinitarian God who reaches out to extend his own community. It also reflects the attitude of Jesus, the one who welcomed sinners and ate with them.

The welcome needs to be warm without being effusive and overwhelming. Many retailers do this so much better than the average parish: they train their staff to be courteous, helpful, customer-centred, with plenty of eye contact. Of course, shop assistants are in the business of selling products whereas the purpose of the welcome in church is to guide a visitor to worship. The trouble is some well-meaning sidespeople can be so busy talking to their friends that they miss the stranger in their midst as they hand out a raft of books and service leaflets. Giving someone our full attention is an art and a discipline that requires us to disengage from what we are doing or from our conversation with a neighbour in order to be present to the other.

We all think we know how to welcome people, but experience shows that this may not be the case. If it were straightforward, major retailers would not give so much time and effort to training their staff. It really does help if a person smiles, looks you in the eye, and at least says hello or good morning. It also helps if the welcomer comes towards you and greets you, rather than hides behind a table of hymnbooks and expects you to go to them.

No good will come of a vicar haranguing his or her congregation to be more friendly. All that succeeds in doing is making everyone feel guilty. By far the best approach is to identify a small number of people who are naturally warm and personable, and set them up as a team. Most parishioners will benefit by having at least some rudimentary training. It can be a useful exercise for them (or a PCC) to think back to an occasion, not necessarily in church, when as strangers they felt welcomed or well treated, and to reflect on the experience. Why was it I felt noticed, acknowledged or listened to? Why did I feel I counted? How can I translate that experience into our church and make it happen for those who come here?

Children

It is rightly said that children are not tomorrow's church – they are today's. The mark of a truly welcoming church is its capacity to value children as much as adults, and for the whole congregation to be flexible enough and willing to adapt around the needs of children in much the same way as happens in any household. Valuing their presence, allowing them to participate, and catering for them are prerequisites if a congregation is to grow. But their behaviour should not be allowed to tyrannize a congregation or destroy the atmosphere of a service. It is entirely possible to combine a generous welcome to children and infants, while maintaining some semblance of order. If all a child can see are the backs of adults, they will get bored and fractious.

Ideally, there needs to be a crèche for parents with very young children or babies where they can retreat to when the going in church gets tough.

Preferably, it should be somewhere where they can still see or at least hear the service. With modern technology it is perfectly possible to relay a service to the room. That way both parents and congregation are able to follow the sermon and the prayers.

Where Sunday School or Junior Church runs in parallel with the main service, it is good practice for the children to be in at the beginning of the service, returning in time for a blessing or communion. In some churches this is also an opportunity for the children to share with the congregation what they have been studying. If orchestrated well, this can be very effective.

Older people

Older people are more likely to be represented in our congregations than the young. In our desire to attract children and young families it is all too easy unwittingly to make older people feel unwanted and useless. Where would the church be without the energy and wisdom of the retired? They shoulder the bulk of the burden of administration and leadership in our communities, and they deserve generous acknowledgement. How would we manage without the prayers and financial giving of the housebound who form the backbone of many of our parishes? Older people are regularly stereotyped as being resistant to change, but in practice they are often more tolerant of contradictions than the middle-aged and may be less fixated about discovering 'the right answer' to problems. With less to prove (and lose) they can be remarkably free. Many are open to new things and embrace the younger generation gladly. They can draw upon deep wells of experience and play a significant part in the life of our churches. Time-rich, they often carry their wisdom lightly, but bring ballast and stability to the Christian community.

Sadly, many young people in our society today have little to do with the elderly, and many older people feel they have nothing to contribute to the aspiring young. This is tragic because older people have much to offer, not least sharing the secret of their resilience. Aside from family gatherings, one of the few places that young and old do come together is in our churches. This is something we should be proud of. It is also something we should give energy to cultivating. Having two people leading the prayers, one young and one old, can be a powerful testimony as well as a moving experience for a congregation.

Older people invariably bring a different set of expectations to worship than the parents of young children, but they also have specific needs that need to be met. Most churches these days are equipped with a loop system to aid the hard of hearing, but few provide service sheets or hymnbooks in big print for those whose sight is failing. The last third of life is very much about the quest for personal integration, a time to explore the essence of life, not merely its accessories. As the years pass the accent falls increasingly on being rather than doing. The prayer of reminiscence becomes a regular

way of praying, nourished by familiar words and much-loved liturgical texts. Many older people value opportunities for reflection in a service. They savour contemplation and, if encouraged, will form the prayerful heart of a parish.

Aftercare

The liturgy can be beautiful, the sermon thought-provoking and the singing of the choir uplifting, but it can all be undone in a matter of minutes at the back of church by an over-zealous busybody collecting the hymnbooks. Equally, the self-preoccupied vicar or Reader who is too busy chatting to a regular member of the congregation to notice, let alone shake the hand of, a visitor will lose bonus points.

Coffee after church can be an excellent opportunity to welcome newcomers, but it can also be a painful and alienating experience. When we come together, particularly after an interval of a week or more, we instinctively gravitate to our friends to exchange news. It is entirely natural, but it can result in a visitor being confronted with a sea of people's backs and strangers chatting. Far from feeling welcomed and included, they feel ostracized. One archdeacon described visiting a church where coffee was only served *after* all the visitors had left! It can help, therefore, if in addition to welcoming people to church at the beginning, some members of

the congregation are designated *not* to talk to their pals afterwards, but to circulate and spot the visitor. John Wimber points out that people go to church for a variety of reasons, but they only stay if they make friends. Not everyone will agree with him, but he does have a point. Churches describe themselves as welcoming and friendly, but do people actually make friends there?

Creating space

Being matey and joining in is not everyone's cup of tea. The steady increase in cathedral worshippers in recent years speaks a different story from that of the all-embracing welcome. Cathedral worship offers space and anonymity. It caters for those who value privacy more than fellowship. For some, intimacy with God is not dependent on engagement with others. They fear being dragged into intrusive conversations or being pressurized into signing up for things they are not inclined to do. The virtue of dim religious light is that at least it allows people to hide in the shadows.

Translating this into a parish context means that we need to give permission to people to hide behind pillars. Those who attend 8 o'clock Holy Communion according to the *Book of Common Prayer* or who prefer Compline by candlelight to Messy Church should not be made to feel second-class parishioners. In services that permit a degree of anonymity, and in worship that requires minimal participation, many find not only refuge but real nourishment. We need to be careful that in our style of worship and in our zeal to be welcoming we do not send out the message that to be a fully paid-up Christian you have to be an extravert or to 'participate', and as a result unwittingly exclude a whole raft of people.

Questions for reflection

1 How can you improve the visual appearance of your church and raise its profile in the neighbourhood?

2 Have you got the timing of your service(s) right in the parish / across the benefice?

3 Most congregations insist that they are friendly – by which they mean friendly with other members of the congregation. How do you know if they are friendly with occasional members of the congregation or with visitors? How can you raise awareness of the need to really welcome people into the life of the congregation?

4 Why not invite a mystery worshipper to come to various services and events, and then write a report of their experiences which can be discussed at the PCC?

5 How are your sidespeople / welcomers trained? What is the basis of your confidence that they are genuinely welcoming and helpful to visitors? Do you undertake training on a regular basis?

6 Have you undertaken a review of your facilities for the disabled, the partially sighted and the deaf?

7 What is your aftercare like? In your concern to get the welcome right, are you giving equal attention to what it feels like for a visitor at the close of worship?

8 Where in your church life are you creating space for the anonymous worshipper or those for whom the prospect of 'fellowship' is not an attractive proposition?

Worship Audit

I appeal to you, therefore, brothers and sisters, by the mercies of God, to present your bodies as a living sacrifice, holy and acceptable to God, which is your spiritual worship. Do not be conformed to this world, but be transformed by the renewing of your minds.

Romans 12.1–2

A worship audit can be a useful tool in enabling a church to take stock of its worship and renew its spiritual life. A parish can expect to be both changed and challenged by the exercise, not least by being forced to reflect on the experiences and perceptions of visitors, not all of which may necessarily be welcome. To be effective, a review needs to enjoy the support of the PCC, not just the clergy or ministry team. It need not be overly burdensome, but it does need to engage with the regular congregation, particularly those who do not normally have the confidence to voice their opinions. If handled wisely, the conversation within a Christian community that such a review generates can be hugely energizing.

Aims

Fundamental to an audit are the following questions:

- Is our worship meeting the needs of God's whole family in this place?
- Is our worship accessible and attractive to those who are not yet part of our church?
- What do we do well and what can we do better?

Process

- The PCC appoints a working group who can commit time and energy to undertake a review of the parish's worship on its behalf.
- The group meets to plan its work.
- The group gathers information, seeking honest answers to its questions. This can be done by:
  - conducting a survey of worshippers after the principal service(s),
  - members of the group meeting with a representative selection of groups within the congregation (such as Sunday School, young people, choir, music group, servers, older people, disabled people),
  - inviting mystery worshippers to visit the parish on different occasions and report back,
  - personal conversations with parishioners, including occasional attenders and those on the 'fringe'.
- The group prepares a report and makes recommendations.
- The PCC discusses the report and decides if, how and when to implement its recommendations.

Overleaf is a list of potential questions a parish might like to incorporate in a survey of worshippers as part of a worship audit. Depending on the style and churchmanship of your parish, you will need to select and tailor the questions you ask. On subsequent pages is printed an example of an audit tailored to a parish where the principal service on a Sunday is the Parish Communion according to *Common Worship* (Order One).

AUDIT SURVEY QUESTIONS

Before the service

- If you were a visitor, what would you know about the date, time and nature of this service from the church noticeboard and/or website?
- How were you welcomed when you arrived in church?
- How would you describe the atmosphere in church before the service?

During the service

- Did you have any problems seeing or hearing in church?
- How easy was the service book / leaflet / hymnbook to use?
- Did you find the print large enough to read?
- Could you see the overheads clearly? Did they help or hinder your worship?
- What are your observations about each of the people who were leading the worship (clergy, Readers, musicians, servers)?
- Did you find the ceremonial and symbolism of the service helpful?
- Was there anything that irritated you or which you found distracting?
- Did you know when to sit, stand or kneel? Were there too many or not enough changes in posture?
- Was the leadership of the service reverent, helpful and clear?
- Did the service have a coherent theme?
- Did the music fit with the theme and style of the service?
- Were you generally happy with the music / mix of musical styles?
- Were any of the hymns or songs unfamiliar? If they were unfamiliar, how did it make you feel?
- How was the Bible reading introduced and read?
- What did you think about the sermon?
- To what extent did the sermon deepen your knowledge and love of God?
- To what extent did the sermon connect with your daily life?
- Were the prayers (intercessions) audible / appropriate / helpful?

- Did the service allow you times of silence for your own prayer and reflection?

Visitors

- If you were a visitor, what were the best aspects of the worship?
- To what extent did you feel part of the worshipping congregation or merely a spectator?
- Did anything during the service make you feel excluded, embarrassed or stupid?
- What was the aftercare like? If there was coffee after church, were you invited to stay? Did you feel included or ignored?

General

- Was the length of the service about right or too long?
- If you could change just one thing about the service, what would it be?

PARISH EUCHARIST AUDIT

The context we set

- How long before the beginning of a service are preparations completed? Is there a cut-off point by which time everything must be in place?
- Does the choir or music group rehearse in church before the service; and if so, how long is the gap between their rehearsal and the beginning of the service?
- How long before the start of a service are people encouraged to arrive? What happens when they do arrive?
- Are there designated welcomers? Where are they situated and what do they actually do? What is given to worshippers on entering the building? How can we give them sufficient information without overloading them?
- When does music begin to be played and by whom? Is there ever any silence before the beginning of worship?
- Is the sound system adequate? Can people hear clearly in every part of the building?
- Is the lighting appropriate and adequate? Are there ways in which it could be improved?
- What provision is made for children? Is there a crèche facility? If children go out for separate activities, when and how are they welcomed back into the service?
- How do those leading worship (clergy, servers, choir, musicians, Readers) prepare to do so? Does anyone pray with the church-wardens, sidespeople, welcome team before the service?
- Where do the notices and the Banns of Marriage take place in the service? How can these be done in such a way as to enhance the worship, not interrupt it?

Music

- Is the music traditional or contemporary or a mixture? Is there a music group or an organ or both? Is the music wholly congregational? If there is a choir, does it lead or dominate?
- To what extent does the music of the church suit the style of service?
- Is the current repertoire of hymns and worship songs satisfactory? If not, how can it be improved?
- Is a congregational setting of the Eucharist used? If so, is it 'owned' by the congregation or is the music too ambitious?
- If your parish has a strong choral tradition, do you feel the choir is genuinely part of the congregation or a separate body? If the latter, how can be the choir be more integral to the life of the parish?

The Gathering

- Are there ways in which the entry of the ministers (choir and servers) can be improved?
- As the congregation gathers for worship, how can the President better draw them into worship?
- Are there ways in which informal words of greeting and the introduction to the theme of the service could be better dovetailed with the liturgical greeting?

The Liturgy of the Word

- How and when are people coached to read the scripture clearly and sensitively? Do they know how to introduce the reading? Do they know how to use the microphone? Do they know how to conclude the reading?
- Are the readings typed out in a pew sheet or is the congregation provided with Bibles? What translation is used? Does this need to be reviewed?

- If the normal practice in your church is to preach on the readings set in the lectionary, have you considered having a sermon series, for example during Lent? Alternatively, if your normal practice is to have sermon series, have you considered preaching on the lectionary readings for a period?
- How long is a sermon on average in your church? Is this too long, too short or about right?
- If your custom is to have a short sermon or homily, when and where in the life of your church will people have opportunities for systematic learning about the Christian faith?
- Who leads the prayers (intercessions) and do they ever receive any training? If so, by whom? How integrated into the rest of the service are the prayers?

The Liturgy of the Sacrament

- To what extent does the way the Peace is shared enable the congregation to come to the altar in unity? Or to what extent does it interrupt the movement of the liturgy?
- If there is a procession to bring up the bread and wine, are there ways that it might be done differently to enhance a sense of offering our lives to God?
- What do you like about the way that your parish priest presides during the Eucharist? Is there anything you wish he or she did differently?
- Are you content with the choice of Eucharistic Prayers that are used in your parish?
- Do you need to review the place and the manner in which Holy Communion is distributed in your church? Are there ways in which you can make the reception of Holy Communion more prayerful?

The Dismissal

- How does the ending of the liturgy prepare the congregation to go out and proclaim the Gospel and serve others?
- How are visitors identified and greeted at the end of the service? Are sidespeople or the welcomers trained to talk to them? – and take them to coffee?
- How are visitors given the opportunity to provide their contact details for follow-up?
- How can the parish priest be released to make sure that no visitors are missed?

General

- If you could change just one thing about your parish's worship what would it be?
- How can lay people be affirmed in their ministry as readers of scripture, intercessors, servers, welcomers and musicians?

3

BRINGING TEXTS TO LIFE

If we can image a whole liturgy – not just a homily – that disrupts as much as it consoles, that offers us alternative images, that reshapes the way we imagine, that enables us to react violently against the forces, internal and external, that enslave us, then we shall be on the way to a new state of seeing and being.

Richard Giles, *Creating Uncommon Worship*

INTRODUCTION

There are few places in society where we say or sing things together. Church is one of them. National Citizen ceremonies provide immigrants with a secular liturgy to cement their new status and nationality during which they sing the National Anthem. Remembrance commemorations may include the singing of 'O God our help in ages past'. But these are exceptions to the rule. For most people today the occasions when they unite with others in word or song, beyond singing 'Happy Birthday' to a member of the family or a colleague at work, are few and far between. It is one of the things that makes church distinctive in the twenty-first century. Put another way, it's what makes church odd.

The word 'religion', as we have noted earlier, derives from the Latin *religare,* meaning to bind. Religion is that which binds us to God and binds us to one another. In this enterprise liturgy is the glue. It provides familiarity, structure, words, song, music, rituals, patterns of worshipping and movement. The Church of England has a treasury of liturgical experience upon which to draw, but things are changing. Today congregations at a funeral

are more likely to know the words of Frank Sinatra's song, 'I did it my way', than the words of the twenty-third psalm. How do we enable people to re-connect with the riches of Christian liturgy and spirituality? There is an architectural quality to liturgy. How do we enable people to re-inhabit its spaces? 'Thou hast set my feet in a large room,' says the psalmist (Psalm 31.8, *BCP*). How do we encourage a new generation to explore the salons and attics of God's mansion?

The last forty years have seen huge changes in both society and the church. There has been considerable liturgical experimentation and an explosion of new services, but texts need to be brought to life. Congregations can easily become disheartened by yet another liturgical innovation, overwhelmed by an avalanche of esoteric but unfamiliar words. The menu of worship on offer in churches is rich, but diversity creates problems of its own. The titles of services can confuse the occasional worshipper. What exactly is 'Messy Church'? What is a 'Story Telling Service'? Meanwhile newly ordained priests, unfamiliar with the rubrics and cadences of sixteenth-century English, trip up when presiding at Prayer Book Holy Communion, much to the irritation of their older parishioners.

Basic principles

The gathering for worship begins long before the first hymn or song is announced, or the opening greeting is given. Preparing the building for worship, ensuring that it is clean, tidy and de-cluttered of junk is a task in itself. Printing service sheets, liaising with musicians, arranging rotas of readers and servers, all take time. Getting it right is worthwhile because attention to detail will raise the quality of worship. Various issues and questions need to be thought through as follows:

- Make sure the building, including the toilets, are clean and tidy.
- Organize the way people are welcomed and train up a team of welcomers.
- Get the lighting and the seating right.
- Make sure people can hear.
- Minimize the number of hymnbooks, leaflets and bits of paper that are given out.

- Are your Orders of Service user-friendly? Better to have a series of book-lets, incorporating seasonal variations, than one big complicated book. *Common Worship* also provides the service with section headings to give the liturgy shape. If you are producing your own booklets, don't ditch these headings and observe the typology. It will help people better understand what is going on.
- Think through the congregation's posture during the service. Worship is – or should be – more than just listening passively. A change in posture can help people engage more fully in the worship and praise of God.
- If you have a crèche ensure that it is clean, tidy and well-resourced if you want young families to stay.
- Start the service on time.
- Without rushing, make sure the service doesn't normally go beyond an hour and ten minutes – people will get restless.
- Organize the 'aftercare' so that, as far as possible, no one feels excluded.
- Make sure the contact details (including email addresses) of new people are taken so that they can be followed up.

Before the service

'Talk to God first and to each other later' encapsulates a traditional approach to church. Cut out the chat and focus on God: you can catch up with your friends *after* the service. There is wisdom in this. It ensures that the atmosphere in church before a service is quiet and reflective, and that a congregation is recollected. Incidental music, whether played by an organ or a music group or a CD, can help focus people's thoughts and set the tone for the worship that follows. Orders of Service can carry 'prayers to help you prepare' as well as the weekly notices. Carefully chosen overheads can aid reflection.

However, in parishes where there is a concerted effort to engage those for whom church is a foreign land the gathering for worship is likely to be more informal, perhaps even noisy. Some take this philosophy one stage further and have their refreshments *before* the service, not after. This approach is designed to facilitate the welcoming of newcomers, and allow young chil-dren to blow off steam and (hopefully) settle before the service begins.

Leading worship

The ethos of a church is shaped by those who lead its worship. Humility may not be a virtue greatly admired in a culture of self-assertion, but it is all-important in clergy and those who lead worship. Of equal importance is body language. Good posture, self-confidence, and the ability to pause and hold people's attention is important. Presence is something that can be recognized in a person, but not easily taught. What can be taught is competence. It is incumbent on clergy and all who regularly lead worship to inhabit the liturgy. They need to know their way round the *Book of Common Prayer* and *Common Worship* so that they don't get lost. They need to know the text intimately, and wherever possible learn the invariable parts of the liturgy by heart so that they are fluent and can be free to look at the congregation from time to time, rather than have their nose stuck in the book. When a priest knows the service well, he or she is better able to *pray* it, and instinctively this communicates to a congregation.

Worship is not just a cerebral thing. It involves our bodies and therefore our senses. It is why music and movement, touch and indeed smell can all have a part to play. Communication is as much by our gestures and facial expressions as by the words we speak. Clergy need to inhabit their bodies as well as the text of the liturgy, so that they offer their 'souls and bodies as a living sacrifice'. Gestures need to be natural and performed with conviction and confidence, not half-heartedly or furtively. A self-conscious priest unsettles people. An anxious priest leaches tension into the congregation.

Without being prissy, it is also sensible if those leading worship take a minute to look in the mirror before walking into church. The liturgy is akin to a drama, with its participants actors on a stage. Ministers who look a mess, whose robes are dirty and dishevelled, or who amble around the place in a daze are not an edifying spectacle. Kneeling at the communion rails, people notice clergy with dirty fingernails or scruffy jeans poking out from under their cassocks. If we want to raise the quality of worship in our churches, it will start when the clergy raise their own game. Clergy set the benchmark for others leading worship, including a choir and servers. Bored servers and disaffected musicians are bad news.

In all this there is no substitute for personal preparation. If a congregation needs to be still and expectant before worship, so do those who lead it, particularly those who are privileged to preside at the Eucharist. Spending five minutes waiting on God in quiet prayer in a side chapel before a service is time well spent. Words of St Bernard of Clairvaux come to mind, from his commentary on the Song of Songs:

> If you are wise, you will show yourself more a reservoir than a canal. A canal spreads abroad water as it receives it, but a reservoir waits until it is filled before overflowing, and so without loss to itself communicates its superabundant water. In the church of the present day we have many canals, but few reservoirs.

Guidelines

Although there is little uniformity across the breadth of churchmanship (was there ever?) there is still a recognizable 'shape' to Anglican worship and a body of wisdom that applies to most, if not all, churches. This section garners good practice in relation to the most common Sunday services. A step-by-step guide is offered to Holy Communion according to the *Book of Common Prayer*; Holy Communion celebrated according to *Common Worship* (Order One); All-Age worship; and Evensong said or sung from the Prayer Book. There follows practical advice on occasional offices: baptisms, confirmations, weddings and funerals. Each service outline ends with a checklist, designed to assist clergy, servers and other ministers.

Finally, there is guidance on leading public worship for churchwardens and lay people who can find themselves taking services, sometimes at short notice, in the absence of their vicar or local Reader. What can you and can't you do? There is also a note about processions, including protocols to be observed when the bishop comes or when welcoming civic representatives to worship.

Holy Communion according to the *Book of Common Prayer*

The Country Parson being to administer the sacraments, is at a stand with himself, how or what behaviour to assume for so holy things. Especially at Communion times he is in a great confusion, as being not only to receive God, but to break and administer him. Neither finds he any issue in this, but to throw himself down at the throne of grace, saying 'Lord, thou knowest what thou didst when thou appointedst it to be done thus; therefore do thou fulfill what thou didst appoint; for thou art not only the feast, but the way to it.'

George Herbert (1593–1633), *The Country Parson*, XXII

Nobody today celebrates the Holy Communion as Cranmer conceived it or as the Prayer Book of 1662 stipulates. To the occasional worshipper, when handed a copy of the *Book of Common Prayer* upon entering a church, the published text (assuming he or she can find it in the book) is difficult to follow. Few young people know their way round the service and there are as many variations as there are parsons and parishes. Sometimes whole sections are shortened or omitted. Different local customs may be observed, for example in relation to where and when people sit, stand or kneel. The vesture of the minister may vary. Rubrics are not always followed. Additional 'customary' responses may be inserted into the liturgy. Adaptations proposed in the ill-fated 1928 Prayer Book, though never authorized by Parliament, may nevertheless be observed. For all these reasons it makes sense to provide congregations with a booklet in which the actual text of the service as used in a parish is set out plainly.

The majority of clergy these days have not been brought up on the Prayer Book and, unlike earlier generations, have consciously to learn 'how to do it'. A priest must learn *how* to preside, so that word and action are in harmony. It is incumbent on all clergy, but especially a younger generation of ministers, to familiarize themselves with the text until they are fluent. A priest who lacks confidence sets a congregation on tenterhooks. For example, there is a skill to starting a prayer in such a way that expects the congregation to join in. But the liturgy is more than words – beautiful and sonorous though sixteenth-century English may be. It includes movement and action. The priest stands to lead the prayers, to exhort, to read and to preach, whereas the basic posture of the congregation throughout is kneeling. This gives a very different feel to worship.

By custom the service is divided into two halves: Ante-Communion and Communion, with the offertory at the midway point. Although the rubrics of the Prayer Book instruct a priest to preside from the 'north side' of the communion table, in most parishes the priest will be expected either to face east with his or her back to the people, or to face west looking across the holy table at the congregation. In either case it is likely that the communion vessels will have been placed on the altar in advance of the service, covered with a burse and veil according to season, with bread and cruets of wine and water on the credence table (as shown on p. 205). It is always advisable for visiting clergy to arrive in good time in order to familiarize themselves with the customs of a parish.

Given the variety of usage, what is described here may best be described as a guide to the Prayer Book service *as customarily used.*

ANTE-COMMUNION

The Preparation

Assuming the celebration is at the main altar with the priest facing east, upon entering the sanctuary and reverencing the altar, the service begins with the Our Father. This is all that remains of the prayers of preparation said by priest and server in the medieval rite. Cranmer instructs the priest to say the prayer alone, as well as the Collect for Purity that follows which he designed as a prayer of preparation for the congregation. If this traditional pattern is observed, then the priest may stand or kneel at the bottom of the steps of the sanctuary facing the altar to recite the Lord's Prayer audibly, but quietly; and then (standing) in a slightly louder voice the Collect for Purity, at the end of which the priest ascends the steps for the Ten Command-ments. In some churches, priest and people say together both the Lord's Prayer and the Collect for Purity; in others, the priest says the Lord's Prayer alone, but the Collect for Purity is said by all.

Summary of the Law

Following the pattern of the 1928 Prayer Book, in many parishes the Ten Commandments are replaced by Our Lord's Summary of the Law, the priest facing the people and saying as follows:

Our Lord Jesus Christ said: 'Hear, O Israel, the Lord our God is one Lord; and thou shalt love the Lord thy God with all thy heart, and with all thy soul, and with all thy mind, and with all thy strength. This is the first commandment. And the second is like, namely this: Thou shalt love thy neighbour as thyself. There is no other commandment greater than these. On these two commandments hang all the Law and the Prophets.'

The congregation may give one of two responses according to local custom: 'Lord, have mercy upon us, and incline our hearts to keep this law' or 'Lord, have mercy upon us, and write all these thy laws in our hearts, we beseech thee.'

The Collect

The minister then turns east for the Collect(s). Up to three collects may follow, beginning with the Prayer for the Queen, two alternatives of which are printed in the Prayer Book. In some parishes this Collect is omitted. Then follows the Collect for the Day, supplemented in Advent by the Collect for Advent Sunday; and in Lent by the Collect for Ash Wednesday. Some priests preface the Collect with the greeting, 'The Lord be with you', to which the congregation replies, 'And with thy spirit', after the pattern of the 1928 Prayer Book.

The Readings

The congregation sits for the first reading which is usually from the Epistles or (following the usage of the *Book of Common Prayer*), occasionally from the Old Testament. In some parishes modern translations of these portions of scripture may replace those printed in the Prayer Book. In other parishes, particularly where a priest is also preaching at a later service, the readings from the *Common Worship* lectionary may be substituted. Unlike *Common Worship,* the Prayer Book provides the congregation with no response to the reading. It does, however, direct the congregation to stand for the Gospel, and in some churches the acclamations used in the 1928 Prayer Book ('Glory be to thee, O Lord' and 'Praise be to thee, O Christ') to accompany its reading have been adopted. In some churches it is also customary for the priest to stand at the south side of the holy table (the right-hand side from the congregation) when reading the Epistle, and move to the north side for the Gospel, or else to read it from the chancel steps.

Creed and Sermon

What invariably catches out clergy used to *Common Worship* is the positioning of the Creed *before* the sermon instead of after it. The Prayer Book also omits the adjective 'holy' in relation to the church. The Creed is said by all standing. If the sermon is customarily given from the pulpit or from the chancel steps, then some clergy like to leave the sanctuary and move to the pulpit during the closing lines of the Creed. By the same token, at the end of their address, many like to read from the pulpit one or more of the prescribed 'Sentences' to begin the offertory before returning to the altar.

COMMUNION

The priest prepares the elements while the collection is taken. In some parishes, although not stated in the rubrics, it is customary for the priest to add a few drops of water to the chalice – the so-called 'mixed chalice' (see Glossary, p. 260). A lavabo may also be provided (see Glossary, p. 256). If other ministers or servers are to assist in the distribution of holy communion, then ideally they need to move into the sanctuary at this point. If there are communion rails or gates, they should now be closed in readiness for the subsequent distribution of communion.

Prayer for the Church Militant

In some parishes, before beginning the intercession, it is customary for the priest to face the congregation and introduce specific intentions for prayer or mention individuals by name, concluding with the words, 'Let us pray for the whole state of Christ's Church militant here in earth.' The priest then turns east and begins the prayer. In some parishes, at the point where the sick and departed are commemorated in the prayer, it is customary for their names to be inserted. Some clergy, mindful of changes in the meaning of words over the centuries, will substitute the phrase 'impartially minister justice' for 'indifferently minister justice'. Some may also say 'all bishops, priests and deacons' in preference to 'all bishops and curates'.

In most parishes the 'Exhortations' are omitted, requiring priest and people to turn over a number of pages.

Confession and Absolution

The priest turns to face the congregation, invites them to confess their sins saying, 'Ye that do truly and earnestly repent you of your sins ...', turns east and kneels to lead them in the general confession that follows. At the end, the priest stands and pronounces the absolution and, if customary, makes the sign of the cross over the people.

Comfortable Words

Still facing the congregation the priest recites the Comfortable Words.

Sursum corda ('Lift up your hearts')

Still facing the congregation, he or she then says the *Sursum corda*, the ancient exchange between priest and people that begins the Eucharistic Prayer. The priest may choose to raise his or her hands at the same time. Some priests preface the words, 'Lift up your hearts', with the greeting, 'The Lord be with you', to which the congregation replies, 'And with thy spirit', after the pattern of 1928. The priest then turns to face east and recites the Preface. The Prayer Book provides a number of 'Proper Prefaces' to be used on certain Holy Days and/or in the week that follows them, known as their 'Octave'. The 1928 Prayer Book expands and supplements this provision. The Preface concludes with the recitation of the *Sanctus* in which the congregation join.

Prayer of Humble Access

The Prayer Book directs the priest to kneel before the holy table and say this prayer 'in the name of all'. This rubric has led most congregations to join in the prayer, but in some places the priest may be expected to recite the prayer alone. A visiting priest would do well to check this out before the service.

Prayer of Consecration

Standing before the altar, the priest says the Prayer of Consecration as directed. There is no prayer invoking the Holy Spirit (*epiclesis*) as such in the *Book of Common Prayer*. Nevertheless, some clergy (following the direction of the 1549 Prayer Book and modern usage) like to hold out their hands in invocation, palms facing downwards over the elements at the words, 'Hear us, O merciful Father'; and then make the sign of the cross over the elements at the words 'partakers of his most blessed body and blood'. The rubrics of the Prayer Book direct the priest to break the bread, and to 'take the cup into his hands' during the Words of Institution. This is sometimes referred to as 'traditional manual acts'.

Distribution of Holy Communion

It is important that all ministers commit the full words of administration to memory so that they can more easily be recited as a prayerful litany while distributing communion. Custom has made this a solemn moment and communicants are justly irritated when words are muddled or forgotten. The reason the formulae are so long is because they represent the conflation of two texts that were brought together in 1662. One emanated from the 1549 Prayer Book, the other from the 1552 Prayer Book. Most clergy will not use the full formula to each communicant because it slows the administration down, but will instead split the words between two or more communicants.

Ablutions

In the custom of the Prayer Book, what remains of the consecrated elements are placed upon the holy table, 'covering the same with a fair linen cloth'. The elements are not consumed until the end of the service, 'immediately after the blessing'. Two variations in this traditional ordering may be encountered. In some parishes the consumption of the remaining consecrated elements is delayed until much later in order to permit the vicar to go to the back of the church and greet parishioners. In other parishes the ablutions are carried out immediately after all have communicated but before the Lord's Prayer. For different customs, see 'Ablutions', p. 233.

Post-Communion Prayers, *Gloria* and Blessing

After communion, the priest leads the people in saying the Our Father. In contradistinction to the opening Lord's Prayer, this is definitely said by all. There then follows one of two Post-Communion Prayers, the first of which originally formed the second half of the Eucharistic Prayer in the 1549 rite, the so-called 'Prayer of Oblation'. The 1928 Prayer Book transposed this prayer back into its original place, and some clergy do this, in which case the second 'Prayer of Thanksgiving' is always used. The Prayer Book prescribes the *Gloria in excelsis* now to be said. In some churches people remain kneeling throughout; in others they stand, and then kneel again for the blessing. By custom (though there is no rubric to this effect in the Prayer Book) the canticle is omitted in Advent and Lent. The service concludes with the blessing, the priest, if customary, making the sign of the cross over the people. The priest (along with the server if there is one) reverences the altar before going to the door to greet parishioners.

CHECKLIST

Remove dust-cover from altar

Prepare communion vessels

- If a burse and veil are customary, check you have the right liturgical colour according to the season.
- Check the burse has a clean corporal in it.
- Put one large priest's wafer on the paten.
- If a burse and veil are customary, set up the vessels as shown on p. 205, and place either directly on the altar or on the credence table according to custom.

Prepare credence table

- Cover with a cloth.
- Fill cruets/flagons with wine and water.
- Check the wafer box is full, or if bread is used, that it is fresh and covered.
- If a ciborium is used, it may be charged in advance with the anticipated number of people's wafers, and then placed on the credence table in readiness.
- If a lavabo is customary, place the bowl and lavabo towel on the table.
- Have a spare purificator in case of spillage.

In the vestry or sacristy beforehand

- Set out the vestments according to local custom.
- Ensure the sound system is switched on, and that radio microphones have charged batteries and are switched to mute.

In church beforehand

- If a large-print/altar copy of the *Book of Common Prayer* is used, ensure that markers are in the right place, particularly for the Collect, Epistle and Gospel.
- Place a bookstand or cushion on the altar with the *Book of Common Prayer* open at the appropriate page.
- Light the candles.

Holy Communion (Order One) according to *Common Worship*

When a performance is over, what remains? Fun can be forgotten, but powerful emotion also disappears and good arguments lose their thread. When emotion and argument are harnessed to a wish from the audience to see more clearly into itself – then something in the mind burns. The event scorches on to the memory an outline, a taste, a trace, a smell – a picture. It is the play's central image that remains, its silhouette, and if the elements are highly blended this silhouette will be its meaning, this shape will be the essence of what it has to say.

Peter Brook, *The Empty Space*

THE GATHERING

Common Worship directs that the President should preside. Certain parts of the Eucharist can appropriately be delegated to other ministers, but the custom of a Reader or assistant minister 'leading the first half of the service', with the priest taking over at the Peace, undermines the unity of the Eucharist. It is important to find other ways of incorporating and affirming the ministry of others without dismembering the service. Generally speaking, if the rubric says, 'The President says …' it means either a priest or a bishop. If the rubric does not specify or says, 'A minister says …' then what follows can be delegated to a deacon, a Reader, or another person involved in leading the service.

The Greeting

The President sets the tone for the service and it helps if he or she actually looks at the congregation when greeting them. Faces communicate and eye contact helps bring a congregation together. It also helps if the President smiles – not in a false Cheshire Cat way, but in a way that is natural and warm. Grumpy clergy do little to advance the kingdom of God. The opening words should be a liturgical greeting – not 'Good morning everyone' – to remind us that we are in the God business, not gathering for a social. It may then be appropriate to add words of welcome, including an informal greeting, or briefly to introduce the liturgy.

For example, if the Eucharist is to include a baptism, the President might specifically want to welcome the family and godparents. On another occasion the President may wish briefly to set out the theme of the service. *Common Worship: Times and Seasons* provides certain days in the church's year, such as Candlemas, Palm Sunday or the Easter Vigil, with liturgical introductions. There is no reason why this custom should not be a regular feature of the Parish Eucharist. In an age that values informality this approach can 'soften' the liturgy. The President can then move directly either into the Collect for Purity or the Prayers of Penitence as appropriate.

Gloria in excelsis

The *Gloria* is meant to be sung, not said, at least on Sundays and festivals except during Advent and Lent when the *Kyries* may be substituted. In the 1950s the Parish Communion Movement benefited from having two congregational settings of the Prayer Book texts, one by Merbecke, the other by Martin Shaw, both of which had widespread appeal. Today no congregational setting of the modern English text has succeeded in securing either their coverage or affection. There are a variety of congregational settings of the Eucharist of varying quality and 'sing-ability'. In selecting one, it is vital that it is pitched sufficiently low that men in the congregation are not inhibited from joining in. Too many settings and hymn tunes are geared to trained singers and, as a consequence, are pitched too high for the average congregation. Of course, it helps if the parish boasts a good choir. A choir or singing group is a huge asset, provided it animates the congregation rather than dominates it. Singing is important because song feeds the memory.

THE LITURGY OF THE WORD

The *Revised Common Lectionary* provides three readings for every Sunday and Greater Holy Day. On some Sundays between Trinity Sunday and Advent, often referred to as 'Ordinary Time', the lectionary provides alternative first readings. One track selects an Old Testament reading in relation to the Gospel of the day; the other track provides for a sequential reading from the Old Testament. Some parishes have just two scripture readings rather than three. If that is the case, the Gospel must always be read. When time is pressured this is understandable. However, we need to be alert to the danger of a policy that may result in the Old Testament never or rarely being publicly read.

It is good to print out the full text of the readings in a pew sheet to enable a congregation better to absorb the teaching of scripture. 'Read, mark, learn and inwardly digest', as the Prayer Book says. Even better is to provide a congregation with pew Bibles so that they can follow the passages themselves. We are in danger of breeding a generation that no longer knows its way around the Bible. We need to resist a sound-bite culture.

In some parishes the readings are not listened to because they are read so badly. Not everyone knows how to introduce the reading or how to close it, let alone how to pronounce key words. Some readers may be nervous and read too quickly; others may be unfamiliar with using a microphone and end up booming. Of course, sometimes the culprit is not the reader at all, but the sound system operator who is slow on adjusting the decibel level until the reading is almost over. Rather than encourage everyone in the congregation to go on the reading rota, it is far better to identify those who are good at it. This is particularly important at big services and festivals when there are likely to be larger congregations together with a number of visitors. One solution is to earmark key services as occasions when only 'designated readers' are used. All people, young and old, need to be coached to read the scripture clearly and sensitively. Many parishes find that the best time to rehearse people is straight after the main service on a Sunday a week in advance.

Gospel Procession

A reading from one of the Gospels marks the climax of the Liturgy of the Word. For centuries there was little seating in churches. A congregation would stand throughout the liturgy or 'go to the wall' where there might be a bench for the infirm and elderly. Even so, all would stand for the Gospel, giving special honour to its reading, containing as it invariably does words of Jesus himself. In some parishes the reading of the Gospel is accompanied by a degree of ceremony. Two acolytes may stand on either side of the lectern, or lead the reader in procession to the middle of the church where it is proclaimed. The procession may be accompanied by the singing of a hymn or an 'Alleluia' to mark its importance.

Sermon

Charles Simeon, the great Evangelical Divine, had carved on the inside of his pulpit in Holy Trinity Church, Cambridge, where only the preacher could see, words from John 12.21. When Philip brought a party of Greeks to meet Our Lord, they said to him, 'Sir, we would see Jesus.' These words should be a constant reminder to every preacher to focus on making Jesus Christ known. A good sermon should relate both to the Bible readings of the day and to the theme of the service. It should have real content with clear teaching. Most parishes expect a sermon at the Parish Eucharist to be between ten and twelve minutes. It cannot afford to be much longer without the service over-running. A five minute 'thought for the day' will not do.

It is impossible to please all the people all the time. Some respond to exegetical sermons that are biblically based, methodical and analytical; others prefer the poetic. Some people are predominantly visual and warm to a preacher who paints pictures and tells stories; others savour open-ended questions and scorn the didactic. Given people's varied needs and tastes, how can they be accommodated within the constraints of a parish? It is a constant challenge, but worth reflecting on from time to time. What is certain is that boring sermons, which are poorly prepared and badly delivered, insult a congregation.

Preachers give a lot of thought about how best to begin their sermons, but rarely how best to end them; and endings can be as significant as beginnings. Should it end with an application for everyday life? Would some sort of challenge be best? What about ending with a question? Would ending with a prayer or silence work best?

Creed

Common Worship provides a number of authorized 'Affirmations of Faith', but these are not intended to be the normative expression of faith of a congregation to the exclusion of the so-called 'Catholic Creeds'. On occasion it may make sense to omit the Creed if, for example, the service is to include a baptism; or at an All-Age Eucharist to substitute a responsorial

Affirmation of Faith. The trouble is there are few occasions when Christians stand up and proclaim what they believe, and in a multi-cultural society we should not underestimate the formative role this action has in the life of a Christian community. Saying the Creeds in the context of public worship is part of our Anglican heritage and identity, and there is a strong argument that every Anglican should be able to recite from memory the Lord's Prayer, the Creed (either Nicene or Apostles'), the Ten Commandments and the Beatitudes as foundation texts of the Christian faith.

Prayers of Intercession

Leading a congregation in prayer is a gift, and people deserve support and training to help them do it well. Ideally their prayers should relate to the theme of the day and its readings, and this means that it is good practice for priest/preacher and intercessor to liaise more than five minutes before the beginning of a service at the back of church. If different responses are to be said or sung from those that are usual, they need to be stated clearly at the outset of the intercession and repeated by the congregation. A Cook's world tour of trouble spots should be avoided.

There is a difference between biddings and intercessions, and the two should not be confused. Biddings are addressed to people, encouraging them to pray. Intercessions are addressed to God. Intercessions should never be directed horizontally at a congregation in an attempt to inform or improve them, or as an alternative way of giving the notices. Consideration should also be given about where in the church the intercessions are best led from. The lectern is an obvious place, the person facing the people. But equally effective can be the back of the church, the person facing the altar in company with the rest of the congregation.

Notices

In some parishes the notices and Banns of Marriage take place after the intercessions, but before the Peace, forming an informal bridge between the Liturgy of the Word and the Liturgy of the Sacrament. There is sense in this, but it is not ideal because it can break up the movement of the liturgy. Also, if the children and their helpers are in Sunday School at this point, they will miss out. In some parishes notices are given out before the service begins which gives the President an opportunity to speak informally to the congregation, concluding with the announcement of the first hymn. Which is fine, provided people aren't late. In other parishes, notices are given out at the end of the service immediately before the Dismissal. This has the advantage that everyone is there and the priest can encourage visitors to stay for refreshments. There is no perfect solution. Whatever option is chosen, notices are best kept short. What is the point of repeating what is already written in the pew sheet?

THE LITURGY OF THE SACRAMENT

The Peace

The purpose of the Peace is not to say hello to our friends, but to celebrate our belonging to one another in Jesus Christ. In the New Testament we read that Christians greeted one another 'in the name of the Lord' and with a 'holy kiss' (Romans 16.16; 2 Corinthians 13.12). Later this became known as the 'kiss of peace' and was a sign of reconciliation and of the peace that is both Christ's gift to us and his will for us. Too often visitors are left standing and embarrassed while regular members of the congregation rush round the church embracing their pals. The President needs to make a judgement about how long the Peace is to go on for, and with whom he or she will share it.

Preparation of the Table

The President or other ministers prepare the altar table while the collection is being taken. It is usual in most parishes for a hymn to be sung at this point. Ideally it is good practice to place communion vessels on the credence table before the service rather than on the altar itself, so there is a real sense of the 'table being laid' at this point in the liturgy. But with large congregations and therefore multiple ciboria and chalices being required, this may not be possible. *Common Worship* makes optional provision for prayers to be said at this point, but on a Sunday their use can lengthen the service and slow the movement of the liturgy down.

The Eucharistic Prayer

The great Prayer of Thanksgiving forms the core of the service and it is good practice for a congregation to maintain the same posture throughout it, though this may not be practical, particularly in churches with a choral tradition where the choir sing elaborate (and long) settings of the *Sanctus* and *Benedictus*. The President is offering prayer and praise to God in the name of the congregation, not instead of them; and familiarity with the text of the Eucharistic Prayer enables a congregation to pray with their priest.

There are a number of authorized Eucharistic Prayers, but rather than use all of them in rotation, it makes better sense to be selective and to allocate different prayers to different seasons of the church's year, not least because some Eucharistic Prayers cannot accommodate seasonal Prefaces. Striking a balance between variety and sameness is the art of good liturgy.

All modern Eucharistic Prayers include a petition to the Holy Spirit (*epiclesis*), though this was omitted in the 1552 and 1662 Prayer Books. Some clergy like to hold out their hands in invocation at this point, palms facing downwards over the elements, and conclude by making the sign of the cross over the elements.

The Words of Institution have a natural solemnity. Although Anglican theology recognizes no 'moment of consecration', they deserve to be spoken with special dignity. The rubrics of the Prayer Book direct the priest to break the bread at this point and to 'take the cup into his hands'. In *Common Worship,* as in most other modern rites, the breaking of the bread occurs later in the rite as a separate liturgical action, often accompanied by the singing of the anthem *Agnus dei.* Although the bread is not broken during the Eucharistic Prayer, many clergy will instinctively want to pick up the bread/paten and cup, or gesture towards them during the Words of Institution. Clergy nurtured in the Catholic tradition may also wish to bow or genuflect at this point. Others may prefer to lift the bread/paten and cup at the conclusion of the Eucharistic Prayer and then reverence.

Administration of Holy Communion

Whether holy communion is administered kneeling at the altar rail or standing at the back of the church, it needs to be done reverently and efficiently. *Common Worship* provides ministers with various pairs of authorized words of administration. It is not good practice to mix them up, with the person administering the consecrated bread using one formula, and the person administering the cup saying something different. The custom of receiving communion by intinction has become more widespread in recent years, partly in response to the flu epidemic, but this needs to be regulated with sensitivity. Receiving communion by intinction is one thing; dipping the wafer plus your dirty fingers into the consecrated wine is another.

A large congregation will grow restless if the administration of communion is protracted or done inefficiently. Not only do big services require special planning, but the choice of appropriate instrumental music or devotional hymns during communion will be crucial to maintaining a reflective atmosphere.

Prayer after Communion

Common Worship provides one or two collects at this point: the first variable to be said by the President alone; the second congregational to be said by all. Even if the first prayer is not said, it can still be helpful if it is printed in the Order of Service. Although provision is made for a variety of congregation prayers to be said at this point, there is a strong argument for saying the same thing each week to give to the Eucharist a strong structure. If everything is different each week, liturgy loses its power to shape heart and memory.

THE DISMISSAL

The service concludes with the blessing, the priest, if customary, making the sign of the cross over the people. The 'sending out' of the people of God is one of the great acts of the Eucharist. Indeed the word 'Mass' comes from the Latin words that concluded the medieval rite: *Ite missa est,* meaning 'Go, be sent into the world'. The force of this was encapsulated for me by the text printed at the bottom of an Order of Service:

> The worship is ended. Now the service begins.

CHECKLIST

Remove dust-cover from altar

Prepare communion vessels

- If a burse and veil are customary, check you have the right liturgical colour according to the season, and that the burse has a clean corporal in it.
- Allow one purificator per chalice.
- Put one large priest's wafer on the paten.
- If a burse and veil are customary, set up the vessels as shown on p. 205, and place either directly on the altar or on the credence table according to custom.

Prepare credence table

- Cover with a cloth.
- Fill cruets/flagons with wine and water.
- Check the wafer box is full, or if bread is used that it is fresh and covered.
- If a ciborium is used, it may be charged in advance with the anticipated number of people's wafers, and then placed on the credence table in readiness.
- If a lavabo is customary, place the bowl and lavabo towel on the table.
- Have a spare purificator in case of spillage.

If a procession of gifts is customary, then a second table may be prepared at the back of the nave on which is placed a ciborium and a flagon of wine (and water) ready to be brought up at the offertory.

In the vestry or sacristy beforehand

- Set out the vestments according to local custom and according to season.
- Ensure the sound system is switched on, and that radio microphones have charged batteries and are switched to mute.

In church beforehand

- Position the President's chair and assistant ministers' seating. Check books, hymnbooks and service sheets are all set out.
- Check the Bible or *Revised Common Lectionary* is on the lectern and open at the right place.
- If it is customary to have a Gospel Procession, mark up the reading in the Gospel Book in readiness.
- If a large-print/altar copy of *Common Worship* is used by the President, ensure that markers are in the right place, particularly for the Collect, Eucharistic Prayer and any proper Preface.
- Place a bookstand or cushion on the altar with *Common Worship* open at the appropriate page. If the Liturgy of the Word is conducted from the nave, then the altar is normally left bare until the offertory.
- Light the candles.

All-Age Services

Why is All-Age worship so often shallow and patronizing? Can we not envisage a rich, textured worship that blows the minds of people of all ages with the beauty and goodness of God; a worship that gives us space to weep as well as to laugh, to lament as well as to celebrate? Can we not find music, words and drama that will fuel our anger at injustice, unsettle our cosy complacency and rouse us to action?

Anonymous worshipper

'All-Age' services have become increasingly popular, irrespective of the churchmanship of parishes. Their popularity is generated by a healthy desire to be genuinely inclusive in worship and accessible to fringe members. There has also been a reaction to the over-use of the concept of 'family' in relation to worship in some quarters. The Parish Communion Movement in the 1950s saw a worthy emphasis on the church as family and on worship that was family-oriented. In its heyday it was transformative of Anglican worship, but the limitations of this approach became increasingly clear with the passing of the decades. Critics were not slow to point out that the dominant image of the church in the New Testament is not that of the family, but of the Body of Christ – a living, co-ordinated, diverse community of people united by their common baptism into Christ. Allied to this change in theological emphasis, the impact of increasing numbers of divorced people, single-parent families, and older people in congregations, and the fact that many single people, far from feeling 'included' by such services, felt decidedly excluded, combined to make the concept of 'Family services' feel decidedly outmoded.

All-Age worship operates with a different philosophy. To be worthy of the name, the planning and delivery of such worship must embrace the entire age-spectrum: toddlers, Primary (non-reading) School children, Primary (reading) School children, Secondary School children, sixth-formers, students, adults of all ages, and the elderly. A wealth of resource material is available, much of it online. Even so, constructing a service is a huge challenge for any minister or worship leader, requiring careful planning.

A Service of the Word

If the worship is to follow the pattern of a Service of the Word, it is important to include all the required elements to ensure that the service has substantial content and doesn't descend into a glorified 'hymn sandwich'. *Common Worship* sets out the following structure:

Preparation

- Opening Greeting.
- Call to Worship (This may include the *Venite,* an opening set of responses, and/or a hymn).
- Authorized Prayers of Penitence (either at this point or during the prayers).
- Collect (either at this point or to conclude the prayers).

The Liturgy of the Word

- Reading(s) from scripture.
- Psalm or a scriptural song.
- Sermon.
- Authorized Creed or Affirmation of Faith.

Prayers

- Intercessions and thanksgivings.
- Lord's Prayer.

Conclusion

- Blessing and Dismissal.

All-Age Eucharist

In theory a Eucharist is always an all-age event, but it can feel very staid. It may help to substitute one of the *Additional Collects* authorized for use, if the Collect of the Day provided in *Common Worship* is too Cranmerian in taste. Similarly, it is possible to use one of the special Eucharistic Prayers authorized for services when a large number of children are present. Encouraging children and young people to participate and to lead, with perhaps

intercessions led by two people, one young and one elderly, or to deliver a dramatized reading, can engage them as well as enrich the worship of the whole congregation. Creating an altar frontal or banners invites those with artistic gifts to contribute to the worship. Research has discovered that the single biggest reason teenagers leave the church is because they are not given opportunities to contribute. Too often we do young people a disservice by assuming that they are living, breathing consumerists, whereas we might unearth the next raft of church leaders by giving them more roles in which they can give rather than receive.

All-Age services of whatever kind often attract occasional worshippers. It helps, therefore, if a specially printed Order of Service is produced so that they are not juggling innumerable bits of paper and books. It may be good to illustrate the text with appropriate clipart. Short lines and generous spacing of the text on the page makes for a less intimidating appearance. In a non-book culture the use of overheads or video or PowerPoint can also help. But if these are employed, they do need to be operated efficiently and unostentatiously so that the liturgy of the overheads doesn't supplant the worship of God! Visibility is always an issue with overheads. So be alert to the needs of the poorly sighted, the short and those who have to remain seated while others stand.

Much of what applies to all worship applies equally to All-Age services, but here are some guidelines.

Planning

- Focus on one strong theme for the service and build around it.
- Aim for the service to last around 45 minutes.
- Have a variety of people of all ages and abilities involved.
- Maintain a balance between the role of the person leading the worship and other participants so that the service holds together.
- Ensure the service includes a teaching element and is not merely entertainment.
- Avoid having 'adults speaking' and 'children holding things up'.
- Don't attempt to have silences if you have lots of toddlers present, but don't be afraid to have pauses for thought or prayer.
- Think about having a dramatized biblical reading, with the text split into parts for a variety of voices.
- Ensure there is lots of congregational participation, both said and sung.
- Ensure there is congregational movement at regular intervals (standing up, sitting down or moving around).
- Are all the elements of penitence, intercession, affirmation of faith, thanksgiving and praise included?

Liturgy

- Use short sentences.
- Where there are alternatives, use responsorial versions, preferably where the congregation says the same response so that those who can't read can still participate.
- Don't do the intercessions in the same way at every All-Age service.
- If there hasn't been much participation, the intercessions are a good place to introduce it.

Music

- Try to have a mixture of hymns and worship songs that are appropriate to your congregation.
- Toddlers like action songs. Older children and some adults tend to be embarrassed by them.
- If you have a church school, make sure their repertoire of hymns and songs is reflected in what you sing. Ensure you sing something they know.
- Have at least one traditional hymn.
- Don't have too many verses in any one hymn or song.
- If there is a chorus, it might be worth practising it so that non-readers can join in with that part of it.

Leading All-Age worship

- Be clear about what page you are on and what you want the congregation to do.
- If using a long or 'theological' word, think about explaining it. For example, 'the Passion of Christ' – the suffering of Jesus, especially in his trial and death. For example, 'the Incarnation' – Jesus becoming a human being. Don't necessarily print this in the Order of Service, but add it as you lead, not every time, but as an occasional aside.
- If there is a set response for one section, such as during the Intercessions, practise it at the beginning even if it is printed in the Order of Service. For example, 'After each section of the prayers, there is a response. When I say, "Lord, hear us", please reply, "Lord, graciously hear us."' Tip: don't make the first section of the prayers too long or children will have forgotten the response.

Evensong

The day thou gavest, Lord, is ended,
    The darkness falls at thy behest;
To thee our morning hymns ascended,
    Thy praise shall sanctify our rest.

John Ellerton (1826–93)

Evensong is one of the best-loved services in the Church of England, though sadly in decline, in part because people prefer to go to church in the morning and dislike going out in the evening, particularly in winter. Its survival often depends on tradition, on whether or not there is a decent choir, and whether the congregation is used to singing.

Cranmer arranged for the one hundred and fifty psalms of the psalter to be sung in sequence every month. Few parish churches follow this arrangement today. Unlike the cathedrals, which still normally sing all the psalms set for the day in the Prayer Book, most parish churches choose just one psalm, either said or sung to Anglican chant. If the minister cannot sing in tune, they can always ask one of the choir to sing the responses on their behalf.

As with a service of Holy Communion from the *Book of Common Prayer*, it is important that the minister is sufficiently familiar with the rhythm and cadences of sixteenth-century prose to be able to lead the office fluently and look at the congregation from time to time, rather than be glued to the book. What follows here is the order for a typical parish church service of Evensong.

Hymn

Introduction

The service begins with the minister reading one or more verses from scripture, as he or she chooses, followed either by the introduction as set out in the 1662 *Book of Common Prayer*: 'Dearly beloved brethren, the scripture moveth us in sundry places …' or the introduction as proposed in the 1928 Prayer Book:

> Beloved, we are come together in the presence of Almighty God and of the whole company of heaven to offer unto him through our Lord Jesus Christ our worship and praise and thanksgiving; to make confession of our sins; to pray, as well for others as for ourselves, that we may know more truly the greatness of God's love and show forth in our lives the fruits of his grace; and to ask on behalf of all men such things as their well-being doth require. Wherefore let us kneel in silence, and remember God's presence with us now.

The introduction is addressed to the congregation; so the minister should look at them and draw them into the text. The congregation and minister then kneel for the confession ('Almighty and most merciful Father …) after which the minister stands to pronounce the absolution. This is a liturgical act, not just a formula of words, and the minister may choose to make the sign of the cross over the congregation at the words, 'He pardoneth and absolveth all them that truly repent.' If not a priest, the minister says the following Collect instead of the absolution:

> Grant, we beseech thee, merciful Lord, to thy faithful people pardon and peace, that they may be cleansed from all their sins and serve thee with a quiet mind through Jesus Christ, thy Son, our Lord. **Amen.**

The minister kneels and leads the congregation in the Lord's Prayer. There is an art to inviting people to join in, and a visiting minister will need to be alert to local customs. In some parishes the minister says, 'Our Father', and the congregation repeats the opening words before going into the rest of the prayer. In other churches a congregation expects simply to continue, saying, 'which art in heaven'. It is also important to ascertain whether a congregation says a modernized form of the traditional version of the Lord's Prayer, substituting 'who' instead of 'which', 'on earth' instead of 'in earth', and 'as we forgive those who trespass against us' in preference to 'as we forgive them that trespass against us'. Whichever version is preferred, it is vital that the minister is consistent and doesn't inadvertently move from one version of the Lord's Prayer to the other, and throw the congregation.

The minister then stands and leads the congregation in the opening versicles and responses:

O Lord, open thou our lips.
And our mouth shall show forth thy praise.
O God, make speed to save us.
O Lord, make haste to help us.

At this point the congregation also stands.

Glory be to the Father, and to the Son, and to the Holy Ghost:
as it was in the beginning, is now, and ever shall be,
world without end. Amen.
Praise ye the Lord.
The Lord's name be praised.

Psalm

The words of which are printed towards the back of the Prayer Book. Each psalm concludes with the *Gloria* (Glory be to the Father …)

Old Testament Reading

The lectionary designates the portion of scripture appointed to be read. Unlike in *Common Worship,* the readings do not end with a response, but rather, 'Here endeth the first/second lesson.'

Magnificat

Although the Prayer Book prints out the words of *Cantate domino,* most churches tend to use only the *Magnificat* and *Nunc dimittis*. It is traditional to stand to say or sing the canticles.

New Testament Reading

Nunc dimittis

The Apostles' Creed

In many parishes it is customary for the minister (and choir) to turn east when reciting the Creed. Some parishioners may also bow their heads when the name of 'Jesus Christ' is mentioned in the Creed, mindful of Paul's words in the Philippian hymn, 'at the name of Jesus every knee shall bow' (Philippians 2.8).

The Prayers

The minister turns to the congregation and greets them, saying (or singing):

> The Lord be with you.
> **And with thy spirit.**
> Let us pray.

All now kneel.

> Lord, have mercy upon us.
> **Christ, have mercy upon us.**
> Lord, have mercy upon us.
>
> **Our Father …**

If Evening Prayer is sung, the minister may find it easier to stand when singing the responses.

> O Lord, show thy mercy upon us.
> **And grant us thy salvation.**
> O Lord, save the Queen.
> **And mercifully hear us when we call upon thee.**
> Endue thy ministers with righteousness.
> **And make thy chosen people joyful.**
> O Lord, save thy people.
> **And bless thine inheritance.**
> Give peace in our time, O Lord.
> **Because there is none other that fighteth for us, but only thou, O God.**
> O God, make clean our hearts within us.
> **And take not thy Holy Spirit from us.**

Collects

The Collects are to be found in the middle of the Prayer Book, one for every Sunday and major Feast Day. The lectionary states what Sunday or Feast Day in the church's year it is. However, it is easy to fall into a trap at this point because the titles of some Sundays and their numbering is different from that in *Common Worship*. For example, the three Sundays before Lent are called respectively Septuagesima, Sexagesima and Quinquagesima, and the Sundays of Eastertide are numbered differently, beginning on Low Sunday. Also in Advent and Lent the Prayer Book stipulates that the Collects for Advent Sunday and Ash Wednesday respectively are to be said additionally throughout the season, thus making four Collects in all. If the Collects are sung, they are normally chanted on a monotone.

Anthem or hymn

In churches with choirs ('in quires and places where they sing', as the Prayer Book has it) there might now follow an anthem. Otherwise there is usually a hymn.

Intercessions

The Prayer Book prints a number of so-called 'State Prayers' at this point. Sometimes it is appropriate to use one or more of these, but most ministers prefer to use a variety of prayers, traditional and contemporary. Unlike the intercessions in *Common Worship* which usually consist of a series of biddings with congregational responses, Evensong lends itself to set prayers, themed with short introductions with space for reflection. It is common for them to conclude with the Prayer of St John Chrysostom (printed at the end of the State Prayers). The intercessions usually conclude with the congregation joining the minister in saying the grace.

Hymn

Sermon

If there is to be a sermon it is usually delivered at this point. In some parishes, however, the sermon comes after the anthem, and is followed by the intercessions.

Hymn (during which a collection may be taken).

Blessing

CHECKLIST

- Ensure the sound system is switched on, and that any radio microphones have charged batteries and are switched to mute.
- Check prayer books, hymnbooks and service sheets are set out.
- Check the Bible on the lectern is open at the right place for the two readings according to the lectionary.
- Ensure that markers are in the right place in the Prayer Book, particularly for the Collect(s).
- Prepare intercessions.
- Light the candles.

Baptisms

Almighty God,
we thank you for our fellowship in the household of faith
with all who have been baptized into your name.
Keep us faithful to our baptism,
and so make us ready for that day
when the whole creation shall be made perfect in your Son,
our Saviour Jesus Christ. **Amen.**

Common Worship

'Baptism marks the beginning of a journey with God which continues for the rest of our lives, the first step in response to God's love' (*Common Worship*). Few would quarrel with the theology, but the pastoral and liturgical reality of administering baptism today can be challenging. When taking place in the context of the Parish Eucharist or of Morning Prayer, the service requires special orchestration, not least because christenings may involve an influx of sixty or more relatives and visitors unfamiliar with church and with little understanding of what baptism signifies. Some visitors may be uninterested, some openly hostile – not joining in the responses, talking and joking through the prayers. It takes huge amounts of a priest's energy to engage with such a congregation and hold the service together.

Baptisms inevitably lengthen a service, and if they are not organized well, the congregation will grow restless or bored or both. It is advisable, therefore, to slim-down the service without losing the overall shape of the liturgy. Have two readings from scripture rather than three; and omit the Prayers of Penitence, the Creed and intercessions. The one thing that should never be sacrificed is the sermon, which is the one time many visitors will ever hear the Gospel expounded. If things do descend into chaos, it is vital that the priest doesn't allow grumpiness or frustration to spill out on the congregation.

For all these reasons it is unwise to hold baptisms during the main service more frequently than once a month. Parishes that have a large number of baptisms during the year often operate a two-tier system, with the option of baptism in the context of the main Sunday service for regular and committed members of the congregation, and a special non-eucharistic service

usually in the afternoon or later on Sunday morning for those who are not. This may not be theologically defensible, but it does make pastoral sense, relieving the pressure on the Parish Eucharist. The corporate nature of the sacrament can be maintained by having three or four baptism families together, and having a team of representative members of the congregation present to assist and welcome them.

The symbolism of baptism is rich. In addition to water, there is the option of anointing and the presentation of lighted candles. A family christening robe can provide a wonderful mission opportunity to engage with the different generations of a family and draw them into conversation, explaining the significance of white robes in a baptism. In some parishes parents and godparents are invited to make the sign of the cross on the forehead of the child, following the action of the priest. This may be done with oil. If handled well, this can be a powerful moment in the liturgy, emphasizing the family's role in bringing their child to baptism, and giving godparents a tangible way of expressing their commitment to the child's Christian nurture.

An increasing number of parishes make provision for the baptism of adults by total immersion, usually linked with their confirmation. This can be a powerful experience, both for the candidate and the congregation. It has also become fashionable to use portable fonts at the front of church for the baptism of children so that everyone can see what's going on. While understandable, this has the unfortunate effect of abandoning traditional fonts which henceforth stand forlorn, dusty and unused at the back of the church. Portable fonts are small and inevitably cannot contain much water, and this weakens the symbolism of baptism as a ritual washing. Far better to get the *whole* congregation out of their seats and gathered round the old font, and to fill it to the brim. If the parish possesses a baptismal ewer, fill that too so that immediately before the 'Prayer over the Water' the priest can pour some additional water into the almost filled font. This way the congregation can both see and hear the sound of running water. Doing a baptism this way has the advantage of creating an atmosphere of informality which can help put visitors at ease as well as counteract a congregation's restlessness. The drama brings the liturgy alive and gives stronger meaning to the sacrament as 'an outward and visible sign of an inward and spiritual grace'.

CHECKLIST

Before the service

- Ensure the sound system is switched on, and that any radio microphones have charged batteries and are switched to mute.

Prepare the font

- Ensure that the font is clean and that the plug is inserted before filling it with water.
- It is good practice to use the font as it was designed and fill it almost to the brim. A small plastic bowl at the bottom of the font containing one inch of water is a poor substitute. If the font leaks, then get it sorted.
- In winter it is a kindness to take the chill off the water by adding some warm water when filling the font.
- If the parish possesses a baptismal ewer, fill it too so that immediately before the 'Prayer over the Water' the priest can pour some additional water into the partially filled font. This way the congregation can both see and hear the sound of water.
- Provide towels according to the number of candidates to be baptized. Purificators tend to be too small and not sufficiently absorbent.
- Place the baptismal shell (if one is used) on the edge of the font for the use of the priest administering the sacrament, together with a small towel.
- If the parish possesses a Paschal Candle, outside Eastertide this may be lodged near the font in witness to the link between baptism and the resurrection. If so, a taper and matches need to be placed at the ready for it to be lit as directed in *Common Worship.* Alternatively, it may be lit throughout the service.

At the front of the nave beforehand

- Ensure the requisite number of seats for the baptismal party have been reserved and equipped with Orders of Service.
- If the sign of the cross is to be made in oil by the priest, have the oil of baptism, together with a purificator or tissue, at the ready. In some parishes parents and godparents are invited to make the sign of the cross on the forehead of the child too. If this custom is observed, particularly if oil is used, they need to be able to wipe surplus oil off their finger afterwards.
- If a lighted candle is to be presented after the baptism, this needs to be ready, together with a taper or matches, and in the right location in the church where this part of the ceremony will take place.

Confirmation

Almighty and ever-living God,
you have given these your servants new birth
in baptism by water and the Spirit,
and have forgiven them all their sins.
Let your Holy Spirit rest upon them:
the Spirit of wisdom and understanding;
the Spirit of counsel and inward strength;
the Spirit of knowledge and true godliness;
and let their delight be in the fear of the Lord. **Amen.**

Common Worship

A Confirmation is a big event in the life of a parish, but being an infrequent occurrence and the liturgy complex it can be difficult to orchestrate well. In addition to the confirmation of candidates, a service may include the baptism of some of them, the reception of a person into the communion of the Church of England, and/or some who wish to reaffirm their baptismal faith. An increasing number of parishes make provision for baptism by total immersion and where this occurs the choreography of the proceedings can be challenging. For all these reasons, an incumbent will need to draw up a special Order of Service as directed by the bishop and tailored to the day.

As with a christening, a Confirmation invariably involves an influx of relatives and visitors who come in support of the candidates, but who may be unfamiliar with customs in church and have minimal understanding of what is going on. It is vital that the welcome is spot on. *Common Worship* makes provision for the giving of testimonies by one or more of the candidates. If done well, this can be an incredibly powerful moment in the liturgy, enabling people (particularly those on the fringe of the church) to make important connections between faith, life and discipleship, and with the liturgy of Christian initiation itself. The best testimonies tend to be those where a person is interviewed. This ensures that a person does not go off at a tangent or speak for too long. But equally moving can be the inclusion of candidates' reasons for being confirmed in an annex to the Order of Service.

It is always good to encourage candidates to participate in the service, perhaps by reading the lessons or choosing the hymns and music. If the service is held within the context of the Eucharist, as *Common Worship* encourages, then it will also be important to decide whether the candidates come forward to receive communion together in advance of the rest of the congregation, or whether they come up with their friends and families.

The liturgical colour used at Confirmations will vary from parish to parish, and indeed from diocese to diocese. White tends to be the default option, but some bishops encourage red in honour of the Holy Spirit. By custom, if the readings are specially chosen for the service and are proper to the rite, then the Collect will be that for a Confirmation and the liturgical colour white. However, if the Confirmation is held on a Feast Day or Festival such as Easter, Pentecost or a Patronal Festival, then the readings and Collect will be proper to the day, and the liturgical colour appropriate to the season or feast being celebrated.

CHECKLIST

This checklist provides general guidance in the organization of the liturgy which will need to be shaped by the directions of the bishop.

Before the service

- Ensure the sound system is switched on, that any radio microphones have charged batteries and are switched to mute.
- Position the Bishop's Chair as directed. Be ready, if requested, to provide him with a small table or stool on which he can place his books and mitre.
- Check with the bishop where he would like his pastoral staff to be placed when not needed, and at what parts of the service he will require it.
- Ensure the requisite number of seats for the candidates have been reserved and equipped with Orders of Service.
- If the candidates are supported by sponsors, they will need to be seated nearby.
- If any candidates are also to be baptized, they will need to sit together, preferably at the end of a row so that they can easily get out when standing before the bishop.
- If the sign of the cross is to be made on their foreheads with oil, have the oil of baptism ready, together with a purificator or tissue.
- If the parish possesses a Paschal Candle, outside Eastertide this may be lodged near the font in witness to the link between baptism/confirmation and the resurrection. If so, a taper and matches need to be placed ready for it to be lit as directed in *Common Worship*. Alternatively, the candle may be moved to the front of the nave for the whole service and lit there.

If any candidates are to be baptized or if the renewal of Baptismal Promises is to take place around the font

- Ensure that the font is clean and that the plug is inserted before filling it with water.
- It is good practice to fill the font almost to the brim. A small plastic bowl at the bottom of the font containing one inch of water is a poor 'outward and visible sign of an inward and spiritual grace'.
- If the parish possesses a baptismal ewer, fill it so that, if desired, the bishop can pour some additional water into the font before the 'Prayer over the Water'. That way the congregation can both see and hear the sound of water.
- Provide towels according to the number of candidates to be baptized.
- Place the baptismal shell (if one is used) on the edge of the font for the use of the bishop when administering the sacrament, together with a small towel for him to dry his hands afterwards.
- If the candidates are to be sprinkled with baptismal water in preference to them making the sign of the cross themselves, provide the bishop either with an aspergillum or a small bunch of twigs (usually of rosemary) for the purpose.

At the Confirmation

- The bishop will direct whether candidates are to be confirmed individually, in pairs, or in a line. He will also indicate if he prefers to confirm standing or seated. If candidates are to kneel before him, ensure that a kneeler is located by the Bishop's Chair.
- If the candidates are to be anointed by the bishop, have the oil of chrism, together with a purificator or tissue, at the ready. When all have been anointed, the bishop may wish to cleanse his fingers, particularly if there have been a large number of candidates. Ideally have a lavabo bowl and towel ready, the bowl filled with water. A piece of lemon helps remove any surplus oil.

At the Sending Out

- If the candidates are to be presented with lighted candles at the end of the service and perhaps led out by the bishop, choose decent sized candles preferably with a cardboard drip shield so the candidates don't get covered with hot wax. Have them ready, together with a taper to light them efficiently.

Aftercare

- If there are to be photos, it is good to do them at the end of the service at the back of church before people disperse. A note to this effect can be put in the Order of Service for the benefit of relatives and friends.
- If gifts and/or confirmation certificates are to be given to the candidates, the bishop may appreciate being directed to a table where he can speak to the candidates most conveniently and sign certificates.

Weddings

I cannot fix on the hour, or the spot, or the look, or the words, which laid the foundation. It is too long ago. I was in the middle before I knew that I had begun.

Mr Darcy to Elizabeth Bennet, Jane Austen, *Pride and Prejudice*

The steady decline in the number of marriages solemnized in the Church of England led to the commissioning of the Weddings Project. The results of its national survey make interesting reading and its findings are already re-shaping the way clergy engage with couples and conduct marriages. Those who want a church wedding do so for a variety of reasons. Some are faithful Christians. Brought up in the life and worship of the Church, a wedding in the parish church is their natural choice. For others, the choice of a church wedding may be more a matter of tradition or a family connection with a particular church or minister. Others simply want their wedding to be in a pretty country church rather than a posh hotel or a secular venue. Although claiming not to be particularly religious, they value the dignity that the Church of England brings to the occasion.

Research has revealed that it is the quality of the relationship between the priest who will perform the ceremony and the couple getting married that matters most. This finding comes as a huge affirmation of clergy, some of whom have lost confidence in their role. The initial contact with the church or clergyperson will be key to whether a couple, exploring various options, choose a church wedding or take their custom elsewhere. The way the parish administrator answers the phone or responds to an email, and the voice and tone of the message on the vicarage answerphone are all important. For a young couple making the inquiry this is the voice of the church speaking.

Most couples are unlikely to have met or spoken to a priest before. Uncertainty about banns and the legal preliminaries to marriage, combined with a general nervousness of the clergy, can make these early conversations stilted. They want advice and guidance, and value a sense of the priest being alongside them, but will be sensitive to being patronized. Clergy can be intimidating. Social mores have changed since the time when Jane Austen described the courtship of Elizabeth Bennet by the inscrutable Mr Darcy. Today cohabitation before marriage is frequent, and some presenting couples may already have children. Clergy need to watch what they say and indeed their body language so that nothing may be interpreted as judgemental. Whatever a couple's circumstances, they need to know they are special, and they need to hear that from the vicar, certainly if they are to be receptive to any Christian teaching.

Couples bring with them a variety of expectations of their wedding, often with little or no Christian background. In terms of church services, two basic options are open to them: either the traditional Marriage service as set down in the Prayer Book or as modified in 1928; or the modern language service as set out in *Common Worship: Pastoral Services*. Legally, the choice is the minister's, though most clergy will be sensitive to the wishes of the couple. There is little room for manoeuvre in the liturgy. The declarations, texts of the marriage vows, and giving and receiving of ring(s) are all mandatory. There is, however, considerable flexibility in the choice of readings and prayers. It is these that enable a service to be customized to suit the couple.

Music makes a special contribution to the character of a wedding, but couples today are unlikely to be familiar with the traditional church repertoire of hymns and organ voluntaries. If at all possible, it is good to provide a couple with a CD of potential music for them to go away with and listen to at their leisure. Churches with good sound systems can offer a greater degree of flexibility in the choice of music, something that is taken for granted in secular venues.

The majority of the population today instinctively turn to the internet for information. This is particularly the case for a younger generation who will scour the web for the right venue for their wedding. Traditional legal requirements of residency will mean little to them. Parishes that have up-to-date websites are immediately at an advantage here. Church websites need to carry basic information about what options are available, who to contact, what the legal preliminaries are, what a wedding in church costs, *and* what Christians believe about marriage and family life. Basic information combined with good photographs is a winning combination.

Some clergy make the mistake of beginning the service with a list of ten things people are not to do, such as throw confetti, take photographs during the service, use their mobile phones etc. These things are all relevant, but it is important to find ways of saying them without being hectoring. Otherwise we will put the congregation on edge and shut down the chances of them hearing anything about God. Simply standing at the front of the church and smiling helps. Suggest that people are welcome to take photographs of the couple in the church *after* the service, and that confetti is best reserved for the reception when the couple leave for their honeymoon etc. Lightness of touch is essential.

In an age when most people could not read, marriage vows were repeated parrot-fashion after the priest. Today other possibilities present themselves. Some brave couples learn their vows off by heart, reassured by the presence of the priest standing beside them to prompt if they stumble. The advantage of such a venture is that (hopefully) the vows will stay with them for the rest of their lives. It is equally possible for a couple to read the vows to each other from cards, specially produced for the occasion and handed to them by the priest at the appropriate moment in the service. Whichever way a couple elects, what is important is that they turn and face each other for this solemn moment. After all, they are marrying one another, not the vicar!

CHECKLIST

At the rehearsal

- Check that all legalities have been observed and that all documentation is in order. If the marriage is to take place following banns, ensure that the couple has the requisite Banns Certificate(s). It is illegal to proceed without one.
- Check with the couple who they wish to be their witnesses at the Signing of the Registers. Traditionally, this is often the fathers of the bride and groom, but this should never be presumed. To avoid any embarrassment, sort it out in advance.
- Establish the parameters to be observed by photographers and sound recordists. Better to negotiate well in advance of the service, than five minutes beforehand.

Before the service

- Ensure that reserved parking signs are set outside the church early on to safeguard space for the bride's car and those carrying the immediate family.
- Reserve sufficient seating at the front of the church for family and close friends, and ensure their seats are equipped with Orders of Service, including spares for the bridesmaids.
- Some parishes have special chairs or faldstools for the use of the bride and groom. If so, these need to be positioned in advance of the service.
- Ensure the sound system is switched on, and that any radio microphones have charged batteries and are switched to mute.

- If members of the family or friends are to do readings, identify them in advance of the service to ensure they know where they are to read from. Advise them about the sound system as necessary.
- Set out the registers, together with a fountain pen containing Registrar's ink, blotting paper – and a spare pen just in case. Double-check that all the information is correctly entered.
- Light the candles.
- If a Nuptial Mass is celebrated, by custom white vestments are worn.

Funerals

For everything there is a season,
and a time for every matter under heaven:
a time to be born, and a time to die.

Ecclesiastes 3.1

God be in my head,
and in my understanding.
God be in my eyes,
and in my looking.
God be in my mouth,
and in my speaking.
God be in my heart,
and in my loving.
God be at mine end,
and at my departing.

from the *Sarum Primer* (1514)

Funerals are one of the most important aspects of our mission and ministry. It is a huge privilege to be with families in their loss and to journey with them in their bereavement. But attitudes to death and to funerals are changing. The number of non-religious or 'secular' funerals is on the increase. In some urban areas, these now account for 40 per cent of all funerals. A new cadre of humanist 'celebrants' has emerged in recent years, many of whom do a very good job.

Those who continue to look to the church in bereavement do so for a variety of reasons. For some, the choice of an Anglican funeral is admittedly a matter of convention or family tradition. For others, it is a connection with a particular church or, more likely, a particular minister. But many are faithful Anglicans and loyal members of our congregations. Others, although not regular church attenders, still see the Church of England as a benign institution to which they are linked, however tenuously, and which can bring significance in the face of death. But this is a diminishing constituency. Increasingly, people are claiming to be 'spiritual' but not 'religious', though they may not necessarily be ready to tick the box 'no religion' on a census form. And it is this constituency which secular or humanist celebrants are capturing and which we need to win back as part of our mission.

How we engage with this diverse clientele and respond to their expectations will determine many people's future attitude to the church and all things Christian. The bereaved seek comfort and help in their hour of need, but invariably bring with them a clutch of inchoate beliefs, often with little or no Christian background to shape them. Clergy are familiar with funerals, crematoria and cemeteries, but can easily forget that for most people a funeral is an occasional event. Uncertainty about procedure or nervousness of the clergy are amplified in bereavement.

People want advice and guidance, and value a sense of the minister being alongside them, but are sensitive to being patronized, bullied or judged. As with weddings, it is the quality of the relationship with the officiating minister that matters most to the bereaved, and the initial encounter sets the tone for what follows. Even the voice of the recorded message on the vicarage or parish office answerphone is important because for them at that moment it is the voice of the church speaking.

Observations and perceptions

Recent research conducted by the University of Chester into funerals in the Warrington area surveyed both funeral directors and the experience of the bereaved before and after the funeral. There was the occasional horror story of clergy, but by and large the research reveals that Anglican ministers are reliable and do a good job.

That said, a frequent gripe of funeral directors is that clergy, unlike our secular competitors, are slow to agree to conduct a funeral; do not return phone calls promptly and sometimes not at all. By contrast, humanist celebrants respond punctually to the phone calls of undertakers and with generosity to the requests of the bereaved. Typically, they are courteous, well-turned out, and professional in their dealings, recognizing that undertakers are often under huge pressure from a bereaved family to finalize arrangements. Sadly, some clergy will only conduct the funerals of known members of their congregations. In the words of one undertaker, 'There are clergy who serve the public, and those who think the public serve them.'

Most seriously, in company with some of their clients, many of the funeral directors consulted see the Church of England as old-fashioned, tired and inflexible. They report that the funerals conducted by (admittedly) a minority of clergy are woefully *impersonal*. Apparently some ministers still refer to the deceased as 'our dear brother/sister departed' and never mention the person's name. Although a small minority, such ministers fuel the church's reputation for cold formality. Increasingly funerals are bespoke, and in an age where the relational and informality are paramount too many clergy and Readers are not connecting with people. Funeral directors insist that the church must change and adapt, or the growth in secular funerals will continue unabated.

Positively, according to the funeral directors, what distinguishes Anglican funerals from those conducted by humanist celebrants are three things.

- First, a distinctive understanding of death and a belief in the transformative power of the resurrection.
- We offer hope, whereas secular celebrants offer only empathy.
- We offer pastoral care. The involvement of a civil or secular celebrant with a bereaved family finishes at the cemetery gate. A Christian minister is committed to the on-going pastoral care of the bereaved in the months that follow.

At a funeral the bereaved are uniquely receptive to what a minister has to say. We should have more confidence in speaking of God and his love for us in Jesus Christ. Sharing our convictions about death and resurrection is not to be confused with being arrogant. Being confident and being pastorally sensitive are not mutually exclusive.

Obviously if pastoral care is to be a reality and not just a slogan, then we need to identify members of our congregations with good listening skills to be trained as bereavement visitors, mindful of the fact that three months after a funeral is often the low point in bereavement. Following-up on funerals is too big a job and too important a task to be left simply to the clergy. The bespoke nature of funerals these days means that they can be enormously time-consuming. It would be good if over-stretched clergy were more ready to share the load with Readers who have been duly trained and authorized to take funerals, rather than serve up something which is half-baked or rushed. We talk about lay ministry – this is where we need to walk the talk.

Given the findings of this research, one issue that does need to be addressed with urgency is the church's reputation for inflexibility. An Anglican Funeral service, whether held in a church or at a crematorium, no less than a 'secular' funeral conducted by a humanist celebrant, can and should be tailored to the requirements of the bereaved. The funeral of Diana, Princess of Wales, in Westminster Abbey was described at the time as unique 'as befits the unique person she was'. But every person is unique in God's eyes. If we can do it for royalty and the famous, we can also do it for the old gentleman who lived round the corner who ran the newsagents.

Improving the quality of our Funeral services

The Funeral service as authorized in *Common Worship: Pastoral Services* provides an authorized structure with considerable flexibility in how it should be organized. Certain parts of the service, such as the commendation and farewell, and the committal, have authorized words. These are strong moments in the service that require dignity and formality. But elsewhere *Common Worship* provides a choice of prayers, together with suggestions for psalms and readings from scripture which a minister can and should adapt and supplement according to pastoral need.

A well-planned Funeral service should include the sharing of memories and give expression to the variety of feelings that may be present. There may be a mixture of love, grief, anger, guilt, sadness and respect in the congregation. The service should provide a fitting tribute to the deceased in the belief that every person is precious to God, and often this is best done by a member of the family. There should also be an acknowledgement of the finality of death in the belief that Jesus Christ is 'the resurrection and the life'.

The expectations of those wanting a funeral in church, as opposed to those wanting a service just at the crematorium or at the graveside, will vary enormously. A family may request that the coffin be brought into church overnight. They may request that the funeral take place in the context of a celebration of the Eucharist and be a Requiem Mass. Families of African or West Indian descent may request an open coffin, with the whole congregation filing past during the commendation and farewell. By contrast, it is becoming customary in some circles for the committal to take place privately and in advance of the Funeral service which then takes on the character of a Memorial service. In my view, this development should be resisted. This reversal of the traditional order may be designed to meet the needs of hospitality to those who have travelled long distances, but it disables the majority of mourners from coming to terms with their loss. Seeing the coffin brings home the reality of death. Its absence confuses people. When death is tidied away we damage ourselves.

Music

As far as music is concerned, a congregation at a funeral today is more likely to know the words of Frank Sinatra's song, 'I did it my way', than the words of the twenty-third psalm. Re-connecting people with scripture and the riches of the Christian tradition is a challenge, but one that we should not draw back from. Some ministers provide the bereaved with a booklet of twenty or so popular hymns in advance of a funeral to help them decide, and this can be hugely helpful. Churches with good sound systems can offer a bereaved family additional flexibility in the choice of music, something that is taken for granted in crematoria. Unfamiliar with most hymns, some bereaved people fear to voice their preferred choice of music lest it be scorned by the vicar and, as a result, opt for a 'non-religious' funeral conducted by a secular celebrant as the easiest way out. Of course, not all pop music will be suitable in the context of a Christian funeral, but generosity is more likely to win us friends than what may be perceived as cultural snobbishness. We need to draw people in with their choice of music, not alienate them.

What our buildings can offer

Unlike crematoria where the slot allowed for a funeral is strictly limited and seating is restricted, our churches offer huge flexibility. We have far more space available and can allow the service much more time, but we are often shy advocates of what our buildings can offer. When a funeral takes place entirely at the crematorium, a family can ask for a longer slot than is customary and this can be arranged by negotiation, but it is likely to incur additional charges for them. We need to encourage people to come into church for their funeral. This will pay dividends further down the line. Otherwise whole rafts of people will never have had cause to cross the thresholds of our buildings. This should also give added impetus to making our buildings fit for purpose in the twenty-first century.

A church equipped with modern technology and overhead projection can display photographs of the deceased either before or during the service.

Obviously this will not be appropriate in every context, but sometimes it can be very moving. Orders of Service carrying a photograph of the deceased on the front cover, or an enlarged photograph of the deceased on a notice on entering the church, can similarly help personalize a funeral. An Order of Service can also carry information about church services on the back cover, together with contact details, and a brief statement about Christian belief. These are the things that add value to the 'church experience'.

Communication

The majority of the population today instinctively turn to the internet for information, including what to do in the face of death. Parishes that have up-to-date websites are immediately at an advantage here. Church websites need to carry basic information about what options are available when planning a funeral, who to contact, and what Christians believe. A regular and concerted charm offensive with local undertakers will also pay dividends. Whether clergy like it or not, funeral directors will always be the first port-of-call of the bereaved, and we need them on our side. They are the gate-keepers and they have enormous influence on a bereaved family. To put it bluntly, there are few better ways of ensuring that funerals come our way than in making friends with the local undertakers.

A funeral can provide an opportunity to build bridges with the local community many of whom may never have had any contact with the church – or indeed re-build bridges where relationships have come under strain. A 'good funeral' is a good advert for the church. The reverse is also true. In the current free-for-all funeral market we need to have greater confidence in our funeral ministry. We also need to raise our game and be known for the quality with which we conduct funerals and for the care we extend to the bereaved.

CHECKLIST

Given the variety of permutations that are possible, the following checklist relates only to a funeral in church.

- Ensure that reserved parking signs are set outside the church early on for the hearse and cars carrying the immediate family.
- Ensure the sound system is switched on, that any radio microphones have charged batteries and are switched to mute.
- Reserve sufficient seating at the front of the church for family and immediate mourners, and make sure they are equipped with Orders of Service. Try to gauge accurate numbers in advance to avoid over-estimating the seating required, and leaving empty pews behind the immediate family who then feel exposed.
- The coffin is normally placed at the front of the nave, feet facing east. Funeral directors normally come with trestles in two sizes: tall and short. If the custom is to cover the coffin with a pall, tall trestles will be necessary. Otherwise the shorter trestles may be more convenient.
- In addition to flowers and a pall, a Bible or cross may be placed on the coffin, or symbols of the deceased's life, such as military medals.
- In some parishes by tradition the coffin is surrounded by bier lights. There may be two, four or six of these large free-standing candle-sticks, according to custom, set out in pairs. It used to be customary for their candles to be of unbleached wax, but this is now rare.
- In churches that have a Paschal Candle, this may be placed at the foot of the chancel steps or adjacent to the coffin 'in sure and certain hope of the resurrection to eternal life through our Lord Jesus Christ'.
- At the commendation and farewell, it is good practice for the minister to stand beside the coffin, placing his or her hand on it while speaking. The immediate family may be invited to gather round the coffin at this point. If necessary, the bier lights should be moved.

- At the commendation or at its conclusion, the minister may sprinkle the coffin with holy water, walking around it. If this is customary, have the holy water bucket and aspergillum to hand.
- If a body is to be received in church overnight in advance of the funeral, the minister may elect to sprinkle the coffin at this point. If this is customary, the holy water bucket and aspergillum need to be at hand.
- If a Requiem Mass is celebrated, the priest may wear purple, black or white vestments according to local custom.

Leading Public Worship: A beginner's guide for lay people

When things go wrong it's rather tame
To find we are ourselves to blame,
It gets the trouble over quicker
To go and blame things on the Vicar.

John Betjeman (1906–84), 'Blame the Vicar'

In the Church of England all authorized ministers, whether ordained or lay, make a solemn declaration when they are licensed by the bishop that in public prayer [and in the administration of the sacraments] they 'will use only the forms of service which are authorized or allowed by Canon'. Increasingly, however, churchwardens and other lay folk can find themselves thrust into the limelight to lead worship, often with little or no warning. Perhaps the vicar is ill or on holiday, or the Reader from the neighbouring parish scheduled to take Morning Prayer fails to turn up. What then? It is one thing to have sat in the pew for years, but quite another to stand at the front of church and lead the worship.

Here are some general guidelines, together with some tips.

Guidelines and tips

- Before the service, discuss with the organist/music group how you will announce hymns. Some churches prefer minimal announcements; others like everything announced. Some musicians strike up as soon as you announce the number; others will expect you to give a short introduction.
- When people are nervous they tend to gabble or swallow their words. Try to pace yourself. Try not to let your voice drop, particularly at the end of sentences.
- When introducing parts of the service or making links, turn towards the congregation and look at them.
- Write your links on little 'post-it' notes and stick them in your prayer book or Order of Service.
- Try to keep your links short – generally one sentence. For example, 'Our second hymn, number 634, picks up the theme of God's faithfulness.' Try not to preach a sermon before each hymn.
- Don't feel you always have to say something that 'links' rather than simply announce a reading or hymn.
- If you ask people to stand or sit, give them time to do so before you carry on.
- If others are participating in the service, such as leading the intercessions, there may be a theme or something to pick up on, once you become confident enough to *ad lib*.
- Unless you are sure everyone knows their way round the service, you may need to give out page numbers or some guidance without being pedantic. As with hymn numbers, it's best to give the page number before you give the link so that people can be finding their place. For example, 'On page 61 we join in singing the Song of Mary – the *Magnificat*'; *not* 'We are now going to sing the *Magnificat*, the Song of Mary, to be found on page 61.'

Some bad habits to avoid

- Asking a question, rather than giving a direction. For example, 'Shall we pray?' *Or better*: 'Please sit or kneel for the prayers.'

- Becoming a 'salad leader' – be careful not to start every sentence with 'Let us'.
- Being pedantic or bossy.
- Being apologetic.
- Not being ready with the right link at the right time.

What lay people can and can't do in the Church of England

- Absolution – you should use the 'we' and 'us' forms; or else the following Collect at Matins and Evensong:

  Grant, we beseech thee, merciful Lord, to thy faithful people pardon and peace, that they may be cleansed from all their sins and serve thee with a quiet mind through Jesus Christ thy Son our Lord.

- Blessing – you should use the 'we' and 'us' forms; or else simply conclude with the Grace.
- Baptism – lay people cannot conduct baptisms except in life-threatening situations.
- A lay person may not preside at Holy Communion.
- A lay person is not authorized to solemnize a marriage in church.
- Certain lay people, including some Readers, may be trained and given permission to take funerals with the support of their incumbent and the family concerned.
- A lay person may preach on occasions at the invitation of the incumbent, but not on a regular basis. The bishop's licence or permission is required for anyone to preach on a regular basis.

Leading Public Worship: Processions and protocols

A procession is a distinct, significant act of worship. It is not an aimless walk round the church. It must have a definite objective.

Percy Dearmer (1867–1936), *The Parson's Handbook*

Processions have an interesting history. The Bible records several religious processions: the encircling of the walls of Jericho (Joshua 6), the bringing of the Ark up into Jerusalem by King David to the accompaniment of psalms and music (2 Samuel 6.1), and most famously Jesus' triumphal entry into Jerusalem on Palm Sunday. In Christian worship the earliest recorded processions were sung litanies, punctuated by periodic stopping-places or 'stations' for prayer. During medieval times the popularity of such processions multiplied. There were processions of pilgrims to the shrines of saints, Rogationtide processions around fields for the blessing of crops, and processions of the Blessed Sacrament on the Feast of Corpus Christi. Above all, there was a steady stream of pilgrims to the Holy Land, visiting sites associated with Jesus' Passion, real and supposed. By identifying more closely with Christ, particularly in his last and painful journey to the cross, Christians hoped to be able to pray more fervently and more effectively. It is likely that the devotion of Stations of the Cross in humble parish churches across Europe evolved as a conscious attempt to recreate (or perhaps provide a substitute for) this processional route in Jerusalem. As a result, every village and town could walk the *Via Dolorosa*.

The Reformers rebelled against superstition and abuses connected with processions, and in large part abandoned them, together with the litanies that accompanied them. Unusually, Cranmer retained a litany in his new English Prayer Book. Additionally he stipulated the observance of three processions: the procession to the altar in the Marriage service, the procession to the font in Baptism, and the procession at a funeral when the minister leads the coffin into church for the Burial service, and subsequently to the graveside for the committal. These exceptions aside, the reaction against medieval practice meant that Anglican worship soon became largely sedentary.

With the revival of ceremony in the nineteenth century, customs and fashions began to change with the result that today congregations are once again used to getting out of their seats and moving around the church, learning to worship with their bodies and not merely with their minds and hearts. The restrained observances of the Prayer Book have long been supplemented by the revival of the Palm Sunday procession, sometimes complete with donkey, candlelit processions at Christmas and Candlemas, and in rural areas by the ceremony of beating of the bounds at Rogationtide. A public procession of witness on Good Friday, often organized ecumenically, is a regular feature in many towns. Each of these processions has, in the words of Percy Dearmer, its own 'objective'.

Entrance procession

The Church of England is famous for its ordered worship and dignified processions, particularly on state occasions. But how does this 'pomp and circumstance' translate into the life of an ordinary parish church? For example, how should ministers and those leading worship enter church at the beginning of a service? Much will depend on the context, on the geography of the building, and the particular service in question.

At an early celebration of Prayer Book Holy Communion it is not unusual for the entire congregation to sink to its knees when the priest walks in.

This is in marked contrast to most other services. Indeed, in an age of informality where the accent is on dressing-down, some churches have dispensed with all ceremony. Ministers may come into church informally and take their places, the congregation remaining seated. In some high church parishes, perhaps as a corrective to earlier triumphalism, clergy may similarly elect to assemble quietly in church well in advance of the service in order to pray and be properly recollected. Having the President of the Eucharist vested and seated in prayer can certainly be effective in bringing a measure of stillness to a congregation and discouraging endless chatter.

In the majority of parishes, however, clergy, choir and servers process into church in order, often to the accompaniment of the organ or while singing a processional hymn. On high days and holy days, a strong processional hymn such as 'For All the Saints' can inject a burst of energy and create a sense of celebration in the gathering for worship. That said, any dramatic effect will be lost if the first glimpse the congregation has of the procession is the vicar and servers slinking down the side aisle, trying not to be seen. Weather permitting, it is always more effective to go round the outside of the church and come in the main doors. Processions need to keep moving too. The Anglican snail's pace shuffling up the aisle does not exactly communicate vitality.

The virtue of an entrance procession, particularly in large churches, is that it ensures that those at the back of the church feel included. There is a sense of them literally being gathered into the assembly by a procession as they see the ministers who will be leading the worship who might otherwise be disembodied voices. Cathedrals and large parish churches may mark major festivals with a more elaborate procession. In a few churches, somewhat bizarrely, the choir and ministers come in and then embark upon a perambulation around the building. To what purpose, one might ask?

The order of an entrance procession (and recessional) will vary according to the occasion. Some liturgical aficionados, loyal to medieval 'English Usage', observe the convention of the ministers walking before rather than after the choir in a procession, but this is the exception rather than the rule today. Basically, there is no right way. Do what works best. In parishes with robed choir and servers, the entrance procession at a Eucharist may be led by the crucifer, followed by the choir, with the servers and clergy taking up the rear as follows:

Crucifer
Acolytes / taperers
Choir
Readers
Assistant Ministers
President

Alternatively, there may be two processions, with the 'sanctuary party' following the choir into church who have gone ahead to lead the singing of the first hymn. In churches that have a verger, he or she may lead the choir in. The order for a 'sanctuary party' might be:

[Thurifer]
Crucifer
Acolytes / taperers
Assistant Ministers
[Deacon]
President

English Usage has a further variant on this order with the thurifer following the crucifer and acolytes, rather than being out at the front leading the procession. In some servers' manuals, the crucifer and acolytes (also known as taperers) are referred to as 'cross and lights'. The procession may also include a deacon, bearing aloft the Gospel Book, banner bearers, and a senior server known as the 'Master of Ceremonies' or MC.

Civic processions

The protocol for welcoming a Lord Lieutenant, a new mayor or civic dignitary to church is guaranteed to generate anxiety. When dealing with visiting dignitaries it is important to be clear about the order of precedence. The Lord Lieutenant or High Sheriff of a county, as representative of the sovereign, always takes precedence over a mayor, or the chairman of the local or county council. In any procession, the person taking precedence enters the church last and leaves first. If there is any doubt, then it is advisable to consult the Clerk of the Lieutenancy in the county.

By custom, seating for dignitaries is normally reserved in the front rows of the north side of the nave, though some collegiate and historic churches boast a Mayor's Pew. Ensuring that there is adequate reserved parking, that dignitaries are welcomed and personally escorted to their seats is a matter of courtesy. Local conventions will vary with regard to the order of processions. In some ancient boroughs where it is customary for the mayor and corporation to attend an annual civic service, the mayor may lead councillors into church. In others, councillors attending the service may elect to be seated beforehand, the mayor's procession entering separately led by the Mace Bearer bearing the town mace.

When the bishop comes

A visit of the bishop is equally guaranteed to generate anxiety. In general, the organization of the service, particularly if it is a Confirmation or the inauguration of a new ministry, will be shaped by the directions of the bishop, but he will want to be sensitive to the tradition of the parish. With responsibility for a number of parishes, he is unlikely to remember all the customs of a parish and will want time beforehand to familiarize himself with the way worship is conducted. If the bishop is accompanied by his chaplain, he or she will assist in the laying out of the bishop's robes and crozier (pastoral staff). If not, ask the bishop if someone might serve as his chaplain, holding his staff and/or book as requested.

Specifically:

- The bishop may choose to preside from his chair, and this may entail it being moved from its customary position (normally in the north side of the sanctuary) to the front of the nave or chancel.
- Be ready, if requested, to provide him with a small table or stool on which he can place his books and mitre.
- Check with the bishop where he would like his pastoral staff to be placed when not needed, and at what parts of the service he will require it.

In a procession the bishop enters last, preceded by the churchwardens, bearing their wands of office, who walk behind the incumbent, escorting the bishop to his seat before returning to their own places. A bishop's chaplain follows a few paces behind the bishop. During a service the chaplain normally stands just behind the bishop's left shoulder, holding as required the bishop's staff. The reason for this is because a bishop holds the staff in his left hand and blesses with his right hand.

4

ENRICHING THE CHRISTIAN YEAR

All occasions invite God's mercies,
and all times are his seasons.

John Donne (1572–1631)

INTRODUCTION

Human life is rhythmic. Our bodies have cycles, oscillating between activity and sleep, responding to the daily alternation of light and darkness. In relation to this we construct the pattern of our lives, our days and our weeks, our terms and our vacations, our times of work and our periods of rest and relaxation. Much contemporary living distorts or obscures these patterns. Urban living masks the changing seasons. Electric light mitigates our dependence on daylight. The abundance of food on supermarket shelves throughout the year protects us from the vicissitudes of seedtime and harvest. But in the end there is no escaping the fundamental rhythms of nature of which our bodies are a part.

Over the centuries the church has crafted a rhythm of worship and prayer that shapes Christian life. Beginning afresh on Advent Sunday, the liturgical year is constructed around seasons and observances. It sets time against eternity. It celebrates an understanding of the world as the theatre of God's grace, and sees human beings as created beings searching for meaning and purpose in response to his call. To some the church's feasts and fasts are anachronisms, echoes of an antique drum we no longer follow. But if celebrated imaginatively these ancient and trusted landmarks can be powerful signposts in an otherwise barren spiritual landscape by which to plot a course through life.

The Christian annual cycle of commemorations is laid over the rhythm of the week as first shaped by Judaism. 'Remember the Sabbath day, and keep it holy' (Exodus 20.8). There is something unique about the Jewish Sabbath with its strict emphasis upon rest from human effort and achievement. The Sabbath is to be a day of peace and quiet before God, not a day of religious striving to find God. This understanding was incorporated by Christians into their observance of Sunday, with the result that every Sunday became not only a weekly celebration of the Lord's resurrection, but also a Christian Sabbath.

The church's seasons (*temporale*) coalesce into two liturgical cycles celebrating respectively the Incarnation (Advent to Candlemas), and the crucifixion and resurrection of Our Lord (Ash Wednesday to Pentecost). In addition the year is peppered with saints' days (*sanctorale*) which provide opportunities to reflect upon the faithful discipleship of Christians down the ages, giving names and faces to the otherwise unseen 'cloud of witnesses' that surrounds us. With the exception of Easter, this form of personal com-memoration antedated the emergence of the seasons of the Christian Year as we know it today. Taken together, however, the two liturgical forms cre-ate a counterpoint which excites the Christian imagination, enabling people to meditate systematically upon the truth at the heart of the Gospel that 'God was in Christ reconciling the world to himself' (2 Corinthians 5.19).

The sociologist, Andreas Huyssen, describes Western culture as a 'culture of amnesia'.[1] We are losing our corporate memory, and without a corpo-rate memory society will lose its way. So can the church. Wisdom is easily lost in a morass of information. Shameful episodes in history are not con-fronted. Lessons from church history are not learned. Theological insights hard fought over are forgotten. Bereaved of the past, we become impris-oned in the present, vulnerable to the claims of expediency; and when we are selective in what we remember we end up being economical with the truth. In partnership with scripture, one of the functions of the liturgical year is to safeguard the collective memory of the church. As year succeeds year and we reflect on the witness of our forebears, they emerge as a vibrant company of voices which affirm and challenge us. They root our discipleship and give us fresh energy.

The rhythm of the Christian Year affects those who allow themselves to be shaped by it. Historically it has been one of the primary ways in which Christians have appropriated the Christian story and been nurtured by it. In our current state of cultural amnesia, however, this is no longer obviously the case. The challenge is to find ways of enabling a new generation to explore the riches of the Christian Year and to live its rhythm.

There are already numerous collections of prayers and readings either in print or on the web that celebrate the seasons of the church, together with a comprehensive set of authorized liturgical material in *Common Worship:*

135

Times and Seasons, and there is no point in duplicating here what is already freely available. What is offered instead is a selection of innovative examples of how to enrich worship on the feasts and fasts of the Christian Year, and how to bridge the yawning gap between what goes on at church and what happens in the home. Included is some liturgical material, together with commentary and information on a host of practical things from where to get the ash on Ash Wednesday to how you inscribe a Paschal Candle. These rituals and ceremonies are significant because they help us remember; and when we remember we become more open to the transforming power of the grace of God.

Many rural parishes are actively promoting a 'rural cycle' of special services as a way of engaging with local farmers and the wider agricultural community, and are doing so with considerable success. Plough Sunday, Rogationtide, Lammastide and Harvest now shape the rural year alongside the great Christian festivals, and information on two of these celebrations is included here. But we should also note other landmarks in the 'secular' year and see how they too can be Christianized. Valentine's Day on 14 February is big business. Ironically, the greeting card industry and restaurateurs are capitalizing upon a saint's day. Perhaps we might piggy-back on their success and invite people recently married in the parish or who are planning a wedding to a special service, perhaps including the renewal of marriage vows?

Mothering Sunday has long been on the church's radar as the perfect opportunity to reach out to children and parents, but so is Fathers' Day. It is being aggressively marketed, at least to judge by the advertising on television. If card manufacturers and the promoters of 'man-gifts' are on to it, why aren't we? Christians have something important to say about fatherhood, family values and indeed God, our heavenly Father. The football season is over. Why not *invite the Dads*? It would be great to have a special All-Age service that boosted masculinity in the church.

Finally, Hallowe'en continues to gain ground. Along with Santa Claus it is another example of the gradual commercialization and Disney-fication of Western culture. But what are we offering? November is the month of remembrance, and if nothing else it would be good if churches did something special for the bereaved at this season. Ideas for this are included in All Saints and All Souls at the end of the section.

A cursory look at church history reveals how adept our Christian fore-bears were at baptizing pagan rituals and giving them Christian content. There is always risk in such a strategy, but there is also virtue in using society's landmarks in a missional way and turning them God-wards.

Note

1 Andreas Huyssen, *Twilight Memories: Marking time in a culture of amnesia,* London: Routledge, 1955.

Advent Wreath

O Come, O come, Emmanuel!
Redeem thy captive Israel,
That into exile drear is gone
Far from the face of God's dear Son.

Rejoice! Rejoice! Emmanuel
Shall come to thee, O Israel.

from the Latin Advent Antiphons
tr. J. M. Neale (1818–66)

Advent is a time of watching and waiting for the coming of the kingdom of God in power. The word comes from the Latin *adventus,* meaning 'coming' or 'arrival', and referred to Christ's final coming in glory. As a liturgical season it developed in the West as a preparation for the birth of Christ and had a penitential quality. But the readings from scripture reflect a dual aspect. In the early days of Advent they focus upon the coming of Christ as Judge at the Last Day. As the season progresses, they look increasingly towards the birth of the promised Messiah, and focus upon the roles played by John the Baptist, the Lord's forerunner, and of Mary, the Mother of Jesus.

The Four Last Things (Death, Judgement, Heaven and Hell) are traditional themes for meditation and preaching during Advent, but the overriding note of this season is expectation rather than penitence. It shares with Lent a certain spirit of restraint, preparation and penitence, but it is one shot through with confident joy as Christmas approaches. Advent carol services have become increasingly popular in recent years, often attracting large numbers of fringe worshippers. If constructed imaginatively, they can be profound acts of worship.

The introduction of the Advent Wreath represents one of the happier innovations of the twentieth century. Some like to trace the origin of the wreath to Scandinavian celebrations surrounding St Lucy (from the Latin for 'light') whose Feast Day is 13 December, which culminate in the crowning of a young girl with a wreath incorporating four lit candles. It is more likely, however, that the Advent Wreath began as a domestic commemoration in Germany in preparation for the coming of Christ which was transferred into church about the same time as the popularity of erecting Christmas trees in churches was spreading.

The wreath may be large or small, suspended from the ceiling like a chandelier, or more modest but still placed prominently on a stand or table in church where all can see it. Ideally, if it is to have any visual impact and speak of the coming of Christ, it does need to be big. It is constructed from holly and ivy and other evergreen branches. Undoubtedly of pagan origin, the greenery was seen by Christians as symbolic of God's faithfulness, with the holly and its scarlet berries being re-interpreted as tokens of the death of Christ and his crown of thorns, as evidenced by many traditional carols.

The wreath normally has four large white candles, one for each of the Sundays of Advent. The fifth candle, symbolizing the birth of the Christ-child and lit either on Christmas Eve or on Christmas Day, was a later development. Some churches opt for purple candles, in a further variant or use three purple candles and one pink candle on the Third Sunday of Advent (traditionally known as *Gaudete Sunday)* when rose-coloured eucharistic vestments may also be worn, as opposed to violet ones, signalling the midpoint of Advent.

The lighting of the Advent Candles can be done either without ceremony, simply as a visual aid to remind people of the coming of Christ; or they can be lit ceremonially within the context of the liturgy, usually during the gathering for worship. Some parishes take the opportunity to use the lighting of the Advent Wreath as a teaching aid for children about the different aspects of Advent. In *Common Worship*, the scripture readings and Collects for the four Sundays of Advent constellate around the following themes:

Advent 1   The Patriarchs
Advent 2   The Prophets
Advent 3   John the Baptist, the Forerunner
Advent 4   The Blessed Virgin Mary

Some incorporate the singing of a carol or hymn to accompany the lighting of the candles. Various texts are in circulation, but below are two that are commonly used – the first an adaptation of the carol, 'The Holly and the Ivy', and the second a more recent hymn, 'Advent candles tell their story', with the lighting of the Advent candles. Various texts are in circulation, but here are two:

> *The holly and the ivy*
> *are dancing in a ring*
> *with the bright and shining candles*
> *giving glory to our king.*

Author unknown

Advent 1	The first is for God's people in every age and day. We are watching for his coming and the light of God's new day. *Chorus*
Advent 2	The next is for the prophets and for the light they bring. They are candles in the darkness, burning bright for Christ our King. *Chorus*
Advent 3	The third is for the Baptist, he calls on us to sing: O prepare the way for Jesus Christ and the joy that he will bring. *Chorus*
Advent 4	The fourth is for our Lady, 'I hear and I obey'. Her child is Christ our Saviour to be born on Christmas Day *Chorus*

The light of Christ is coming into the world.
Praise God who keeps his promise for ever.

OR

Advent 1	Advent Candles tell their story as we watch and pray; longing for the Day of Glory, 'Come, Lord, soon,' we say. Pain and sorrow, tears and sadness changed for gladness on that Day.

Advent 2   Prophet voices loudly crying,
           making pathways clear;
           glimpsing glory, self-denying,
           calling all to hear.
           Through their message – challenged, shaken –
           hearts awaken: God is near!

Advent 3   John the Baptist, by his preaching
           and by water poured,
           brought to those who heard his teaching
           news of hope restored:
           'Keep your vision strong and steady,
           and be ready for the Lord.'

Advent 4   Mary's gift beyond all telling
           we recall today:
           Son of God within her dwelling,
           born to show the way.
           Who could guess the final story?
           – cross and glory; Easter Day!

Christmas Day   Advent Candles tell their story
           on this Christmas Day.
           Those who waited for God's glory:
           they prepared the way.
           Christ is with us: loving, giving,
           in us living, here today!

Mark Earey (b. 1965)
(tune: 'Angel Voices' by Edwin Monk)

The light of Christ is coming into the world.
Praise God who keeps his promise for ever.

Posada

Unto us a child is born, unto us a son is given,
and his name shall be called the Prince of Peace.

Isaiah 9.6

A South American tradition, marking the journey of Mary and Joseph to Bethlehem, has found its way to Europe in recent years. Taking its name from the Spanish, *Las Posadas,* it designates a 'novena of prayer' observed by families in the nine days running up to the birth of Christ on Christmas Day. The custom traces its origins back four centuries to Spanish Conceptionist monks in Mexico visiting each other's monasteries, bearing statues of Joseph and Mary. Apparently they would knock on the monastery door and inquire if there was anyone to welcome them and make room to receive Christ. The custom was gradually taken up by the local population in their embrace of the Christian faith, emblematic of their own reception of Christ, and it persists to this day.

In the days leading up to Christmas families set out, carrying statues of Joseph and Mary, and visit the homes of their neighbours. They knock on the door and ask, 'Is there anyone within who will make space for Christ? Will anyone welcome him?' Symbolically the doors are thrown open and space is made so that they may receive the Christ. In the course of the novena different families have guardianship of the figures of Joseph and Mary in their own homes en route to their being placed in the crib in their parish church on Christmas Eve.

Clearly, if your church's crib figures are fragile or expensive hand-carved Bavarian statues this may not be a possibility, but there are inexpensive olive wood crib sets (often made in Bethlehem) which are tactile, safe and robust for children to hold. This South American custom can become a way of engaging with local families and drawing them into the worship of the church at Christmas. The idea is to construct a simple domestic liturgy around the notion of the 'Advent Journey' for families to use.

When a family receives the figures of Mary and Joseph (and even a donkey) from whichever family had them previously, they should be encouraged to invite them to join in a little welcome ceremony, an example of which is printed below. Depending on the age of the child(ren) parents can lead the prayers themselves or get the children to read them. The prayers can be adapted or added to as they think best. Parents may like to light a candle as the prayers are said, or read from the Bible, or perhaps sing the carol, 'Little Donkey', or, 'Away in a Manger'. Parents then liaise with the next family on the Posada when and how to pass on the figures. The last family takes them to church on Christmas Eve where they are placed in the crib. The Posada should be designed to enable families with young children to pray together at home and, amidst all the razzmatazz of Christmas, to focus on the spiritual heart of the season.

On the way to Bethlehem

Adults	Welcome, Mary and Joseph, to our home.
Children	**Welcome.**
[Adults	Welcome, faithful donkey.
Children	**Welcome.**]

Adult/Child	We thank you, Father God, for allowing us to share in this special Advent journey, as Mary and Joseph travel to Bethlehem. Help us to travel with them in our hearts.
All	**Come near, Lord Jesus, and make room in our hearts.**
Adult/Child	Bless our home, our family and our friends as we prepare for Christmas.
All	**Come near, Lord Jesus, and make room in our hearts.**

Adult/Child	When Jesus was born, the shepherds brought him a lamb, and the kings brought him special presents. When we share our presents on Christmas Day, help us to remember that Jesus' birth is the best present of all.
All	**Come near, Lord Jesus, and make room in our hearts.**

Little Donkey carol

Our Father …

In our watching and our waiting
All **Come, Lord Jesus.**
In our hearts and in our homes
All **Come, Lord Jesus.**
In our life and in our world
All **Come, Lord Jesus.**

Christingle

Today our Saviour is born. So let us rejoice! This is no season for sadness: it is the birthday of Life! It is a life that annihilates the fear of death; a life that brings us joy with the promise of eternal happiness. Nobody is an outsider today.

Leo the Great (d. 461), *Sermon on the Nativity of Christ*

This ceremony of lighted candles, Moravian in origin and made popular by The Children's Society, may be celebrated at any time from Advent to Candlemas. Each child is presented with an orange, representing the earth, around which has been tied a red ribbon, representing Christ's blood, symbolic of the love with which God enfolds the world. Four cocktail sticks, one for each season, are skewered with fruits and sweets and stuck into the orange, representing God's providential care in providing the fruits of the earth for our use. In the middle of the orange is set a lighted candle, representing the light of Christ shining in the darkness of this world. Hence the name, *Christingle*, literally 'Christ-light'. In Moravia children were encouraged to put their Christingles on a windowsill at home and re-light them for passers-by to see to remind them of the birth of Jesus.

The theme of a Christingle service can be modified according to when it is held. In Advent, a service built around the hope of Christ can be created. At Christmas the service will inevitably focus on the birth of Jesus as the Light of the world. At Epiphany, the theme might be God's light reaching out to every corner of the world, embracing all nations and peoples. Many churches that hold Christingle services do so on Christmas Eve, but this may be wasting an opportunity. There are missional advantages to holding a Christingle service on another occasion and sticking with a traditional Crib service on Christmas Eve. A Christingle service attracts young children and by keeping it in reserve, a parish has a further opportunity once Christmas is over to build bridges with local families.

For many families, however, Christingle constitutes their Christmas observance. Clergy may balk at this, but we need to face reality. This means that it is all the more important that the experience be a good one, that real care is taken not simply over the choreography of the service, but with the choice of music and the theological content of the service. In the end, a Christingle is only a visual aid pointing to a greater reality. As with occasional offices, creating a leaflet that people can take away with them on which are printed details of regular services together with contact details of the church and its clergy will help grow the congregation. Most Orders of Service will end up in the waste basket at home, but some will be kept and in a few cases a worthwhile contact will have been made.

Making a Christingle

- Fasten a red ribbon or a piece of red sticky tape around the middle of the orange.
- Place the orange on a plate to catch any juice and cut a small cross in the top of the orange. Lay a square of silver foil (approximately 75mm/3" square) over the cross.
- Place a candle on top and wedge it firmly into the orange. The purpose of the foil is to stop hot wax running down on to the child's hand.
- Skewer four cocktail sticks with a mixture of raisins, sultanas, cherries or soft sweets (Dolly Mixtures or small Marshmallows are best) and insert them into the orange around the base of the candle.
- Store the Christingles upright in trays in a cool place. Some people cut off a thin slice off the bottom of the orange to give it a flat base, but this is not necessary. An ideal method of storage is to re-use greengrocers' fruit trays.
- On the day have a fire extinguisher ready in case things get out of hand, plus a stash of wet flannels in case a child manages to set fire to another child's hair! It is sensible to cater for all eventualities.

Christmas

It came upon the midnight clear,
that glorious song of old,
from angels bending near the earth
to touch their harps of gold:
'Peace on the earth, good will to men,
from heaven's all-gracious King!'
The world in solemn stillness lay
to hear the angels sing.

Edmund Sears (1810–76)

The celebration of Christ's Incarnation constitutes one of the two great liturgical fulcrums around which the Christian Year pivots. Christians believe that God created the world free, but also immersed himself in it to the point of becoming part of it. In Jesus Christ, the child of Bethlehem, God became human, part of the stream of time. Francis of Assisi is credited with being the first person to construct a Christmas crib as a visual aid to prayer when celebrating Christmas with the brothers at Greccio in Italy in 1223. He did so with 'live' actors taking the various roles in the story and set tableaux. From Italy the custom spread worldwide and today there are few churches that do not have their Christmas crib, albeit with models and statues.

Nativity plays and Crib services are held in many churches, with readings, carols and prayers geared to children and families. Typically Crib services are held on Christmas Eve in the late afternoon, but the crib may also be a focus of devotion during a celebration of Midnight Communion. In some

churches the dedication of the crib at Midnight Mass is an elaborate affair involving a special procession of the Christ-child from the altar to the crib during the singing of a carol, followed by a prayer of blessing. In others, the crib is dedicated more simply. In both cases, the dedication is usually performed at the beginning of the service. But a more effective way, after the custom of the Dominicans, is to postpone the blessing of the crib until after the reception of holy communion so that it becomes the grand finale of the service.

Blessing of the crib

While the ablutions are being performed, hand-held candles may be distributed to the congregation and lit. After the Post Communion Prayer(s), the carol, 'O Come All Ye Faithful', is sung, during which the clergy process to the crib. The electric lights in church are then dimmed.

President   The people who walked in darkness have seen a great light.
                Those who dwell in the land of deep darkness,
                on them has light shone.
                Alleluia. To us a child is born.
All   **To us a son is given. O come, let us adore him.**

President   God our Father,
             on this night your Son Jesus Christ
             was born of the Virgin Mary
             for us and for our salvation:
             bless this crib
             which we have prepared to celebrate that holy birth;
             may all who see it be strengthened in faith
             and receive the fullness of life he came to bring;
             who is alive and reigns for ever. **Amen.**

Then by candlelight all sing 'Silent Night'.

> Silent night, holy night.
> All is calm, all is bright,
> round yon virgin mother and child;
> holy infant, so tender and mild,
> sleep in heavenly peace.
>
> Silent night, holy night.
> Shepherds quake at the sight,
> glories stream from heaven afar,
> heav'nly hosts sing alleluia:
> Christ the Saviour is born.
>
> Silent night, holy night.
> Son of God, love's pure light
> radiant beams from thy holy face,
> with the dawn of redeeming grace,
> Jesus, Lord at thy birth.

Joseph Mohr (1792–1848)
tr. J. F. Young (1820–85)

This is followed by the Dismissal.

Before leaving the building, members of the congregation can be encouraged to place their lighted candles in trays of sand around the crib and, as they do so, to pray for someone they love, perhaps a member of their family, a sick friend, a person in need, or someone from whom they are separated at Christmas. This can create a contemplative end to the service, and with a higher number than usual of non-communicants, it helps occasional worshippers feel included, less spectators and more participants in the liturgy.

Make sure that somewhere on your special Christmas service sheets are printed the times of the following Sunday's services. Never presume that you won't see any of the occasional worshippers till next Christmas!

Candlemas

Mary the blessed, Joseph the just, Simeon the devout, Anna the religious, all in today, secular and religious, of all sexes and orders; all come in today, as at the end of Christmas; like the chorus to the angels' choir to bear a part in the angels' anthems, to make up a full choir of voices to glorify God for this great present which brings peace to earth and goodwill among men. And this day first it is given into our arms.

Mark Frank (c.1612–64), *First Sermon on the Purification of the Virgin Mary*

The great liturgical cycle celebrating the Incarnation, which began in Advent, culminates on 2 February with the Feast of the Presentation of Christ in the Temple, bringing the Christmas season to a close. The child Jesus, who had been manifested to the magi at his birth as saviour of the Gentiles as well as of the Jews, is now recognized by Simeon and Anna when he is presented in the temple by his parents Mary and Joseph. According to Luke's Gospel, the occasion of the presentation was Mary's ritual purification following childbirth; hence the medieval title of the feast retained in the *Book of Common Prayer*, 'The Purification of the Blessed Virgin Mary'. This ancient title is no longer in common use. Today it is more commonly referred to as Candlemas because of the custom of lighting candles in honour of the Christ-child who, according to Simeon, would be both a 'light to lighten the Gentiles' and 'the glory of God's people Israel'.

Recent liturgical revision has restored the feast to a pivotal place in the Christian calendar with the result that it now forms both the finale of the incarnational cycle and the prelude to Lent and the forthcoming Passion. Simeon's closing words to Mary that a sword would pierce her own heart point us to the foot of the cross where Mary, as an older woman, would one day stand and watch as her son died. The new calendar allows for Candlemas to be observed on a Sunday; and if this option is chosen, the various themes of the service offer the possibility of rich exploitation and are particularly suitable for All-Age worship. For example, the Gospel reading lends itself to dramatic presentation, and with Simeon and Anna both being older people – indeed Luke specifically mentions that Anna is 84 – there is an ideal opportunity to affirm the witness of older people to Christ and to bridge the gap between the generations.

Candlemas can also provide the backcloth for a Christingle service, and The Children's Society provides excellent worship resources for this. Otherwise the ceremony of the blessing and lighting of candles, and carrying them in procession, can be a dramatic reminder of our calling to bear the light of Christ in the world.

CHECKLIST

In addition to the usual setting up for a Eucharist, the following may also be required:

- Prepare the requisite number of hand-held candles for the congregation, together with drip-shields.
- Ensure that there are sufficient tapers for the efficient lighting of candles.
- Have a fire extinguisher ready in case things get out of hand, plus a stash of wet flannels in case a child manages to set fire to another child's hair!
- If the candles are to be sprinkled with holy water in blessing, provide either a holy water bucket and aspergillum or small bunch of rosemary twigs.
- The liturgical colour is white or gold.

Ash Wednesday

It is not plain dust that is used on Ash Wednesday, but ashes – those of the palms which were carried in procession on Palm Sunday the year before. It is the dead remains of something we can remember as a living thing not so very long ago; the embers of glory. The symbolism of that is plain and hackneyed enough: the ashes are a foretaste of the dust that will rattle, one day, on our coffin. And by a kind of grim irony, spring, early or late, is the moment chosen for this importunate reminder. Just when earth is beginning to put out its first shy promise of green, we are plucked by the sleeve and reminded that we are dust.

Ronald Knox (1888–1957), *Stimuli*

The word 'Lent' derives from the Old English *lencten*, meaning 'lengthen'. It referred to the lengthening of daylight and hence the arrival of Spring. In time and by association the word came to refer to the period of spiritual preparation for the celebration of Easter. The origin of the word reminds us of the way the Christian Year, at least in the northern hemisphere, has evolved in close association with the natural world, its seasons and rhythms. And this gives a unique spiritual flavour to the observance of Lent which is easily overlooked. Lent is a season of penitence and self-discipline, but it should also be a season of growth and spiritual renewal. Lenten observance should never be joyless. It should be a springtime of the heart for every Christian.

Liturgically, the season of Lent originated in the period of preparation that candidates underwent before their baptism and which took place at

Easter. In the early church Lent was also a time when those who had been excommunicated for grave and public sin prepared to be readmitted to the church's sacramental life. It was not long before the church came to realize the benefit to all Christian people of such a period of intense preparation for the celebration of the death and resurrection of Christ at Easter. As a result, Lent came typically to be marked by penitence, fasting, almsgiving and prayer. Fasting was not only about self-denial. Like anointing with oil, it was thought to be a purifying and strengthening practice – a preparation for some challenge yet to come. Significantly, the idea of 'giving things up for Lent' was balanced by the requirement to give to the poor: you cannot love the God whom you have not seen if you do not love the poor at your door whom you do see.

We see the character of Lent emerging as early as the fourth century. John Chrysostom, the great Patriarch of Constantinople, identified five paths of repentance.[1] First and most obviously, repentance involves admitting one's sins and failings, and repenting of them. Second, it necessitates letting go of anger and resentment, and forgiving those who have wronged us. 'Nursing resentment', to quote a modern author, 'is like eating poison and waiting for the other person to keel over.'[2] Thirdly, there needs to be a renewed commitment to be constant and dedicated in prayer. The fourth path of repentance he identifies is almsgiving. As children we were given little cardboard Lent Boxes to put in money from our pocket money. That custom seems quaint and old-fashioned, but it was teaching us about the importance of giving: life is not all about me or having a great time.

Generosity expands the human heart and makes us bigger people. Lastly, John Chrysostom says that we grow in humility through acts of service. What can I do for that lonely person? How can I help that elderly neighbour? Where can I make a difference?

In addition to fasting, Chrysostom's five-fold teaching on repentance has shaped the Christian observance of Lent for generations. If the liturgy of Ash Wednesday is to come alive then it needs to be re-connected with Christian spirituality. We need to find contemporary expressions of these disciplines and see how this ancient spiritual currency can be re-minted for a new generation. How do we understand the call to sanctification and how can we excite our congregations to give energy to it?

The ancient custom of shrouding crosses, statues and pictures with veils during Lent – either for the whole season or just for Passiontide – is still observed in some cathedrals and parishes. This can be quite a performance, but the effort is worthwhile, signalling an austerity suitable for Lent. It seems odd to veil the cross during Lent – of all seasons in the church's year. But the visual impact on people when they walk into church on Ash Wednesday and see it stripped of decoration, devoid of flowers, and complete with Lenten veils is very dramatic. Lenten veils may be violet in colour or, following old English custom, may be made of unbleached linen or sackcloth. Special Lenten hangings may be painted with symbols of the Passion, and taken together form what is termed a Lenten Array. They give a radical simplicity to the interior of the church.

Like sackcloth, ashes are an ancient sign of penitence. Since at least the tenth century, Christians have observed the beginning of Lent by marking their foreheads with the sign of the cross in ash, hence the name 'Ash Wednesday'. Indeed in medieval usage it was simply called, 'The Day of Ashes'. The ashes used may be purchased in advance commercially, but (in theory at least) are produced by burning the previous year's palm crosses which members of the congregation have previously returned to church for the purpose. Some parishes take this one stage further, burning the crosses publicly during the liturgy to symbolize the way God deals with our sins and forgives us in Christ. This dramatic action can be a very effective visual aid in school assemblies for teaching children about the meaning of Ash Wednesday.

Notes

1 John Chrysostom, *Homily 'On the Devil the Tempter'* 2, 6.
2 Anonymous – source unknown.

CHECKLIST

- Prepare or purchase ashes from a church supplier in advance of the day.
- Prepare the church according to local custom, including removing all flowers.
- Change the altar frontal and hangings to either purple or the Lenten Array.
- The ashes should be placed in a small bowl on the credence table in readiness for the ceremony of the imposition of ashes. Some people mix the ashes with a tiny amount of water or oil which can help them to adhere better during the ceremony of the imposition.
- After the imposition, the celebrant will need to cleanse his or her fingers which are likely to be badly stained. Prepare an additional lavabo bowl with water and slices of lemon, and towel. Alternatively, have two large slices of fresh lemon in a dish ready, together with some bread to absorb the residue. In combination this may be more effective than plain water.

Palm Sunday

Let us go together to meet Christ on the Mount of Olives. Let us spread before his feet not garments or lifeless olive branches which delight the eye for a few hours and then wither, but ourselves, clothed in his grace. We who have been baptized into Christ must ourselves be the garments that we spread before him. Let our souls take the place of the welcoming branches as we join today in the children's holy song: 'Blessed is he who comes in the name of the Lord. Blessed is the King of Israel.'

Andrew of Crete (c.660–740), *Oration*

Nails were not enough to hold God-and-man nailed and fastened to the cross, had not love held him there.

Catherine of Siena (1347–80), *The Dialogue*

Passiontide normally designates the fortnight before Easter, beginning on the Fifth Sunday of Lent, though some people restrict the term to Holy Week itself. It is the most solemn season in the church's year, rehearsing the events leading up to Jesus' arrest and crucifixion. The consensus among biblical commentators is that the Passion Narratives, the accounts of Jesus' last supper with his disciples, his betrayal, trial and subsequent execution, were the first parts of the Gospels to be written down. They are called 'Passion Narratives' because they record God's passionate love for the world revealed in and through the crucifixion of Jesus, the Latin root of the word, *passio,* meaning 'suffering'. The Fifth Sunday of Lent was called 'Passion Sunday' in the medieval church because the readings of scripture began to anticipate the story of Christ's suffering and part of the Passion Narrative was read. The title continues even though in modern usage the Passion is now read on Palm Sunday which is why (confusingly) in some circles, Palm Sunday may also be called Passion Sunday.

In the common revised lectionary the Passions according to Mark, Matthew and Luke are read in succession in a three-year cycle on Palm Sunday, and the Passion according to John on Good Friday. *Common Worship: Times and Seasons* sets out the liturgy for Palm Sunday, including the option of reading the Passion dramatically with different members of the congregation speaking the parts. Arrangements for the liturgy will vary according to local custom, primarily in relation to whether or not there is a procession commemorating Our Lord's entry into Jerusalem, and where and how it is staged.

CHECKLIST

In general

- Prepare sufficient palm crosses in advance, including sufficient for the housebound and children, and place in basket(s) in readiness.
- Decorate the sanctuary with palms.
- Vestments are normally Passion Red.

For the procession

- Provide ministers participating in the Palm Procession with decent sized palm branches. In some areas, it is customary to cut willow branches as a substitute or in addition to palm branches.
- If the palm crosses are to be blessed using holy water, provide the President with the holy water bucket and aspergillum.
- If the route of the procession is outside the church, ensure that some palm crosses are available to members of the congregation who remain in church, unable to participate by virtue of age or infirmity.

For the reading of the Passion

- This is a solemn moment and it is customary that this not be marked by a Gospel Procession or by Gospel acclamations.
- If the Passion is to be read dramatically, readers need to be rehearsed and positioned in the building where they can at least be heard, even if they cannot be seen. If the congregation is to be 'the crowd' it is advisable to have rehearsed a core of people in advance who can then lead the congregation's participation otherwise the whole thing may fall flat.
- It is customary in some churches when the evangelist reads the words commemorating Jesus' death ('and he gave up his spirit') to pause, or indeed for the congregation to genuflect/kneel briefly.
- It is appropriate for there to be silence at the end of the Passion in order to allow the congregation to digest the impact of the narrative before the sermon.

Maundy Thursday

Go up with our Lord into the large upper room that is prepared for supper, and be happy to share the delights of the meal that brings us salvation. Let love overcome your shyness, affection drive out fear, so that our Lord may at least feed you with some of the crumbs from the table when you beg him for something. If you prefer, keep your distance and like a poor man dependent on a rich benefactor, stretch out your hand to receive something. Let your tears declare your inner hunger.

But when he rises from the table and girds himself with a towel and pours water into the basin, consider what majesty it is that is washing and drying the feet of mere mortals. Look at the graciousness with which his sacred hands touch the feet of a traitor. Watch and wait and, last of all, give him your own feet to wash because those whom he does not wash will have no part with him.

Why are you in such a hurry to leave? Can you not wait a little while? Do you see? Who is that, I wonder, who is reclining on his breast and bending back his head to talk with him? Happy is that guest whoever he may be. Oh, I see: his name is John. O John, tell us what sweetness, what grace and tenderness, what light and devotion you are drawing from that fountain.

In this upper room are indeed to be found treasures of wisdom and knowledge, the fountain of mercy, the place of loving kindness, and the honeycomb of eternal sweetness.

Aelred of Rievaulx (1109–67), *A Rule of Life for a Recluse*

Our English word 'maundy' derives from the opening words of the Latin anthem, traditionally sung on this day: *Mandatum novum do vobis* ('A new commandment I give you', John 13.34). According to the Fourth Gospel, these words were spoken by Jesus to his disciples as they shared what proved to be his last supper. The commandment to 'love as I have loved you' lies at the core of Christian discipleship and of the Eucharist itself which Christians have celebrated down the ages 'until he comes again'.

St John tells us that at the end of supper Jesus girded himself with a towel, and assuming the role of the house-slave washed his disciples' feet, much to their amazement. It was more than a gesture. It was a deliberate act to cement into the memories of the disciples Christ's self-giving love, for 'the Son of Man did not come to be served, but to serve and to give his life a ransom for many' (Mark 10.45). Jesus himself told his disciples that he was giving them an example. By ancient custom, therefore, the liturgy of Maundy Thursday often incorporates the washing of feet by clergy and others as a sign of Christ's call to serve.

Additionally, at the end of the Eucharist, in some parishes there is a special procession to a side chapel bearing what remains of the consecrated bread and wine which will be distributed at the end of the Good Friday Liturgy. It is a widespread custom for there to be no celebration of the Eucharist on Good Friday. The altar on which the Blessed Sacrament is reserved overnight is called the 'Altar of Repose' and it is often adorned with flowers and candles to symbolize the Garden of Gethsemane where Christ went with his disciples to pray.

There is then held a vigil of prayer, mindful of Christ's plea to his disciples: 'Could you not watch with me one hour?' By custom, the solemn watch ends at midnight when the narrative of Christ's betrayal by Judas in Gethsemane may be read, the candles extinguished, and the congregation disperse into the night, just as Jesus was abandoned by his disciples.

The other ceremony that may be observed on Maundy Thursday is known variously as the 'Stripping of the Sanctuary' or the 'Stripping of the Altars'. After the reception of communion, the lights of the church are gradually extinguished and one of the great Hebrew psalms of lament is read: either Psalm 22 ('My God, my God, why have you forsaken me') or Psalm 69 ('Save me, O God, for the waters have come up even to my throat') or Psalm 88 ('How lonely sits the city that once was full of people!'). During the recitation of the psalm the sanctuary is gradually stripped of its remaining hangings and furnishings, echoing the interior desolation that came upon Christ as he confronted the reality of his imminent death.

CHECKLIST

In addition to the usual setting up for a Eucharist, the following preparation may also be required.

The Altar of Repose

- Prepare a side altar on which will be placed what remains of the consecrated elements after all have received communion, and where a solemn watch may be maintained until midnight.
- The altar should be furnished simply, but with greenery and flowers, and normally illuminated only by candlelight.

Foot-washing

- In those parishes where this ceremony is observed, 12 people representing the 12 Apostles may be invited to have their feet washed by ministers. In some parishes an invitation is extended to the entire congregation. According to local custom, therefore, appropriate seating needs to be provided at the front of the church. If the entire congregation is invited to participate, it is best to provide at least two 'stations' to expedite matters.
- Prepare sufficient bowls, towels, and jugs of water for the ceremony.
- Ministers participating in the foot-washing will need to remove their vestments, and may choose to wear simple linen or cotton aprons during the ceremony.
- Ministers will need to wash their hands with soap and clean water at the end of the ceremony before continuing with the Eucharist.

The Eucharist

- By custom the liturgical colour is white – the 'best' vestments are reserved for Easter Day.

- If there is to be a watch at the Altar of Repose, with general communion from the reserved sacrament on Good Friday, additional wafers (and wine) will need to be prepared for consecration.
- If there is to be a procession to the Altar of Repose, the priest may use a humeral veil when carrying the Blessed Sacrament.

Stripping of the sanctuary

- At the end of the service, if it is customary for the sanctuary to be symbolically stripped of hangings and furnishings, this is a profoundly moving ceremony but it does need to be carefully rehearsed. It is most effective if the President remains motionless in front of the altar while servers and others remove the furnishings during the recitation of the psalm. If possible, the lights in church should be gradually dimmed until the church is left in semi-darkness.

Easter Vigil

Yesterday I was crucified with Christ;
   today I am glorified with him.
Yesterday I was dead with Christ;
   today I am sharing in his resurrection.
Yesterday I was buried with him;
   today I am waking with him from the sleep of death.

Gregory of Nazianzus (329–89)

It is unclear when Christians first began to make an annual, as opposed to a weekly, memorial of the death and resurrection of Christ. The fact that the dating of Easter is fixed according to the Jewish (lunar) calendar whereas every other Christian feast depends on the solar calendar suggests that, like Sunday, it was a custom observed from apostolic days. Unsurprisingly, for the first three centuries there was no uniformity in the observance of Easter, but increasingly in the West, and especially in Rome, it became the tradition that Easter should always be celebrated on a Sunday, and gradually this custom prevailed.

The English word 'paschal' comes from the Greek word for Easter, *Pascha*, which in turn derives indirectly from *pesach*, the Hebrew word for 'Passover'. From at least the second century, *Pascha* was observed by an all-night vigil, with Christians meditating on scripture and the mighty acts of God. This was followed by a celebration of the Eucharist at cock-crow at which point Christ's resurrection was proclaimed. It was a single great festival which celebrated both the Passion and the resurrection of Christ all in one.

By the time of Tertullian (c.160–c.225) this annual liturgy also included the baptism of candidates.

Initially all the great themes of redemption were included in this one great Easter liturgy, but with the development of the liturgical year in the years that followed the reign of the Emperor Constantine (d.337), the celebration of the *Pascha* began to differentiate, admittedly in a haphazard sort of way, into a series of commemorations. Gradually the structure of Holy Week and Easter services that we know today emerged as a coherent liturgical presentation of the events of the last week of Jesus' life.

The Easter Vigil, as it is usually known, is thus the church's oldest liturgical observance. Today it may be held either on Easter Eve or very early on Easter Sunday morning, but in either case it is invariably dramatic. Its central act is the kindling of the new fire and the lighting of the great Easter Candle symbolizing Christ, the Light of the world, rising from the darkness of the grave. As the Easter Candle passes through the darkened church, the light of Christ is passed progressively to all present, culminating in the singing of the *Exultet* – the ancient Easter hymn of praise, linking Christian redemption to the Passover night of Israel's escape from slavery in Egypt.

The Easter Candle is marked symbolically with the cross; with the first and last letters of the Greek alphabet, a reminder that Christ is the beginning and end of all things; with the numerals of the current year, a reminder that Jesus, the Lord of the ages, is present here and now; and finally with five grains of incense fashioned in the shape of nails and inserted in the shape of a cross, symbolizing the wounds of Christ.

In the early church baptism and Easter were intimately linked. Indeed, Easter was the only season in the year when baptisms were regularly administered. The catechumens, who had been preparing for their baptism, sacramentally entered into Christ's redeeming death and resurrection at the same time as the whole Church celebrated its memorial of those saving events. It thus became customary for the Easter Liturgy to include within it, at the very least, the renewal of baptismal vows by the congregation, marking the completion of their Lenten observance and an affirmation of their union with Christ, crucified and risen.

If the Easter Vigil concludes with a celebration of the first Eucharist of Easter, the Gospel reading is of the women going early to the tomb as the dawn is breaking, there to find it mysteriously empty. Up goes the great shout 'Alleluia! Christ is risen!' to which the ancient reply is 'He is risen, indeed. Alleluia!'

CHECKLIST

In addition to the usual setting up for a Eucharist, the following may also be required.

Prepare the church

- Remove any remaining Lenten veils or Passiontide hangings.
- Change the altar linen.
- Altar hangings and frontals should be gold or best white.
- The church should be decorated with flowers and equipped with new candles, and if the Easter Vigil is to begin in darkness, it is good to disperse around the building lots of small candles or tea-lights which can be lit during the singing of the *Exultet*.
- If the sacrament is to be reserved for the communion of the sick and housebound, then it is customary to leave the door of the aumbry ajar, with a new sanctuary lamp ready to be lit once the Eucharist has been celebrated, and new consecrated elements set aside.

Prepare the 'new fire'

- Set up the 'new fire' in a brazier or wherever it is to be lit.
- Ensure that beside the brazier are matches, waxed tapers, tongs to remove lighted charcoal if incense is to be used, and a fire extinguisher in case things get out of hand!
- It is also good to have a torch to hand in case the President cannot read the text in the gloom.

Prepare the Easter (Paschal) Candle

- Move the Paschal Candlestick into position and decorate as appropriate.

- Prepare the Easter Candle in the customary way with the sign of the cross, the Greek letters Alpha and Omega, and the date of the year. Traditionally these marks are made by the President during the Vigil, but nowadays the priest is more likely to trace over a transfer either with a stylus or with his or her finger, while saying the prayer (see p. 174). Check that the new candle fits comfortably in its stand *before* the service begins.
- Prepare five nails or grains of incense which the President can insert in remembrance of the five wounds of Christ.
- Prepare the requisite number of hand-held candles for the congregation, together with drip-shields.

Prepare for the renewal of baptismal promises

- If there is to be a baptism or if the congregation is to gather around the font to renew their baptism promises, follow the usual setting up for a Baptism. It is good practice to clean the font thoroughly once a year, and Easter Eve is the ideal day to do so.
- If the congregation is to be sprinkled with baptismal water, provide either a holy water bucket and aspergillum or small bunch of rosemary twigs.

MARKING THE EASTER CANDLE

The Easter (Paschal) Candle is presented to the President who traces first the sign of the cross, then the Greek letter *Alpha* above it, and then the Greek letter *Omega* below it. The numbers of the current year are then traced in the spaces between the arms of the cross, as shown below.

The following words are said by the President as he or she does this:

As the vertical of the cross is traced:
    Christ, yesterday and today,
As the horizontal of the cross is traced:
    the beginning and the end
As the Alpha is signed at the top of the cross:
    Alpha
As the Omega is signed below the cross:
    and Omega.
As the first number of the current year is traced on the candle:
    All time belongs to him,
As the second number of the year is traced:
    and all ages;
As the third number of the year is traced:
    to him be glory and power,
As the last number of the year is traced:
    through every age and for ever. **Amen.**

```
              A
              1
        2     |     0
              2
    4 ━━━━━━━━┿━━━━━━━━ 5
        [0]   |   [0]
              |
              |
              3
              Ω
```

Five nails or grains of incense are then inserted by the President into the Paschal Candle, symbolizing the wounds of Christ, at the four points of the cross and finally in the centre, using the words:

By his holy / and glorious wounds / may Christ our Lord / guard us / and keep us.

Rogationtide

The Country Parson is a lover of old customs, if they be good and harmless; and the rather because country people are much addicted to them, so that to favour them therein is to win their hearts, and to oppose them therein is to deject them. If there be any ill in the custom, that may be severed from the good, he pares the apple and gives them the clean to feed on. Particularly, he loves procession, and maintains it, because there are contained therein four manifest advantages.

First, a blessing of God for the fruits of the field. Secondly, justice in the preservation of bounds. Thirdly, charity in loving walking and neighbourly accompanying one another, with reconciling differences at that time, if there be any. Fourthly, mercy in relieving the poor by a liberal distribution and largesse, which at that time is, or ought to be used.

Now love is his business and aim; wherefore he likes it well, that his parish at good times invite one another to their houses, and he urgeth them to it, and sometimes, where he knows there hath been or is a little difference, he takes one of the parties and goes with him to the other, and all dine or sup together.

George Herbert (1593–1633), *The Country Parson*, XXV

Along with Palm Sunday, Rogationtide presents a golden opportunity to take liturgy outside the church building, to re-connect with the local community and witness to Christ. As the name implies, Rogationtide is linked to the Latin verb *rogare,* meaning 'to ask'. Traditionally three Rogation Days were observed in the run-up to Ascension Day, and the Prayer Book describes the Sunday before Ascension as 'commonly known as Rogation Sunday'. In part this was because the Gospel reading set for that day included part of Jesus' farewell discourse to his disciples with the words, 'Whatsoever ye shall ask for in my name, he will give it you' (John 16.23).

It is likely that the observance of Rogation processions had its origins in paganism, in the ancient Roman festival of *Terminalia* or 'boundaries'. In Graeco-Roman days an annual procession invoking the blessing of the gods upon the crops was undertaken, and over the centuries this was adapted and Christianized into the ceremony of 'beating the bounds' that we know today. In medieval times a procession around the boundaries of a parish, complete with litanies and the singing of the *Benedicite*, the great Song of Creation, was undertaken for the blessing of the land. People knew where they belonged, and this ceremony helped bond the community together. The Reformers were no lovers of litanies and processions (see p. 126), and the custom was repressed, only to be restored during the reign of Queen Elizabeth I in response to a groundswell of opinion. A generation later the priest and poet George Herbert, in his book *The Country Parson,* noted the addiction of country people to this ancient custom, but did so with approval. Herbert had the wisdom to see the worth of such traditions and provided a justification for their continued observance.

Today many rural parishes promote a 'rural cycle' of special services as a way of engaging with local farmers and the wider agricultural community, and do so with great success. Plough Sunday, Rogation, Lammas and Harvest now shape the rural year alongside the great Christian festivals. The rationale of George Herbert for Rogationtide services continues to hold good, but the theological emphasis has shifted somewhat. Their scope has broadened to encompass stewardship of the planet, our responsibility for the countryside and the environment in general, the world of work, as well as seeking God's blessing on our communities whether we live in the town or the country. The fact that Rogationtide often precedes Christian Aid Week also picks up on the fourth of George Herbert's reasons for such processions; namely, 'mercy in relieving the poor by a liberal distribution and largesse'.

Inevitably and appropriately in rural areas the focus continues to be on the land. Pitched midway between Plough Sunday and Harvest, Rogation takes place in spring when the countryside is greening. It marked the time of year when the soil was warmer and when traditionally in arable farming seed was sown, though nowadays sowing tends to be done all the year round. But Rogation services can equally be used in areas where livestock farming predominates. Coming just after lambing time, they are an opportunity to pray for the growth of the next generation of cattle and sheep. The key to their success is worshipping outside or at least in a different place from the church building. In a country parish a Rogation procession can provide the structure for an extended day of celebration and include a parish picnic, children's activities, as well as enjoying hospitality in homes and farms along the way. George Herbert noted that people love simply walking and chatting together. Things haven't changed. If planned imaginatively, a Rogation procession can be both profound and fun.

A Rogationtide Blessing

May God bless you in winter and summer,
at your ploughing, at your sowing and at your reaping.
May God give you sunshine and rain in due season.
May God, who gladdens the face of the earth,
give you joyfulness of heart,
and perseverance in times of difficulty.
May God, who has called you to work on the land,
set your affections upon Him.
And may God the Holy Trinity,
the Father, the Son, and the Holy Spirit,
shower down his blessing of peace upon you
and all whom you love, today and always.
Amen.

Lammastide

So Naomi returned with Ruth the Moabite, her daughter-in-law, who came back with her from the country of Moab. And the two of them arrived in Bethlehem at the beginning of the barley harvest.

Ruth 1.22

We are used to holding Harvest Festivals in October when 'all is safely gathered in'. But for many people living in rural areas the beginning of the harvest is as important as its completion. In the Old Testament we read that the Jews offered the 'First Fruits' of the land to God, and our Anglo-Saxon forebears, in company with most of northern Europe, observed 1 August as the beginning of the barley harvest. The word 'Lammas' derives from the Anglo-Saxon *hlaf-mas,* meaning 'loaf mass', so-called because it was customary to bring to church a loaf of bread, baked from the new crop, to be blessed. In a way it was a Christian version 'Feast of the First Fruits'.

Today one-sixth of the English population lives in rural areas. Over the next twenty years this population is projected to increase by four million people. Rural churches – often the Cinderella of the Church of England – are once again growing in importance. There is a strong sense of 'place' in the countryside and an attachment to 'their' parish church. Some families will have farmed the same land for generations. Their forebears are buried in the churchyard and they expect to be buried there themselves. Rural communities tend to be more traditional than their urban cousins, and are more attuned to the rhythm of the seasons and the soil. Traditions that have long since disappeared in most parts of the country, like Plough

Sunday and Rogationtide, survive in the countryside and these customs generate a strong sense of identity and belonging in a community.

The revival of Lammastide celebrations can be a fresh way of connecting with the local farming community and (equally important) of bringing newcomers and long-established villagers together. One rural parish has adapted the ancient tradition to a modern setting by asking the local bakery, which also served as a café and general meeting place in the village, if they would bake a Lammas loaf using traditional methods and present it in church to ask God's blessing on the village. The bakery was delighted to be asked and generously donated not one but two huge cottage loaves as large as they could make in their ovens. A local farmer brought a sheaf of barley and asked God's blessing on the local farming community. The barley is grown using modern methods, but the Lammastide barley is harvested by hand. This has now grown into an annual event in the village, and a time of great celebration.

Traditionally, the Lammastide service would have been a Eucharist, and if this custom is followed then part of the Lammas loaf may appropriately be used as eucharistic bread. Alternatively, a short liturgy or Service of the Word can be designed, perhaps celebrating Christ as the Bread of Life. Other smaller loaves or buns in the tradition of 'blessed bread' could be distributed to members of the congregation at the end of the service. A sample of prayers used at the offering of grain and bread are printed here.

Offering of grain and bread

Farmer   In the name of the farmers and farm workers of our community, I bring this sheaf of corn, the first fruits of our harvest. We offer it to Almighty God and pray for his blessing on the gathering of all our crops.

The sheaf of corn is presented

Baker   In the name of the people of our community, I bring this loaf made from ears of ripe corn. We offer it to God, and pray for his blessing on our homes and our families, on the food we eat and the work we do, and on the daily life of our village.

The loaf of bread is presented at the altar

Yours Lord is the greatness, the power, the glory,
the splendour and the majesty,
for everything in heaven and on earth is yours.
All things come from you and of your own do we give you.

O God, who made heaven and earth,
and all that is in them,
bless these fruits of harvest
and multiply them abundantly.
We pray for seasonable weather
that this year's harvest may be a plentiful one.
Rejoicing in your gifts, we offer our thanks
to your divine Majesty, through Jesus Christ our Lord. **Amen.**

The Staffordshire Seven

A Lammastide carol

In the fullness of the summer time,
Grapes are ripening on the vine,
And the grain is swelling in the field:
First fruit of the harvest time.
Now the Lammas Bread is given,
Now the wood has made the wine;
God has opened nature's store.

On a hillside of the Galilee,
Hungry people gathered to hear
Words of hope from the Messiah:
Love and trust; and never you fear.
Fish and bread and wine a-plenty,
Peace and fellowship divine,
In the presence of the Lord.

Jesus Christ the Son of Mary:
Bread of heaven, living and true:
Bringing all into community;
By his Spirit, living anew.
Faithful shepherd of his people,
Gave his life to save us all
From the shadows at the door.

Now, two thousand years have come and gone,
Countless millions honour his name;
Bread is still the food of fellowship,
Oil and wine together proclaim:
Joy and healing to the nations,
Darkness yields to life again,
At his table evermore.

© Stephen Southgate TSSF, 2012. Tune: 'Of the Father's Love Begotten'
Corde Natus (Divinum Mysterium) 87 87 87 7

All Saints and All Souls

The church of all the first followers of Christ awaits us, but we do nothing about it. The saints want us to be with them, and we are indifferent. The souls of the just await us, and we ignore them. Come, let us spur ourselves on. We must rise again with Christ, we must seek the world which is above and set our mind on the things of heaven. Let us long for those who are longing for us, hasten to those who are waiting for us, and ask those who look for our coming to pray for us. We should not only want to be with the saints, we should also hope to possess their happiness.

Bernard of Clairvaux (1090–1153), *Sermon 2*

The Feasts of All Saints and the Commemoration of the Faithful Departed, commonly known as All Souls' Day, are two sides of the same theological coin. Through baptism we are all members one of another in Christ, and that bond transcends death. These two days in the Christian calendar celebrate that reality.

O blest communion! Fellowship divine!
We feebly struggle, they in glory shine;
Yet all are one in thee,
for all are thine.
Alleluia, alleluia!

As Bishop Walsham How's famous hymn, 'For All the Saints', testifies, the church militant here on earth enjoys communion with the church triumphant in heaven. In Christ we are one because we are His.

From its earliest days, the church recognized as its foundation stones the apostles and martyrs, heroes of the faith whose lives have excited others to holiness. The Feast of All Saints began to be observed in the fourth century, initially on the Sunday after the Feast of Pentecost, but from the eighth century its celebration was transferred to 1 November. Currently it may be observed either on the day itself or on the Sunday that falls between 30 October and 5 November when it is termed 'All Saints' Sunday'. It celebrates those women and men in whom the church recognizes the transforming grace of God at work. Collectively, the company of saints form a gigantic prism, refracting the white-light of God's grace into a spectrum of colour. They demonstrate by their lives different ways of being disciples of Jesus Christ. They are role models for the rainbow people of God. In this context, the Litany of 'Thanksgiving for the Holy Ones of God' in *Common Worship: Times and Seasons*, adapted from a Franciscan original, has proved to be a popular and meaningful way of honouring the 'great cloud of witnesses' that surrounds us.

The Commemoration of the Faithful Departed on the day following All Saints' Day began in the tenth century as a monastic custom at the great Abbey of Cluny in France. From there it spread across Europe via the network of Cluniac houses until by the thirteenth century the day was universally observed throughout the West. Although the observance did not survive the liturgical changes of the Reformation, largely because it had got muddled up with the abuses surrounding the 'unscriptural' medieval doctrine of Purgatory, the commemoration was reinstated in the calendar of the 1928 Prayer Book in response to the weight of grief following the carnage of the First World War.

Many Anglicans are ambivalent about praying for the dead, though united in their belief that all the faithful, both living and departed, are bound together in a communion of prayer. As with all prayer, the content of prayer for the departed is love, not knowledge. The commemoration of All Souls' Day enables us to celebrate the saints in a more intimate and reflective way. We remember with thanksgiving those whom we have known personally: those who gave us life, who sustained us by their love and loyalty, or who taught us the faith and 'whom we love, but see no longer'.

Bereavement is a journey and the season of All Saints and All Souls provides an important opportunity to reach out to the families of those who have had funerals taken by the parish clergy during the year or who have lost loved ones. Many, perhaps most, will not necessarily relate to a traditional Requiem Mass, but will relate to a shorter non-eucharistic Bereavement service. At a personal level, they will value the opportunity of seeing again

the minister who took the funeral. Tea and refreshments after the service can provide a relaxed setting in which they can share memories with the minister and catch up. If the parish has a Book of Remembrance, it could be presented and placed open on the altar during the Bereavement service while suitable music is played. The names of the recently departed could be printed in the Order of Service. Alternatively, their names could be read aloud, providing there are not too many of them, and candles lit in their memory 'in sure and certain hope of the resurrection of the dead through our Lord Jesus Christ'. The service needs to be quiet and not rushed, with opportunities for stillness and reflection, without being solemn.

> Bring us, O Lord God, at our last awakening into the house and gate of heaven, to enter into that gate and dwell in that house, where there shall be no darkness nor dazzling, but one equal light; no noise nor silence, but one equal music; no fears nor hopes, but one equal possession; no ends nor beginnings, but one equal eternity; in the habitations of thy glory and dominion, world without end. **Amen.**

> John Donne (1572–1631)

5

BEHIND THE SCENES

The Country Parson hath a special care of his church that all things there be decent and befitting his Name by which it is called. Therefore first he takes order that all things be in good repair; as walls plastered, windows glazed, floor paved, seats whole, firm and uniform, especially that the pulpit, and desk, and communion table and font be as they ought, for those great duties that are performed in them.

Secondly, that the church be swept and kept clean without dust or cobwebs, and at great festivals strawed and stuck with boughs and perfumed with incense.

Thirdly, that there be fit and proper texts of Scripture everywhere painted, and that all the painting be grave and reverend, not with light colours or foolish antics.

Fourthly, that all the books appointed by authority be there, and those not torn or fouled, but whole and clean and well bound; and that there be a fitting and sightly communion cloth of fine linen, with an handsome and seemly carpet of good and costly stuff or cloth, and all kept sweet and clean in a strong and decent chest with a chalice and cover, and a stoop or flagon; and a basin for alms and offerings, besides which he hath a poor-man's box conveniently sited to receive the charity of well-minded people, and to lay up treasure for the sick and needy.

And all this he doth, not as out of necessity, or as putting a holiness in the things, but as desiring to keep the middle way between superstition and slovenliness.

George Herbert (1593–1633), *The Country Parson*, XIII

INTRODUCTION

Whether a church is large or small, in a city centre or tucked down a quiet country lane, lots of practical things need to happen before a service. Most obviously, the church must be opened, cleaned and the flowers arranged. Service sheets need to be prepared, the toilets checked, and the lights and sound system switched on. In winter it helps if the boiler has been switched on more than five minutes before the start of the service. If there is to be a celebration of Holy Communion, then bread and wine must be in place, communion vessels prepared, service books opened, candles lit, and (if they are customary) vestments laid out. The list of jobs is extensive.

The oversight of worship is the responsibility of the clergy working in partnership with Readers, musicians, servers and lay officers. In large urban parishes a number of people may be involved, all of whom require co-ordination and direction, and most importantly, acknowledgement. Good communication is essential if tasks are to be done on time and done well, particularly when dealing with a series of volunteers on a rota who may or may not know one another well, if at all. It helps if people have clear job descriptions and, when volunteering for the first time, are given adequate guidance and training. Otherwise their volunteering will be short-lived.

With fewer people on the ground, preparing for a service in a rural church presents a different set of challenges. People will know one another better, but that can have its minuses as well as its pluses. Co-ordinating worship across a multi-parish benefice can be a Herculean task. The ministry of lay people becomes crucial, not least because with a priest travelling from parish to parish, sometimes turning up with barely five minutes in hand to preside at a service of Holy Communion, he or she is dependent on the home team to have everything ready. Things that in urban parishes are shared around a team, in a rural benefice more often than not devolve upon the churchwarden.

The more jobs can be shared round a congregation the better. Teamwork militates against 'empire building' and generates a sense of ownership and participation in the worshipping community. Problems behind the scenes will arise from time to time. Parish life would be dull without its share of high-octane characters. Friction and emotion are guaranteed, and from time to time things will go bang. On such occasions good leadership, whether by clergy, Readers or churchwardens, will demand patience, a steady hand on the tiller plus a certain lightness of touch.

Clergy get worn down when they feel everything is on their shoulders. Such moaning is understandable and legitimate if true. But sometimes clergy are their own worst enemies, hugging jobs to themselves which in fact could be delegated to others. The 'Father/Mother knows best' mentality disables a congregation. Some lay people are only too willing to help, but may be shy or fearful of making mistakes, and need encouragement not censure. No one can get it right all the time. Which is why having a sense of humour will be as important as being able to draw up a three month rota. The late Cardinal Hume's advice to his clergy remains as pertinent as ever: 'Always take God seriously, but never yourself.'

The Sacristan or Verger

All may of thee partake;
Nothing can be so mean,
Which with this tincture, 'for thy sake,'
Will not grow bright and clean.

A servant with this clause
Makes drudgery divine,
Who sweeps a room, as for thy laws,
Makes that and the action fine.

George Herbert (1593–1633), 'The Elixir'

In some churches much of the preparatory work behind the scenes is undertaken by a sacristan or verger, working under the authority of the vicar and churchwardens. He or she may be assisted by a team of helpers and have significant responsibility for the good ordering of the liturgy. Whether or not there is such a person in a parish, and in rural churches many tasks cascade on to the broad shoulders of the churchwardens, it is still helpful to list what needs doing:

- Ordering and storage of bread and wine for Holy Communion.
- Cleansing and polishing of communion vessels, ensuring their secure storage, and preparing them at times of Holy Communion.
- Supervising the cleaning, ironing and storage of altar linen.
- Supervising the storage, repair and cleaning of vestments and robes.

- Setting out appropriate vestments in good time for a service.
- Preparing microphones, including checking that there is a new battery in place.
- Ordering supplies of candles, palm crosses, Paschal Candle, incense, charcoal, flowers for Mothering Sunday, etc.
- Storage and setting out of liturgical books.
- Changing altar frontals and hangings according to liturgical seasons.
- Maintaining the cleanliness of the font and requisites for baptism.
- Keeping the sacristy or vestry in good order.
- Buying a copy of the new lectionary in good time for Advent each year.
- Assisting the churchwardens in their annual inventory of church plate.

Communion Vessels

You should look upon all the utensils of the monastery and its whole property as you would the sacred vessels of the altar.

Rule of St Benedict, 31

Christians have set aside vessels for use in worship from the earliest days. Rummage around a typical parish church and you may come across a handsome brass dish for alms, a ewer for baptismal water, flagons and cruets for wine, cruses for holy oil, and even the occasional thurible and incense boat. All of life is holy and to be offered to God, but these objects are significant by virtue of the use to which they are put. Unsurprisingly communion plate is accorded the greatest respect and manufactured with more care and artistry than other liturgical vessels because of the centrality of the Eucharist in the life of the church.

Fashions change, and form invariably follows function. During the latter part of the Middle Ages, the separation of liturgical action from everyday life and the custom of withholding the wine from the laity at communion resulted in the production of elegant but small chalices. The restoration of the cup to the laity at the Reformation meant that chalices had to be large enough to communicate an entire congregation, not merely the priest. Many ancient parish churches are the proud custodians of these wonderful heirlooms, though sadly insurance requirements often mean that they are locked away in a bank vault or deposited in a cathedral treasury and rarely used.

Just as the design of chalices has changed over the years, so the size and style of patens or plates for the communion bread has altered too. In early centuries these were large and circular, holding sufficient bread for an entire congregation. However, as the use of unleavened wafers in Western Europe became more common, and as the frequency with which lay people received holy communion declined, so by the late Middle Ages a paten might need to hold only one wafer-bread for the priest. Patens became

small, made of the same material as the chalice and designed in proportion to it. From this developed the custom of placing the paten on top of the chalice before and after communion.

At the Reformation there was a desire to recover the communal setting of the Eucharist and people were urged to receive holy communion 'in both kinds' on a regular basis, and not be passive spectators in the liturgy. There was also a return to using leavened bread which necessitated the production of larger communion plate. Today a parish might opt to use either leavened bread or unleavened wafers at Holy Communion. If the latter, then it is likely that the parish will also have a wafer box for storing unconsecrated wafers, together with a ciborium for their distribution during the service.

Prior to the fourteenth century a ciborium was exclusively an architectural term designating a canopy above an altar. Gradually the term came also to be applied to certain communion vessels, shaped like chalices but fitted with lids, which were used to hold consecrated wafers. Clergy, now as then, like ciboria because they are convenient to use in the administration of holy communion. Wafers easily slip off a flat paten. Unfortunately ciboria do look like drinking cups, not bread plates, and ecclesiastical fashions are once again changing.

Roman Catholic practice since Vatican II has seen a move to use either slightly larger and thicker individual people's wafers, or else very large wafers which the priest can break up during the Eucharist to reinforce a sense of sharing in one bread. Desirable though this liturgical development may be, it will necessitate the design and purchase of yet another range of bigger communion vessels, and many parishes will hesitate before going to the additional expense.

Anglican Canon Law states that communion plate should be made of precious metals, not least because they do not break easily (Canon F3). Pottery is not only fragile but porous, and potentially unhygienic. Even with metal chalices it is still important to maintain high standards of hygiene by cleansing them with hot water after communion and drying them thoroughly. Tarnished communion vessels make their own statement about the lack of care with which a church celebrates the Lord's Supper. On the other hand, over-zealous polishing will damage silver and may leave unsightly marks on a purificator. It is good practice, therefore, to store communion vessels in felt bags to minimize tarnishing and stop them scratching one another in the safe. Even with these precautions, re-gilding may still be necessary at some point.

Bread and Wine

The bread, whether leavened or unleavened, shall be of the best and purest flour that conveniently may be gotten, and the wine the fermented juice of the grape, good and wholesome.

Canons of the Church of England

Love is that liquor sweet and most divine,
Which my God feels as blood; but I, as wine.

George Herbert (1593–1633), 'The Agonie'

Only the best is good enough for God. So why in so many parishes is cheap white bread the preferred choice? In the custom of the Church of England either leavened or unleavened bread may be used at celebrations of Holy Communion, but both have to be of the best quality. Given that a sacrament is 'an outward and visible sign of an inward and spiritual grace' we do not aid worship by outward signs that speak more of consumerism and chemicals than of God. David Scott, in his poem, 'A long way from bread', makes the point forcefully.

In Roman Catholic churches wafers of unleavened bread called 'hosts', often marked with a monogram or cross, are normally used. The term comes from the Latin *hostia*, meaning 'victim'. Medieval theology stressed the sacrificial nature of the Eucharist and, as a consequence, the term came to be applied to the consecrated bread. In the Orthodox Church leavened bread is more usual, baked specially for the purpose.

If individual people's wafers are used for convenience, it is good for the President to be provided with a larger priest's wafer in order that he or she may more easily break the bread and be seen to do so. Breaking the bread, the characteristic action of Jesus by which the disciples on the Emmaus Road recognized him after the resurrection, provided one of the ancient titles for this sacrament. The significance of sharing in the one bread is lost if it is replaced by the invisible snapping of a tiny wafer, or if the bread is stale and too hard to break in a seemly manner.

In some parishes a member of the congregation may undertake to bake the bread for the Eucharist. A traditional recipe for this is on p. 200. The rise in numbers suffering from Coeliac Disease and who require a gluten-free diet is an additional factor to be borne in mind when preparing for celebrations of the Eucharist. Gluten-free wafers are readily available, and are usually square to distinguish them from ordinary wafers. A note to this effect should be made in the service sheet for the benefit of visitors to save embarrassment. Gluten-free wafers should always be stored separately from ordinary wafers to avoid contamination.

In the custom of the Church of England, 'The bread shall be brought to the communion table in a paten or convenient box' (Canon B17.3) – not a plastic bag. In some parishes this action may be elaborated into an offertory procession, with members of the congregation ceremonially bringing up the bread and wine, usually at the same time as the collection. In other churches the elements may be placed in readiness on a credence table in the sanctuary.

The wine for the Eucharist must be the fermented juice of the grape, the 'fruit of the vine' (Luke 22.18). It is important that it is kept in good condition and not allowed to turn to vinegar. For this reason, many parishes prefer to use a fortified wine which keeps better. Normally the colour of wine is red because it is a better 'outward and visible sign' of Christ's blood, but there is no reason why white wine should not be used. What is not permitted in Anglican custom is grape juice.

A long way from bread

by David Scott
written for the Hilfield Families' Camp

We have come so far from bread.
Rarely do we hear the clatter of the mill wheel;
see the flour in every cranny,
the shaking down of the sack, the chalk on the door,
the rats, the race, the pool,
baking day, and the old loaves:
cob, cottage, plaited, brick.

We have come so far from bread.
Once the crock said 'BREAD'
and the bread was what was there,
and the family's arm went deeper down each day
to find it, and the crust was favoured.

We have come so far from Bread.
Terrifying is the breach between wheat and table,
wheat and bread, bread and what goes for bread.
Loaves now come in regiments, so that loaf
is not the word. *Hlaf*
is one of the oldest words we have.
I go on about bread
because it was to bread
that Jesus trusted
the meaning he had of himself.

It was an honour for the bread
to be the knot in the Lord's handkerchief
reminding him about himself. So,
O bread, breakable;
O bread, given;
O bread, a blessing;
count yourself lucky bread.

Not that I am against wafers,
especially the ones produced under steam
from some hidden nunnery
with our Lord crucified into them.
They are at least unleavened, and fit the hand,
without remainder, but it is still
a long way from bread.
'Better for each household to have its own bread,
daily, enough and to spare,
dough the size of a rolled towel,
for feeding angels unawares.
Then if the bread is holy,
all that has to do with bread is holy;
board, knife, cupboard,
so that the gap between things is closed
in our attention to the bread of the day.'

I know that
'man cannot live on bread alone'.
I say, let us get the bread right.

Communion Bread

Sift together into a large bowl:
2½ lbs (1.12 kg) whole wheat flour
8 teaspoons baking powder
4 teaspoons salt

Mix together:
½ pint (250ml) milk
½ pint (250ml) vegetable or other light oil
½ pint (250ml) water
16 oz (450g) honey (1 jar)

Pour the liquid into the dry ingredients and mix until thoroughly blended. The dough should be stiff and moist, but not sticky.

Turn the dough out on to a lightly floured board and knead briefly, using additional flour as necessary. For ease of handling, divide into two portions and work one at a time.

Roll out on to a lightly floured board not more than ½" (1cm) thick, and cut into rounds of appropriate size, but no larger than 6½" (16cm) diameter. Stamp firmly with floured mould or incise with cross, using a sharp, thin knife dipped in cool water.

Place the dough on an oiled baking tray and bake at gas mark 6 or 200°C for 12–14 minutes, depending on your oven's temperature. Allow the loaves to cool on a wire rack and wrap well before refrigerating. The bread may be reheated in a microwave (ever so briefly to avoid drying) before use.

This recipe yields several medium (3" approx. 7cm) and large (6" approx. 16cm) diameter loaves which will communicate between 16 and 24 people each respectively.

Altar Linen and Frontals

The Table, at the Communion-time having a fair white linen cloth upon it, shall stand in the body of the church, or in the chancel, where Morning and Evening Prayer are appointed to be said.

1662 *Book of Common Prayer*

In the ancient world Egypt was prized for its linen. Made from the stalks of flax plants, it was exported throughout the Mediterranean world including Jerusalem where it was used to make the hangings and vestments of the temple. Linen was valued for its beauty and durability. It was used for clothes, curtains, sails, and even the shrouds of the dead. From the earliest times Christians covered the table at which they celebrated the Eucharist with a linen cloth. It was placed on the altar at the start of the service and removed at the end.

By the year 1000, Christian communities were leaving this cloth on the altar table permanently. It was also becoming customary to place the altar against the east wall of a church, often with a retable or hanging behind it. Congregations went to great lengths to commission lavish frontals to cover the altar, often heavily embroidered and in different colours according to the liturgical season. Some styles of frontal required an additional super-frontal: a narrow strip of the same fabric and design as the frontal, hung at the top to disguise the way the altar frontal was held in place. Whatever the preferred design, on the top of the altar table was always placed a white linen cloth, in England known as the 'fair linen', typically long enough to hang to the floor on either side.

At the Reformation medieval stone altars were replaced by communion tables. Initially these were placed in the body of the church. The Reformers wanted to move away from an understanding of the Mass as sacrifice and to recover a stronger sense of the Eucharist as a communal sacred meal. Although altar frontals became redundant and were discarded or cut up for clothes, Cranmer insisted that the ancient custom of covering the holy table with 'a fair white linen cloth' at every celebration of the Lord's Supper should be retained.

In the early seventeenth century during the reign of King Charles I, liturgical fashions changed once again, and not without controversy. Following a directive of Archbishop Laud, communion tables were returned to the sanctuary behind communion rails for safe keeping and in order to provide for the more seemly reception of holy communion by congregations. In addition the holy tables were to be dignified with a covering down to the ground on all four sides; hence the title 'Laudian' for this style of altar frontal.

In the nineteenth and early twentieth centuries, under the influence of the Oxford Movement, parish churches were re-ordered yet again and often beautified. Under the guidance of Anglo-Catholic clergy such as Percy Dearmer with his best-selling book, *The Parson's Handbook,* a new benchmark in worship was set. Interiors of parish churches were restored to a quasi-medieval appearance, complete with altars, hangings and frontals. It became fashionable once more for the priest to face east with his back to the people during celebrations of the Holy Communion rather than to preside from the 'north end' – the liturgical position favoured by the *Book of Common Prayer,* and still retained by some evangelical clergy.

'North end celebration' made total sense when communion tables were placed lengthwise in the chancels of churches, but the custom looked bizarre when the tables went back into the sanctuary, and positively antiquarian in comparison to the modern convention of the priest facing the congregation across the altar table. Over the last fifty years, in the wake of the Liturgical Movement, matters have come full-circle. Some churches have introduced nave altars – free-standing communion tables – at the top of the nave in a desire to maximize the participation of congregations, much in the way that the Reformers attempted to do in the sixteenth century.

The furnishings of parish churches reflect the chequered history of liturgical fashions. In addition to a stock of fair linen, embroidered altar frontals, complete with matching pulpit falls, a church will also have a store of linen cloths used in the administration of Holy Baptism. Each item of linen has a name designating its use. There are as many ways of ironing and arranging the linen as there are ways of ironing tablecloths and napkins. There are no 'rights' and 'wrongs' in this, but the customary ways, together with their names and uses, are as follows:

Corporals

In addition to the main altar cloth, in most churches it is customary to spread immediately under the communion vessels, either before the service or at the offertory, a large square piece of linen known as a 'corporal'. The term comes from the Latin *corpus,* meaning 'body', because in the medieval rite, during the Prayer of Consecration, the priest would place the host directly on the linen corporal and slide the paten underneath it. The corporal is folded in on itself into nine equal squares both for convenience and to safeguard any particles of the consecrated bread (see Figure 1 i–iv). There is often a small cross embroidered in the middle of the corporal or in the middle of the edge of the linen facing the priest.

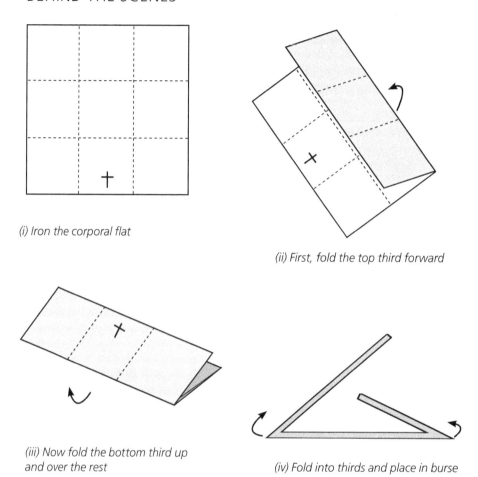

(i) Iron the corporal flat

(ii) First, fold the top third forward

(iii) Now fold the bottom third up
and over the rest

(iv) Fold into thirds and place in burse

Figure 1 i–iv: Folding the corporal

In medieval times, and again in the nineteenth century when the custom was revived, the corporal might have been stored in a fabric-covered case or envelope known as a **burse** to keep it flat and clean. Still in many churches, the communion vessels, particularly at 8 o'clock Holy Communion, are placed in readiness on the altar or on the credence table under an embroidered square of material known as a **chalice veil**, with the burse containing the corporal resting on top of it. The burse and veil are usually made of matching materials and a parish may have several sets of them in different liturgical colours.

When assembling the vessels, first drape a **purificator** over the chalice. Now place the paten, containing a priest's wafer, on top of the chalice and purificator, followed by a pall on top of the paten. Finally, the veil is draped over the vessels, and the burse, containing the corporal, placed on top (see Figure 2).

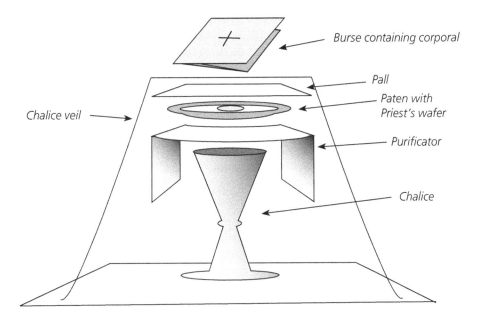

Burse containing corporal

Pall

Paten with
Priest's wafer

Chalice veil

Purificator

Chalice

Figure 2: Chalice and paten, covered by burse and veil

In churches where it is customary for the ablutions to be performed at the end of the service rather than immediately after the reception of holy communion, the consecrated elements may be covered with a simple white linen veil and set aside. In Anglican custom consecrated elements not required for the purposes of holy communion must be consumed reverently, never discarded.

It is good practice for the size of corporals to correspond to the dimensions of an altar and the number of communion vessels that are customarily placed on it. Large corporals are unlikely to fit into ornate burses, and this may have contributed to burses and veils going out of fashion in recent years. Some parishes do not supplement their fair linen with a corporal, but most do if only to protect the fair linen from stains. It is easier to wash a corporal than to change an entire altar cloth. In most churches the fair linen is changed three times a year: Christmas, Easter, and Michaelmas. During the week it makes sense to protect the fair linen with a dust-cover.

Credence cloth

Some medieval and Victorian churches have recesses cut into the side wall in the sanctuary area in which can be placed communion vessels and other requisites required for the celebration of Holy Communion. Other churches rely on a credence table, adjacent to the altar and covered with a simple white linen cloth. In addition to cruets of wine and water, in churches where it is customary for the priest to wash his or her hands ceremonially before beginning the Eucharistic Prayer, the credence table will also have a small bowl, jug and towel placed in readiness.

In modern liturgical practice, emulating the practice of earlier centuries, the communion vessels are not placed on the altar during the Liturgy of the Word, but remain on the credence table until after the Peace. Only then are they placed on the holy table. *Common Worship* in the section 'Preparation of the Table' provides optional 'table prayers' at this point. After all have received communion, the vessels should be cleansed and returned to the credence table, rather than left on the altar. In large parishes this means that a credence table needs to be big enough to do the job, as well as unobtrusive.

Purificators

A purificator is a liturgical napkin, used to wipe the chalice during the administration of holy communion. It is also used during the ablutions at the end of the service for drying the vessels. One purificator should be provided per chalice. Like other cloths, purificators are normally made of linen, but left unstarched to aid their absorbent quality. Traditionally the material is folded twice in on itself to form a long strip. This gives it added absorbency and makes it easier for the person administering the cup to use.

Pall

Because pall means 'cover', this word has two uses. At funerals the word designates a large cloth that may be draped over a coffin. In the Eucharist, however, pall designates a square (usually) of cardboard, covered in an envelope of linen, which can be washed as necessary. It is placed on top of a chalice to keep insects out, and is particularly useful in summer or at outdoor celebrations of the Eucharist.

Towels

Liturgical towels can be made either of linen or other textiles, provided they are absorbent. A **lavabo towel** may be used at the offertory in the ceremony of the washing of fingers. After receiving the collection, but prior to the Eucharistic Prayer, a server pours water over a priest's hands into a bowl, and then offers a small towel for drying. In churches that use incense, the lavabo is customarily taken after the priest has censed the altar. The bowl and towel should be large enough to presume the washing of hands, not merely fingertips.

Towels are also used at baptisms. Their size will depend on the age of the candidates and whether they are being baptized by having water poured over the heads or by total immersion. Large white towels will also be needed on Maundy Thursday in those parishes that undertake the foot-washing. Some churches also provide the clergy officiating with simple linen aprons to protect their robes during the ceremony.

Lenten veils

The word 'veil' has already been used in reference to the simple white linen cloth that may cover the elements after all have received communion until the ablutions can be performed; or to a larger embroidered chalice veil with matching burse that may cover the communion vessels. There is a third usage that applies to the ancient custom of veiling crosses, statues and pictures during Lent – either for the whole season or just for Passiontide. This custom is still observed in some parishes. It can be quite a performance, often requiring the services of more than just the sacristan or verger, but the effort is worthwhile. The visual impact on people when entering church on Ash Wednesday can be dramatic, signalling an austerity suitable to the season. Lenten veils may be violet in colour, but in those parishes that follow medieval English custom, unbleached linen or sackcloth is used. This picks up the biblical theme of 'sackcloth and ashes' in token of repentance. Lenten hangings may be painted with symbols of the Passion, and taken together form what is called a **Lenten Array** (see p. 158). By custom the veils are removed on Easter Eve in time for the Easter Vigil and the celebration of the resurrection.

LAUNDRY

As with domestic laundry, getting rid of stains on material is a challenge. After communion, it is advisable to rinse used purificators in cold water immediately, or else leave them to soak in a bowl of water until they can be washed. Lipstick and red wine stains are notoriously difficult to get out, but a combination of very hot water and bleach usually does the trick.

Candle wax

Candle wax is another challenge. Many churches take the precaution of putting a large piece of thick white paper under candlesticks, particularly in draughty churches where candles are wont to gutter, in order to protect their fair linen from damage. Wax needs to be left to harden before any attempt is made to remove it from the fair linen or any other textile. A blunt instrument that will not cut into the fabric can then be used to prise off excess wax. Smaller spots can be ironed off by placing plain brown paper over the fabric. The linen will then need to be washed in hot water with bleach added.

Storage

In most churches, because linen easily creases, it is best ironed slightly damp using a steam iron. Altar cloths are usually starched and best kept rolled on acid-free tubes and stored in large drawers.

IRONING

Corporals

All linen is best ironed damp. Iron a corporal flat, finishing with it right side up. By custom, it is then folded into nine equal squares (see Figure 1 i–iv, p. 204). First, fold the top third toward you (ii). Now fold the bottom third up and over the top third of the corporal (iii). Finally, fold the corporal in thirds again so that it appears like a square (iv). This should now fit neatly into the burse where it can be stored flat.

Purificators

Purificators tend to be smaller than corporals with a cross in the middle, and rectangular in shape rather than square. They too need to be ironed flat and then folded into nine equal parts, right side to the outside, ending with the cross on the top. These folds make it easy to use when wiping a chalice during the administration of holy communion. Store flat with the cross on the top.

Liturgical Colours

We love the place, O God,
Wherein thine honour dwells;
The joy of thine abode
All earthly joy excels.

William Bullock (1798–1874)

The Christian Year has evolved over the centuries. Gradually it became customary (at least in the West) for the church's seasons to be marked by different liturgical colours for vestments and hangings. The first reference to a sequence of liturgical colours does not occur until the twelfth century in Jerusalem. It is likely that the association of particular colours with different seasons developed as much for psychological reasons as theological. Red was the colour of blood; gold was richness and festivity; white was purity; and green signalled growth. In spite of the early Christians' preference for white at funerals in celebration of the resurrection and in sharp contrast to the custom of their pagan neighbours, violet and black once again became the colours of death and mourning.

It took some centuries before the use of liturgical colours was standardized. In medieval England there was no uniformity. The custom of Salisbury Cathedral, known as 'Sarum Usage', was widely followed but this differed in notable respects from continental Europe. For example, green was never used. Instead red vestments were worn during the period after Pentecost until Advent. Yellow was used on many saints' days. Dark blue, as opposed to violet, was the preferred colour of Advent. In Lent an array of unbleached linen was used, often bearing symbols of the Passion, with pictures and crucifixes veiled (see p. 158).

In the decades following the Reformation, the use of liturgical colours largely lapsed in the Church of England. Meanwhile successive popes enforced a high degree of uniformity in the Roman Church. In the nineteenth century, in the wake of liturgical revival in the Church of England, liturgical colours were reintroduced in many cathedrals and parish churches. Some adopted the new Roman sequence of colours; others reverted to a version of Sarum Usage to display their loyalty to the ancient customs of the church in England as distinct from 'Romish' custom.

Common Worship sets out the following standard sequence of liturgical colours during the Christian Year, but there are as many variants as there are parsons.

Advent

Begins four Sundays before Christmas and marks the beginning of the church's year. It ends on the afternoon of Christmas Eve.

Colour: Purple (technically known as 'Violet') or Dark Blue (if following the Old English sequence).

Note: Some churches use Rose vestments on Advent 3, the mid-point of Advent also known as 'Gaudete Sunday'.

Christmas–Epiphany

The Christmas–Epiphany Season, celebrating the Incarnation of our Lord, begins with Evening Prayer on Christmas Eve and finishes after Evening Prayer on the Feast of the Presentation of Christ in the Temple (Candlemas) when Simeon and Anna greet the child Jesus and recognize him as the long-awaited Messiah. Christmastide lasts 12 days, with the Feast of the Epiphany (The Manifestation of Christ to the Gentiles) celebrated on 6 January. However, in recent years it has become increasingly customary to translate the Feast of Epiphany to the nearest Sunday in order to ensure that it is observed. The Sundays that follow are designated 'Sundays of

Epiphany', the first of which by custom commemorates Christ's Baptism in the Jordan by John.

Colour: White or Gold.

Note: Some churches, following Roman custom, retain White only until the Feast of the Baptism of Christ (the Sunday following the Epiphany) and then go into Green until the beginning of Lent.

Ordinary Time before Lent

The length of the period from Candlemas to Shrove Tuesday varies from year to year. The date of Easter follows the lunar calendar with the result that this period can be as little as a few days or last a month. In Roman custom, Ordinary Time begins the day after the Baptism of Christ.

Colour: Green.

Note: Churches loyal to the Old English sequence may wear Dark Blue vestments during this season.

Lent

Lent begins on Ash Wednesday and concludes with the celebration of the Lord's Supper on Maundy Thursday evening. It marks the 40 days in which Jesus fasted in the wilderness in preparation for his public ministry.

Colour: Purple (Violet) or Lenten Array.

Note: Some churches use Rose vestments on the Fourth Sunday of Lent, the mid-point of Lent also known as 'Mothering' or 'Laudete' Sunday.

Passiontide

Passiontide normally designates the fortnight before Easter, beginning on the Fifth Sunday in Lent, though some people restrict the term to Holy

Week itself. It is the most solemn season in the church's year, rehearsing the events leading up to Jesus' arrest and crucifixion. The Fifth Sunday of Lent was called 'Passion Sunday' in the medieval church (and still is in some churches today) because the readings of scripture began to anticipate the story of Christ's suffering and part of the Passion Narrative was read. In modern usage the Passion is normally read on Palm Sunday which is why (confusingly) in some circles, Palm Sunday may also be called Passion Sunday.

Colour: Purple (Violet) or Lenten Array; Passion Red from Palm Sunday.

Holy Week

Holy Week honours the last week of Jesus' life. It begins on Palm Sunday with the commemoration of Jesus' triumphal entry into the city of Jerusalem with his disciples, and climaxes with the **Paschal Triduum** – or Triduum for short – the term for the 'Three Days of Passover'. For Jewish people, Passover celebrates the event when God delivered the people of Israel from slavery in Egypt. For Christians, it commemorates the saving death and resurrection of Our Lord Jesus Christ. The Triduum designates Maundy Thursday, Good Friday and Holy Saturday.

Colour: Passion Red.

Maundy Thursday

The day on which is commemorated Jesus' last supper with his disciples and the institution of the Eucharist.

Colour: White.

Good Friday

The most solemn day in the Christian Year marking the crucifixion. By custom, all hangings are removed. Some parishes may use Black vestments at liturgical services.

Easter

Eastertide is 50 days: seven weeks plus one day, a week of weeks. It begins on Easter Day with Christ's bursting from the tomb, and climaxes on the Day of Pentecost (Whitsun) with the coming of the Holy Spirit upon the disciples in Jerusalem.

Colour: White or Gold, with Red on the Day of Pentecost.

Ordinary Time

From the Monday after the Day of Pentecost until Evening Prayer on the Saturday before Advent Sunday.

Colour: Green.

Note: Except for the Feast of Christ the King (Sunday before Advent) when some churches use Red. Some churches also use Red during November, from after the Feast of All Saints till Advent Sunday.

Trinity Sunday, All Saints' Day, Feasts of Our Lord, Feasts of the Blessed Virgin Mary

Colour: White or Gold.

Feasts of Apostles, Evangelists and Martyrs

Colour: Red (except the Feast of St John the Evangelist which by custom is White).

Saints other than martyrs, Dedication Festival

Colour: White or Gold

Candles

Hail, gladdening Light, of his pure glory poured
who is the immortal Father, heavenly, blest,
holiest of holies, Jesus Christ our Lord.

Now we are come to the sun's hour of rest,
the lights of evening round us shine,
we hymn the Father, Son, and Holy Spirit divine.

Worthiest art thou at all times to be sung with undefiled tongue,
Son of our God, Giver of life, alone,
Therefore in all the world thy glories, Lord, they own.

Phos hilaron, third century
tr. John Keble

Oil lamps and candles have been used in Christian worship from earliest times, though initially without symbolic meaning. We know that candles were ritually lit in the temple in Jerusalem long before the birth of Jesus, and that they were used not only at night but during the day as well. When Christians first began to hold their meetings for worship, many of which took place at night, these were illuminated by some form of oil lamp or groups of candles.

The first reference to their ritual use in Christian worship does not emerge until the third century. At Evening Prayer in the Eastern Church, Christians began to sing the hymn, *Phos hilaron*, during the ceremony of the 'lighting of the lamps' or *Lucernarium*. Provision for this ancient custom has been made in 'The Blessing of Light' as part of Evening Prayer in *Common Worship*.

The custom of placing candles on the altar seems to have developed out of the processional lights which in earlier centuries were placed beside or on the holy table. The declaration in the Gospel that Jesus is the 'Light of the world' provided a theological rationale for something that was probably purely practical in origin. Liturgical embellishment can be seen at its clearest in churches that hold a Gospel Procession during the Eucharist, when the Gospel Book is ceremonially carried into the body of the church, the deacon or reader flanked by two servers (also known as acolytes or taperers) each bearing a lighted candle. A similar procession happens in many Orthodox synagogues when the scroll of the law is paraded around the synagogue before being placed back in the ark.

Over the years liturgical fashions have come and gone. In some churches six candles were put on the altar ('the big six'), in others none were allowed. With so-called 'English Altars', still seen in some cathedrals and greater churches, the holy table was surrounded by four tall riddel posts and hangings, each of which might bear a candle, with two further candlesticks placed directly on the holy table, making six candles in total. In most parish churches, however, two became the norm, and the modern preference for liturgical simplicity has reinforced this convention.

In England the two candles are usually placed at either end of the altar table, but in many churches on the Continent it is now customary to place the candles together at one end, with the priest's missal placed on the opposite side for visual balance. Some churches have been more radical and reverted to the practice of leaving the altar uncluttered to give emphasis to the communion vessels, with two candles positioned on the floor on either side of the altar in free-standing holders.

Easter (Paschal) Candle

The Easter or Paschal Candle (from *Pasch*, meaning the Christian Passover) is lit at the Easter Vigil and at every principal service until and including the Day of Pentecost. It burns for the Fifty Days of Easter in witness to the resurrection of Christ. It has always been the largest candle in the Christian community, made from the finest beeswax and often decorated with great artistry.

During the Easter Vigil the President marks the candle with the sign of the cross, the Greek letters Alpha and Omega, and the date of the year. Five grains of incense are inserted in remembrance of the five wounds of Christ. Traditionally, these marks were made with a stylus, but today it is more likely that the priest will merely trace over a transfer placed on the candle beforehand. (For details see p. 174.)

The Paschal Candle should be displayed on a purpose built stand and placed prominently at the front of the church for all to see. In some churches the base of the candle may be further decorated with flowers. Ideally the candle should be lit long before people arrive in church on a Sunday, and only extinguished after all have left to remind the congregation of the victory of the resurrection.

In order to reinforce the relationship of baptism to the dying and rising of Christ, after Eastertide it is usual for the Paschal Candle and its stand to be placed alongside the font in the baptistery where it can be re-lit at baptisms. It then becomes the source of light for the candles given to the newly baptized. *Common Worship* advocates that the candle should also be lit during a service of Confirmation when candidates renew their baptism promises.

Baptism candles

At a christening candidates may receive a baptism candle in remembrance that they have passed 'from darkness to light'. Special candles can be purchased for this, but any candle will do, provided it is large enough. It is good practice to encourage parents to light the candle on the anniversary of a child's baptism and to pray with their child. In some parishes, as a way of staying in touch with young families, special baptism anniversary services are held, complete with afternoon tea, during which the child's baptism candle may be re-lit.

Votive candles

Most churches provide a means by which parishioners and visitors can leave requests for prayer. Sometimes there is an intercession board where these requests may be left. Many people also like to light a candle for someone as they pray for them. Such candles are known as 'votive candles'. They may either be placed in trays of sand or displayed on purpose-built stands known as 'prickets' because of the spikes or holders for candles. It is advisable to put trays underneath such stands to catch any molten wax, and line them with silver foil for ease of cleaning.

Sanctuary lamps

One of the most obvious lamps in a church is a sanctuary lamp. Some churches suspend one, often on a pulley, in front of the altar. Made of brass or silver, usually with a red glass shield, it may contain a long-burning candle or an oil lamp. In some cases the lamp has been electrified. If so, care needs to be taken lest it look tawdry. Symbolic of the presence of Christ, such lamps echo the lamps maintained in the temple in Jerusalem, or that lit beside the Ark of God at Shiloh which Samuel was charged to maintain (1 Samuel 3.3).

When the sacrament is reserved in order to take holy communion to the sick and housebound, it must be locked securely in a special cupboard designated for the purpose, called an 'aumbry'. An aumbry is usually set into the wall of a side chapel and often has a simple curtain in front of it. As a further mark of reverence, and in order to indicate the presence of the consecrated elements, it is customary to keep a lamp burning perpetually beside it. Like a sanctuary lamp, this may be made of silver or brass, and contain a long-burning candle or oil lamp. The glass is usually clear and therefore it appears white, but in some churches the glass is red. One of the tasks that invariably falls to the sacristan or verger is the cleaning and maintenance of these lamps.

In some churches additional votive lights may be placed beside a statue of a patron saint or of the Blessed Virgin Mary. By convention, the glass of such lights is red for saints and blue for Our Lady.

Bier lights

Bier lights are tall free-standing candlesticks that are placed beside a coffin when it is brought into church for a funeral. There may be two, four or six of these candlesticks, according to local custom, set out in pairs around the coffin. In some churches, the Paschal Candle may also be placed along-side the coffin 'in sure and certain hope of the resurrection to eternal life through our Lord Jesus Christ'. It used to be customary for the tall candles used in bier lights to be of unbleached wax, but this custom is now rare.

Incense

Let my prayer rise before you as the incense,
and the lifting up of my hands as the evening sacrifice.

Psalm 141.2

The early congregations of believers lived in a deeply sensuous world, one in which the presence of God was experienced by means of all the senses working together: the taste of bread and wine, the smell of incense, the touch of the laying on of hands in prayer.

Roger Ferlo, *Sensing God*

Incense is used in many religions and Judaism was no exception. The offering of incense was an integral part of the ritual used in the temple in Jerusalem and was symbolic of the offering of prayer to God. The reference in Revelation 8.3–5 to the offering of incense by angels and 'the prayers of the saints' has been interpreted by some as evidence that incense was used by the early Christians, but there is no undisputed evidence until the fourth century. Thereafter we find numerous references to the censing of altars, churches and people.

At the Reformation the use of incense, along with much medieval ceremonial, was disapproved of and largely discontinued. Censing makes an appearance in the Church of England only occasionally during the next three hundred years. In the nineteenth century, however, it staged a comeback as part of a wholesale revival of ceremonial in parishes and cathedrals,

particularly at festivals and on major Feast Days. Although still disapproved of in some Anglican circles and far from widespread, the use of incense today is generally tolerated and is far less contentious than it was a generation ago.

Censers or thuribles (the technical term for an incense burner) may have been fixtures in the early centuries, but they soon became portable, suspended on chains which permitted them to be swung ceremonially, perhaps in imitation of those carried before Roman magistrates. They usually have three chains, with a central chain to raise and lower the lid. Incense may be used in processions or in services, particularly during the Eucharist. In the few parishes that still have Solemn Evensong, incense may also be offered during the singing of the *Magnificat*. When not in use the thurible is hung from an incense stand, the top being slightly raised to permit both the incense to escape and oxygen to get in, otherwise the charcoal will go out.

Incense grains are kept in an incense boat: a small metal container, usually made of brass or silver, complete with its own spoon for putting the incense on to the burning charcoal in the base of the censer. The person charged with preparing and maintaining the thurible is called a thurifer, who may or may not be accompanied by a young server called 'the boat-boy'.

Norms of ceremony

It is essential that clergy and those who act as thurifer should be confident in the use of the thurible, not least because it is hot. It is all too easy to burn yourself or inadvertently to allow hot charcoal to escape and burn a hole in the carpet. As far as possible, censing should be done silently and without fuss. Clergy and servers who make a great performance, clanking chains, draw attention to themselves and detract from the worship.

The ceremonial use of incense is referred to in terms of the 'swings' of the thurible, which are either single or double. The number of swings is traditionally a mark of the rank of the person or object being censed. Thus the President of the Eucharist may be censed with three doubles, a deacon with two, and others with one double. But this hierarchy of ritual may not always be observed. In processions the thurible should be swung back and forth in line with the direction of walking, allowing the chains to swing to their full length without hitting the person in front or behind. When censing a person or an object, the chains are held a short distance above the lid which should be firmly closed. The censer can then be held up at approximately chest height and swung towards the person or object.

The traditional points during a celebration of the Eucharist when incense is used are:

Processions

According to local custom, the thurifer either leads a procession into church or else follows the cross and servers.

Censing of the altar at the beginning of the Eucharist

At a free-standing altar, the President stands in the middle, facing the congregation, takes the thurible and moves in an anti-clockwise direction around the altar. If there is a crucifix, it is customary to make a 'station' before it: bow, cense the cross three times using double movements, bow, and continue round the altar until the circuit has been completed. The thurifer may then cense the President or wait until the priest goes to the President's chair.

Gospel Procession

The President charges the thurible and blesses the incense, making the sign of the cross over it. Once the deacon or other minister has announced the

Gospel, he or she receives the thurible and censes the Gospel Book three times (doubles), first in the middle, then to the left and then to the right.

Offertory

Once the altar is prepared, the altar book and its stand are normally removed to permit the easier censing of the communion vessels. Chalices should be covered with palls to prevent any grain of incense or pieces of burning charcoal inadvertently dropping into the wine. Traditionally, the President makes the sign of the cross over the elements with incense, and then circles the vessels three times: twice clockwise, and once anti-clockwise. Some clergy follow a simplified usage, censing the elements in the same way as the Gospel Book. The President may then cense the altar in the same way as at the beginning of the service. The thurifer then censes the President three times (doubles), a deacon (if present) twice, then the rest of the sanctuary party, before censing the people. Once the censing of the altar is complete and the collection received, the President takes the lavabo.

Practical tips with incense

1 Lighted charcoal is the best method of burning incense. It is generally available in 'self-igniting' briquettes: discs of charcoal that have
   been treated so that only a brief touch of a flame is needed to
   ignite them.

   Beware: some charcoal gives off sparks when first lit. It is sensible,
   therefore, to light charcoal over a fire-proof surface. Holding the
   briquette in metal tongs against the flame of an old candle is the
   preferred way of most thurifers. It will take longer if the charcoal is
   damp. So store the charcoal in damp-proof containers, preferably
   in a metal cupboard.

2 With most modern charcoals it is only necessary to light them ten
   minutes or so before they are needed. Too early and they will burn
   out and all you get is smokeless fuel. Depending on the size of
   the thurible and the burning time of the charcoal, two or three
   briquettes will be needed. The best charcoal is that which is shaped
   with a small well on one side to cradle the incense grains. The charcoal will not last out for the whole service and the thurible will need
   to be supplemented at the offertory. This means that a thurifer
   usually misses the sermon!

3 Whenever using a charged thurible, it is vital to ensure that the
   chains are not twisted and that the brass ring is sitting securely
   over the top of the censer. Otherwise, the moment the thurible is
   swung, all its contents will be flung out.

4 After the service, the thurible will still be hot. So hang it from a
   hook to let it cool down before cleaning it. Once cool, spent charcoal and incense can easily be disposed of and the detachable bowl
   in the base of the thurible cleaned.

Sanctuary Bells

The sound of the bells will be heard when he enters the holy place before the Lord and when he comes out.

Exodus 28.35

In addition to church bells, some parishes have a sanctuary gong or three or four little brass sanctuary or sacring bells suspended from a hand-held frame. These are rung by a server at significant moments during the celebration of the Eucharist. Customs vary, but in traditional Catholic parishes the bells are rung four times:

- *After the singing of the* Sanctus *and* Benedictus
  To signal the congregation to kneel for the Prayer of Consecration.

- *At the elevation of the host*
  Following the Words of Institution, the priest genuflects, elevates the host, and genuflects again. On each occasion, the bells are rung.

- *At the elevation of the chalice*
  As for the host.

- *Invitation to communion*
  Once the priest and assistants have received holy communion, the bells are rung to invite the congregation to come forward.

Nowadays, where bells have been retained, the custom has also been simplified, mirroring modern Roman Catholic usage. For example, *Common*

Worship encourages congregations to maintain the same posture through-out the Eucharistic Prayer; so there is no need to signal a change of posture to a congregation. With the custom of the priest facing the people across the altar now virtually normative, elevations of the host and chalice (if done) are more restrained, it being no longer necessary to lift the consecrated bread or chalice above the priest's head in order for people to see. Modern Catholic ritual also prescribes only one genuflexion, not two, after the Words of Institution, and many Anglican clergy prefer to bow in any case rather than genuflect at the end of the Eucharistic Prayer. In combination, this has resulted in a more restrained use of sacring bells.

Holy Oils

Are any among you sick? They should call for the elders of the church and have them pray over them, anointing them with oil in the name of the Lord. The prayer of faith will save the sick, and the Lord will raise them up; and anyone who has committed sins will be forgiven.

James 5.14–15

In ancient Israel the king was anointed with oil as a sign of God's blessing and of his future service to the people. In the New Testament the title of 'Anointed One' (*Messiah* in Hebrew, *Christos* in Greek) is famously conferred upon Jesus by Simon Peter at Caesarea Philippi. At his baptism by John in the River Jordan, Jesus is anointed by the outpouring of the Holy Spirit. The New Testament also speaks of the gift of the Holy Spirit as an anointing (1 John 2.20, 27) and of God setting 'his seal upon us' (2 Corinthians 1.21–22). It comes as no surprise, therefore, that from early days it was customary for candidates for baptism (known as catechumens) to have the sign of the cross traced in oil on their foreheads, and to be anointed after their baptism with chrism (olive oil perfumed with balsam) as a sign of their new life in Christ. Through their baptism they were now sharing in the priestly and royal life of Jesus Christ.

We associate olive oil predominantly with cooking, but in the ancient world it was prized more for its healing properties. It was used to soothe aching limbs and cleanse infected wounds. Thus the Letter of James encourages his readers to anoint the sick with oil and to pray over them in testimony of the healing and forgiveness that is God's will for us and his gift.

These are the biblical roots of anointing in the liturgical and pastoral life of the Church, and of the three named oils: of baptism (catechumens), of the sick, and chrism. The oil of chrism may be used at confirmations and ordinations to anoint candidates. It is also used at the coronation of the sovereign, and sometimes in the dedication of new church furnishings, such as a new altar table.

On Maundy Thursday many clergy and lay ministers go to their cathedral to renew their ordination promises at a special Diocesan Eucharist. During the liturgy the bishop blesses the oils for use in the diocese for the forthcoming year, and ministers take back to their parishes fresh supplies. For this reason it is sometimes known as the Chrism Eucharist. The oil is stored in small containers called 'stocks'. Typically, they are metal cylinders with either the letter 'B' (oil used at baptism), 'I' (oil for the sick: *infirmatis* Latin for sickness), or 'C' (oil of chrism), engraved on their lids.

Some clergy keep a smaller stock for their ministry to the sick and dying. Stocks are often stuffed with cotton wool and suffused with the oil to make them easier to use and carry around in the pocket. Stocks of holy oils should be kept in a secure place in the church under lock and key. In parishes where the blessed sacrament is reserved, clergy often use their aumbry to house stocks of oil, though some prefer to designate a separate locked cupboard for their storage.

Statues and Icons

In former times God, who is without form or body, could never be depicted. But now that God has appeared in the flesh and dwelt among us, I make an image of God in so far as he has become visible. I do not venerate matter; but I venerate the creator of matter who became matter for my sake, who willed to make his dwelling in matter, who worked out my salvation through matter. I shall never cease, therefore, to venerate the matter which wrought my salvation.

John of Damascus (d.749), *On the Incarnation and the Holy Icons*

Many of our ancient parish churches bear visible evidence of the chequered history of Christianity in these islands and an ambivalent attitude to art and human representation. Smashed medieval glass, whitewashed walls and defaced statues and crucifixes were the result of the intolerance of the Reformers, and later of the Puritans during the Commonwealth, to any form of human representation. To them any representation amounted to idolatry. In the history of the church there have been similar episodes of iconoclasm in many countries and contexts. However, on balance the instinct of the majority of Christians worldwide has been that the Old Testament prohibition of images of God had been superseded because of the Incarnation: 'the Word was made flesh and dwelt among us, and we have seen his glory'. Today Anglicanism finds itself the inheritor of a complex tradition, caught in a tangle of theological and artistic attitudes, with the result that church interiors may be austere or flamboyant, boasting no statuary whatsoever or an abundance of images, complete with crucifixes and Stations of the Cross.

Contact with the Orthodox East and the increasing popularity of icons has also had an impact on the humble parish church. In addition to a modest statue of the Virgin and Child or Mothers' Union banner in the Lady Chapel, many churches now display an icon, perhaps of Christ in Glory or of Mary or of a patron saint. These days it is more likely to be good taste and funding that determines whether or not a church has such treasures rather than the theological sensibilities of its vicar. Giving thought to the

layout of a church and to the quality of its furnishings and hangings may seem incidental to the conduct of the liturgy itself, but in a visual age what people look at when they come to church can be as important as what they hear. There is a grace in art and architecture which can communicate the beauty of God very powerfully and enhance the worship of God.

6

GLOSSARY

Ablutions The ceremonial cleansing of the eucharistic vessels by the priest, deacon or other minister, from the Latin *abluere*, meaning 'to wash clean'. The ablutions may be performed either immediately after all have received holy communion, or during the final hymn, or at the end of the service. If the ablutions are deferred in this way, it is usual to cover the vessels with a pall or simple linen veil, but not dirty, used purificators! The ablutions may take place either at the altar, or more customarily nowadays at the credence table or in a side chapel. A few clergy, following medieval custom, still use both water and wine to cleanse the chalice, first placing their thumbs and index fingers over the chalice for a server to pour over them wine and water to remove any particles of consecrated bread that may have adhered to them during the administration of communion. The vessels are then washed a second time, but using just water. With the simplification of ceremonial in recent years, this practice has largely been discontinued in favour of using just water.

Absolution The formal act of pronouncing the forgiveness of sins, from the Latin *absolvere*, meaning 'to release' or 'to free an accused person'. The absolution, declaring God's forgiveness, is pronounced by the priest acting upon the commission of Christ to 'bind' and 'loose' (Matthew 16.19; 18.18). An absolution is usually accompanied by the priest making the sign of the cross, and takes place at the end of the general confession in the Eucharist or at Morning and Evening Prayer. It is also pronounced over a penitent following the private confession of sins to a priest, for which the church makes separate liturgical provision.

Abstinence, Days of Special days of fasting, prayer and self-denial such as Ash Wednesday and Good Friday.

Academic hood   The coloured cloth made into a ceremonial hood which hangs over the shoulders and down the back, indicating that the person is a graduate. Traditionally this is worn by clergy and Readers over a cassock and surplice, but under the preaching scarf that hangs round the neck. Collectively, this forms Anglican choir dress.

Acclamation   A brief act of spoken or sung praise. A memorial or eucharistic acclamation may occur half-way through the Eucharistic Prayer, such as, 'Christ has died. Christ is risen. Christ will come again.'

Acolyte   A server who assists the clergy at the celebration of the Eucharist. An acolyte usually bears a lighted candle and will assist at the offertory. Also called a taperer.

Act of Contrition   A prayer of sorrow and penitence said by a person when making a formal confession to a priest.

Advent   From the Latin *adventus,* meaning the 'coming' of Jesus Christ. Advent marks the beginning of the Christian Year and is the season of preparation and expectation that precedes Christmas.

Advent Wreath   A wreath usually made of holly and ivy, with four candles representing the four Sundays of Advent.

Agape   From the Greek, meaning love, but also designating a love-feast – the shared meal celebrated by Christians in conjunction with the Eucharist in the early church.

Agnus dei   From the opening Latin words meaning 'Lamb of God': a devotional anthem introduced in the seventh century to accompany the breaking of the consecrated bread (fraction) during the Eucharist. Originally the text was simply repeated until the action was completed. However, with the use of unleavened bread becoming normative (at least in the West) by about the middle of the ninth century, the number of repetitions became fixed at three. As early as the eleventh century a further variant appeared at requiem masses when the phrase 'grant them eternal rest' was substituted. ***See also Fraction.***

Alb A long white or cream coloured robe, derived from the *tunica alba* (white tunic), the linen tunic worn under civilian dress in Roman times. An alb covers the whole body from neck to ankle, and is worn by priests and deacons under eucharistic vestments, and often by servers as well. Traditionally an alb is made of cotton or linen and has close-fitting sleeves. Underneath it, around the neck, may be worn an amice which sometimes may also have a decorated collar or 'apparel'. A cincture or rope girdle is worn around the waist to gather the alb around the middle. Modern albs tend to be designed to be worn without a cassock or an amice, and are sometimes called 'cassock-albs'. They tend to have looser-fitting sleeves, and may be worn with or without a girdle. In the medieval church the alb was interpreted as a symbol of purity.

All-Age worship Worship designed to embrace the whole Christian community. It is not the same as 'Children's' or 'Family' worship. Such services tend to be highly participative and are attractive to occasional worshippers. They usually follow the framework of *Common Worship* 'Service of the Word'.

Alleluia From the Hebrew *hallelujah*, meaning 'Praise God!' In the Eucharist it is sometimes sung or said in conjunction with a verse of scripture as an acclamation before the reading of the Gospel, or to accompany a Gospel Procession. By custom, alleluia is not sung during Lent when it is replaced by a Lenten acclamation. For the same reason, hymns with alleluia tend to be avoided in Lent, making the first alleluia in praise of the resurrection on Easter Day all the more triumphant.

Alms and almsdish The word 'alms' has an archaic ring, but ultimately derives from the Greek meaning 'mercy'. Gifts of money (traditionally for the relief of the poor) are collected and presented in an almsdish or basin which may be made out of brass, pewter or wood. The importance of generous giving was recognized by the first Christians as a response to Christ's own self-giving (2 Corinthians 8.9). The presentation of such gifts became a regular feature of Christian worship, though the word 'collection' tends to be used today.

Altar The holy table on which is celebrated the sacrament of the Lord's Supper. The eucharistic table may be made of wood or stone. Some altars have a wooden base, but a stone top or *mensa*. The tops of altars are often marked with five crosses, one in each corner and the fifth in the centre, when dedicated with chrism by the bishop. Moveable altars are often used in large churches at the front of the nave to create a more intimate and inclusive feel to the celebration of the Eucharist.

Altar frontal   An ornamental cloth, often heavily embroidered, that covers the front and often the sides of the altar. So-called 'Laudian frontals' – named after Archbishop Laud – are throw-overs covering the entire communion table. Frontals may change with the liturgical seasons.

Altar of Repose   A special altar constructed on Maundy Thursday on which is placed the Blessed Sacrament at the end of the liturgy for use on Good Friday. It is usually decorated with greenery, flowers and candles in token of the Garden of Gethsemane where Jesus went to pray after the Last Supper.

Altar rails   *See Communion rails.*

Alternative Service Book   Known affectionately as the ASB. Published in 1980, it represented the first full-scale revision of the liturgy and psalter of the Church of England in modern English. It was superseded by *Common Worship* in 2000, and is no longer authorized for use.

Ambo   A raised platform or pulpit, often approached with a flight of steps, from which the Gospel was read or a sermon preached in the early church. In the early centuries an ambo was also used by the deacon during the Easter liturgy for singing the *exsultet*.

Ambulatory   From the Latin *ambulare*, meaning 'to walk'. A continuous passageway round the east end of a church or cathedral to facilitate the movement of clergy and servers without disturbing the congregation.

Amice   From the Latin *amictus*, itself derived from *amicio,* meaning 'to wrap around'. An amice is a rectangular piece of linen or cotton worn with a traditional alb to cover the neck, originally to protect other vestments from sweat. It is secured around the top of the body with long tapes. It is sometimes decorated with an ornamental collar or 'apparel' which may change colour with the liturgical seasons. Because it is the first vestment to be donned, placed initially on the head and then pushed back once the alb is on, in the medieval church it came to symbolize 'the helmet of salvation' referred to by St Paul.

Anamnesis   A liturgical term from the Greek but expressing a Semitic concept meaning 'to remember' or 'to make memorial': the central action of the Eucharistic Prayer by which the saving work of Christ is remembered and its effects made present.

Angelus A traditional Catholic memorial of the Incarnation, based on the text of the annunciation in St Luke's Gospel. The first word of the prayer in Latin (*Angelus ad virginem* – the angel brought tidings to Mary) gave the name to the prayer. The Angelus is said three times a day, first thing in the morning, at noon, and in the evening, and is often accompanied by the ringing of church bells.

Ante-Communion The first half of the Communion service leading up to and including the Prayer of Intercession (the Prayer for the Church Militant in the *Book of Common Prayer*). The term may also designate a service where there is to be no communion. The word often appears on Good Friday in conjunction with the litany, designating a non-eucharistic service.

Antiphon A sentence, usually from scripture, sung as a refrain at the beginning and end of a psalm or canticle, particularly in monastic liturgy.

Antiphonal A book containing the plainsong music of antiphons. The term 'antiphonal singing' refers to the custom of singing or reciting psalms and canticles by alternate verses, usually done by two sides of a choir.

Apocrypha From the Greek *ta apokrupha*, meaning 'the hidden things'. The title given to certain late books of the Old Testament which, although appearing in the Greek version of the Bible, were excluded from the Hebrew Bible. They are not printed in all versions of the Bible, and appear variously between the Old and New Testaments, or as an appendix at the end of the Bible. They are more appropriately termed 'Deutero-Canonical Books'. In Anglican custom these books may be read in church for edification and learning, but are not used as doctrinal sources.

Apparel The name given to a strip of fabric that may decorate traditional amices and which appears as an ornamental collar. Colours vary with the liturgical season. Apparels may also decorate the cuffs and the lower front and back hems of servers' albs. The latter are sometimes nicknamed by servers 'kick-plates'.

Apse The semicircular shape of the east end of the sanctuary, roofed with a half dome. This architectural style was very popular in early Christian basilicas and early medieval churches. In some churches it was mirrored at the west end by a baptistery.

Ash Wednesday The first day of Lent. In medieval usage it was called 'The Day of Ashes', so called because since at least the tenth century, Christians have observed the beginning of Lent by marking their foreheads with ashes made from burning the previous year's palm crosses as a sign of penitence.

Asperges   From the Latin *aspergere*, meaning 'to sprinkle'. The word comes from the Latin translation of the verse, 'You will sprinkle me with hyssop and I shall be clean; you will wash me and I shall be whiter than snow' (Psalm 51.7) customarily recited by the priest when sprinkling a congregation with holy water in remembrance of their baptism. This may happen in the context of a Confirmation service when candidates gather around the font to renew their baptismal promises, or more generally during the annual renewal of baptismal promises at the Easter Vigil. An **aspergillum** may be made out of metal (usually brass) and come complete with a holy water bucket, or a priest may use a bunch of fresh greenery (often containing rosemary) for the purpose.

Aumbry   A special cupboard or safe, usually recessed into the wall of a church, in which may be housed eucharistic vessels, precious liturgical books, or the Blessed Sacrament itself, reserved for the communion of the sick and housebound. If the sacrament is reserved, the cupboard usually has a curtain in front of it and a white or red light burning above it. Aumbries may also store the holy oils.

Back To Church Sunday   A designated Sunday in late September on which there is a concerted drive to re-engage the lapsed in the worshipping life of a parish.

Baldacchino   Technically a canopy, but when used as an architectural term, it refers to an ornate canopy built over an altar in the Baroque manner. An altar canopy resting directly on four columns is more correctly referred to as a ciborium, but this can cause confusion because the same term is used for a eucharistic vessel.

Banner   An embroidered panel, traditionally of the Blessed Virgin Mary or the patron saint of a parish, mounted on a long pole so that it could be carried in processions. In many churches today, banners of material are hung from pillars or walls as decorations.

Baptism   The rite by which new Christians are initiated into the church. A person may be immersed in water or have water poured over the head 'in the name of the Father, and of the Son, and of the Holy Spirit' in obedience to the command of Jesus.

Baptismal shell A scallop-shaped shell used to pour water at baptism. The scallop shell, as well as being practical, was also a symbol of the Christian pilgrimage, relating to the ancient shrine of St James at Compostela.

Baptistery The place of baptism. In early churches when adult baptism by full immersion was normative, baptisteries (as at Pisa and Florence) were separate buildings from the church. In English medieval churches, by which time infant baptism had become normative, the place of baptism was within the church building, often at the west end of the church or near the church door, symbolizing it as entry into the fellowship of the church. Nowadays, with adult baptism once again becoming more common, many modern churches are being built with special baptisteries that permit both infants and adults to be baptized, the latter often by total immersion.

Benedicite The 'Song of the Three Children' (*Benedicite omnia opera*) appended to the Book of Daniel, 'O all ye works, praise ye the Lord'. This Song of Creation with its refrain, 'Sing God's praise and exalt him for ever' is included in the office of Morning Prayer in both the *Book of Common Prayer,* and *Common Worship.*

Benediction From the Latin *bene* meaning 'well', and *dicere* meaning 'to speak'. The term is used in two different senses. First, to refer to the blessing given at the end of a service by the presiding minister. Secondly, a service of blessing, usually held in the afternoon or evening, at which the people are blessed with the Reserved Sacrament usually displayed in a monstrance.

Benedictus The word may refer to two things:
1 The Song of Zechariah from Luke 1.68–79, beginning, 'Blessed be the Lord, the God of Israel'. The canticle is said at the climax of Morning Prayer, and corresponds to the use of the *Magnificat* at Evensong.
2 The anthem that is often joined to the *Sanctus* in the Eucharistic Prayer: 'Blessed is he who comes in the name of the Lord.'

Bidding Prayer An invitation to prayer and worship, often specially composed for an important occasion such as a memorial service or carol service. Biddings are addressed to the congregation, inviting them to pray, and may punctuate prayers of intercession.

Bier Some ancient parish churches still boast their own parish bier – the pallet or trolley on which a coffin is transported to and from the church, and then to the graveside.

Bier lights Tall candlesticks that stand beside a coffin during a Funeral service. There may be two, four or six, used in pairs, according to local custom. The candles used were typically of unbleached wax, but this custom has gone somewhat out of fashion.

Biretta A square hat, with three wings and a tassel, worn or carried by traditional high church clergy. The birettas of priests are black; those of bishops are purple, and those of cardinals scarlet. In origin the biretta was part of medieval academic dress: a cap, not dissimilar to the soft hats or 'Canterbury Caps' seen in the portraits of the English Reformers. On the Continent the cap evolved into the present-day biretta, and eventually became part of Roman choir dress. In England the academic cap became flatter and harder, and came to be nicknamed a 'square' or 'mortarboard'. Squares are no longer a normal part of Anglican choir dress, except in some cathedrals and university choral foundations where clergy and choristers still carry them.

Bishop's Chair The bishop has his seat or *cathedra* in his cathedral church. The custom derives from the ancient world where philosophers had a chair on which they sat when delivering their teaching. Modern universities still talk of professors occupying 'chairs' in a given subject. The *cathedra* is thus the sign of the bishop's teaching authority. By custom, each parish church also has a designated chair for the bishop when he comes as the chief pastor. This is normally placed in the sanctuary on the north side.

Blessed Sacrament A term for the Eucharist or more specifically, the consecrated elements.

Boat-boy A young server who accompanies the thurifer, and who holds the incense-container.

Book of Common Prayer The standard authorized Prayer Book of Anglicans, last revised in 1662, and sometimes referred to simply as 'BCP'. The 1928 revision of the Prayer Book was never authorized by Parliament, but many of its innovations and revisions nevertheless passed into common usage. Its Marriage service, sometimes also known as 'Series 1', is authorized for use by General Synod.

Both kinds   A shorthand term meaning people receive both the consecrated bread and wine at Holy Communion, as opposed to 'one kind' meaning (usually) just the consecrated bread. When the sacrament is reserved for communion by extension for distribution to the sick and housebound, it is often reserved only under 'one kind' for convenience sake. The Church teaches that communicants receive the fullness of the sacrament of Christ's body and blood, even if they are only able to receive under one kind.

Bowing   Bowing the head, as a natural gesture of recognition or respect, evolved into a liturgical act of reverence, often made on entering or leaving the church. A 'profound bow' indicates a bow from the waist and is preferred by some clergy to the act of genuflexion. Some Christians have traditionally also bowed their heads at the name of Jesus, for example during the recitation of the Apostles' Creed at Evensong, or during the *Gloria Patri,* the doxology sung at the end of psalms. ***See also Genuflexion.***

Bread box   Also known as a wafer box. A small, chambered box, usually made of silver, containing people's wafers, normally put on the credence table.

Breviary   From the Latin *brevis*, meaning 'short'. The name of the book containing the Liturgy of the Hours in the medieval church which was superseded by Cranmer's *Book of Common Prayer.* The term is still in use in the Catholic Church as shorthand for the Divine Office.

Burse   A flat case consisting of two squares of covered boards or stiffened material joined on three sides to create a pouch in which the corporal is kept when not in use. This keeps the corporal clean and uncreased. The burse is often embroidered, and may match the liturgical colour of the season. If used, it usually has a matching veil. ***See also Corporal.***

Candlemas   The Feast of the Presentation of Christ in the Temple, also known as the Purification of the Blessed Virgin Mary, on 2 February; so called because of the custom of lighting candles in honour of Jesus who would 'lighten the eyes of the Gentiles'.

Canon   The Greek word *kanon* means a rule or measuring rod, and came to be applied to the rules for the ordering of worship, hence the 'Canons of the Church of England'. ***See also Canon of the Mass and Canonical Hours.***

Canon of the Mass   The Greek word *kanon* came also to be applied to the central part of the Eucharistic Prayer, including the Words of Institution. In early liturgical books, where improvisation was permitted, we find the word appearing as a heading, indicating to the priest that the text from this point on was fixed.

Canonical Hours   The times laid down when services are to be held, sometimes just called 'The Hours'. In monastic usage the day was punctuated by prayer and in medieval times seven hours were observed: Lauds, Prime, Terce, Sext, None, Vespers and Compline. In addition monks also said a Night Office, variously known as 'Vigils' or 'Matins'. Prime, Terce, Sext and None are sometimes known as the 'Little Hours', meaning that they were shorter and not as important as the other offices. Modern monastic custom has simplified this arrangement.

Canticle   From the Latin *canticulum*, meaning 'a song'. Over the centuries certain texts from the Bible or the Fathers have been incorporated into the liturgy and are called canticles. In the Eucharist there is the *Gloria in excelsis*, based on the song of the angels at Christ's birth. There is the *Nunc dimittis* (The Song of Simeon, Luke 2.29–32), *Benedicite* (The Song of the Three, from the Apocrypha)*, Te deum*, and the so-called Easter Anthems. The two most famous are the so-called 'Gospel Canticles'. These are the Song of Zechariah (Luke 1.68–79) and the Song of Mary (Luke 1.46–55), known respectively by their Latin titles *Benedictus* and *Magnificat*. In the Western Church these are said at Morning and Evening Prayer respectively.

Cantor   From the Latin *cantare*, meaning 'to sing': a person leading the people's singing, particularly when unaccompanied or in a responsorial psalm.

Cassock   The customary robe of clergy, servers, and members of robed choirs. The colour of the cassocks of clergy is usually black, though many cathedral foundations have distinctive colours (e.g. Hereford wear blue; Salisbury wear green). Royal Foundations and the Queen's Chaplains wear scarlet cassocks. Bishops usually, though not always, have purple cassocks. The cassock comes in two styles, known as 'Sarum' and 'Latin'. The Sarum or English style is the traditional 'flapover' cassock, worn with a belt or cincture. The Latin cassock is single-breasted, sometimes with 39 buttons in symbolic remembrance of the lashes Jesus received before his crucifixion. This style of cassock, particularly if it has a short cape, is also known as a soutane.

Celebrant   The priest or bishop presiding at the Eucharist. The term 'President' is preferred today partly because it is the ancient title designating this role, but also because it is the whole assembly that 'celebrates' the Eucharist, not just one individual.

Censer   *See Thurible.*

Chalice   From the Latin *calix*, meaning 'cup', used to contain the communion wine.

Chancel   From the Latin *cancellus*, meaning lattice or enclosure. The word came to be applied to the eastern part of a church, the most sacred part of the building, which was often separated from the nave by a screen or steps and reserved for the officiating clergy. At the extreme eastern end of the chancel is the sanctuary where the altar is housed.

Chasuble   The outermost vestment worn by a priest or bishop presiding at the Eucharist. It is often richly embroidered and its colour may vary with the liturgical season. In origin, like the cope, the chasuble was an outdoor cloak worn by both men and women in the late Graeco-Roman world, but since the eighth century its use has been restricted to clergy. It is worn over the head in the style of a South American poncho. The Gothic shape was still quite full, but over the centuries it was gradually reduced in size and became more stylized. The Latin or Baroque chasuble lost its sides and the front of the vestment was cut in the shape of a violin; hence its nickname, 'fiddle-backs'. Modern designs favour a return to a more ample cut.

Chimere   A silk or satin gown without sleeves worn over a rochet by Anglican bishops and Doctors of Divinity. It is either black or scarlet.

Chi Rho   The first two letters of the Greek word *christos*, meaning 'Christ'. Together, the letters were adopted by Constantine, the first Christian emperor, as his symbol, and since then have entered Christian iconography.

Choir dress (choir habit)   The term to describe the vesture of the clergy at non-eucharistic services: cassock, with either surplice or cotta, scarf (tippet) and academic hood (optional).

Chrism   One of the oils consecrated by the bishop on Maundy Thursday for use in the church (see oils). It is easily distinguished from others because of the balsam that is mixed with it which gives it a distinctive aroma.

Christening   Traditional title for baptism, particularly used in relation to the baptism of infants.

Christingle   Meaning 'Christ-light'. The ceremony of lighted candles, made popular by The Children's Society, is Moravian in origin. It celebrates the light of Christ shining in the darkness of the world.

Christus Rex   A cross on which is displayed the figure of Christ the King, dressed in royal robes 'reigning from the tree'.

Churchmanship   A term designating a parish or individual's preferred style of worship. The terms 'high', 'low', 'central', 'broad', 'middle-of-the-road' indicate where on the spectrum between simplicity and ritualism a parish is to be located. The term 'evangelical' implies a preference for minimal ceremony, combined with a commitment to strong biblical preaching. This may be qualified by the adjective 'open' or 'conservative', indicating their degree of adherence to traditional approaches to doctrine, hymnody and worship. 'Charismatic' signals a preference for an informal style of worship in which emphasis is given to the work of the Holy Spirit in the life of the church. The term 'liberal' indicates a generous openness to dialogue with others and a non-fundamentalist approach to Christian life and doctrine. 'Catholic' signals a strong preference for sacramental worship. This may be further differentiated. The terms 'Anglo-Catholic' or 'Traditional Catholic' designate a loyalty to a traditional view of church and worship, whereas 'Modern Catholic' or 'Liberal Catholic' indicate a commitment to sacramental worship, but in a contemporary fashion. The term 'papalist' refers to an Anglican whose loyalty to the Church of England goes hand-in-hand with an admiration for all things Roman Catholic, whereas 'Prayer Book Catholic' indicates high church, but an unswerving loyalty to Anglican formularies.

Churchwardens' staves   Churchwarden is the oldest lay office in England. Their staves are symbols of their authority, and are often topped with either a crown or a mitre.

Ciborium   From the Greek *kiborion*, meaning 'a cup'. A container, usually made of silver resembling a cup but with a lid, used to contain wafers at Holy

Communion. For this reason, its cup-shape tends to be specially shaped or flat-bottomed. **See also Baldacchino.**

Cincture   A band of cloth or silk worn at the waist of a cassock instead of a belt. This is purple in the case of bishops. The term may also be used for the rope or cloth girdle that holds in an alb at the waist.

Clerk   A general term for an educated or literate person. A 'clerk in holy orders' designates a clergyperson; a 'lay clerk' is an adult member of a cathedral choir; and a 'parish clerk' is appointed by an incumbent and PCC to assist in the administration of the parish. In the seventeenth and eighteenth centuries, the parish clerk had a liturgical role in leading the congregation in saying the responses in services or reading the lessons, and sometimes read the Epistle.

Collect   From the Latin *collecta* or *collectio* meaning 'collected' or 'summed up'. Both the *Book of Common Prayer* and *Common Worship* provide a short prayer or Collect for every Sunday and major Feast Day of the church's year. The Collect is said immediately before the Liturgy of the Word in the Eucharist, and at the conclusion of Morning and Evening Prayer. It is a very early form of Latin prayer and is a characteristic of liturgy in the Western (Latin) Church.

Collect for Purity   The opening prayer beginning, 'Almighty God, unto whom all hearts be open', said following the Lord's Prayer in the rite of Holy Communion in the *Book of Common Prayer*. Cranmer designated this to be said by the priest alone, but in *Common Worship*, if the prayer is used, it is now said by all as a prayer of preparation following the opening greeting.

Comfortable Words   One of the most loved parts of the Communion service in the *Book of Common Prayer*, where the priest recites four passages from the New Testament, introducing them with the words, 'Hear what comfortable words our Saviour Jesus Christ saith to all who truly turn unto him.' Over the centuries the word 'comfort' has somewhat changed in meaning, but in origin it meant to give strength or to encourage.

Common Worship   The collective title of the revised liturgy and occasional offices of the Church of England, authorized in 2000 in succession to the *Alternative Service Book*. The *Book of Common Prayer* remains the benchmark of all Anglican liturgy.

Communicant   A person in good standing who receives holy communion.

Communion rails   The low rail where people kneel to receive holy communion. Such rails were rare in England prior to the Reformation, but begin to appear during the reign of Elizabeth I. Their installation increased in the century that followed in obedience to directives of Archbishop Laud to return the communion tables to their medieval position at the east end of the parish churches of England and Wales. Often complete with balusters and a little gate, these had the added advantage of protecting the holy tables from being fouled by dogs which were free to wander around churches in earlier centuries. Today, when a more open-plan sanctuary is often preferred, permitting a more flexible use of worship-space, or where a church has been re-ordered and communion is received standing up, communion rails may be made portable or dispensed with altogether.

Communion table   Also known as the holy table. The term is preferred by those loyal to the Protestant Reformation. In the sixteenth century the term 'altar' had become irretrievably associated with the medieval idea that Christ was somehow immolated afresh during the celebration of the Mass. *See also Altar.*

Compline   Pronounced 'com-plin': the last monastic office of the day before bed, often including the recitation of *Nunc dimittis*, the Song of Simeon, 'Lord, now let your servant depart in peace'.

Concelebration   The joint celebration of the Eucharist by a number of priests in which the central section of the Eucharistic Prayer is recited by the priests together either silently or *sotto voce*. A **concelebrant** is a priest participating in such a Eucharist.

Confession   From the Latin *confessio* meaning 'I confess'. In early centuries the term usually designated a confession of faith, but nowadays it more usually refers to an act of penitence and may be used in two principal ways: to denote either a general confession said by all during an act of worship; or a confession of sins to a priest in private, for which the church makes separate liturgical provision. The latter may also be referred to variously as the 'sacrament of reconciliation', 'sacramental confession', or 'auricular confession'. *See also Absolution.*

Confessional   A designated area in a church set apart for the hearing of confessions by the clergy. In Anglican churches a confessional usually consists of a chair for the priest, complete with purple stole ready for the priest to wear, and a prayer-desk beside it at which the penitent kneels. In Roman Catholic churches the confessional is usually a stall with a grill to protect the anonymity of the penitent. Such 'confession boxes' are gradually being replaced by 'Rooms for Reconciliation' which permit a face-to-face encounter of priest and penitent, and the easier giving of counsel.

Consecration   From the Latin *consecratio* referring to the act of setting something or someone apart for sacred use. In the 1662 *Book of Common Prayer*, the final part of the Eucharistic Prayer was called the 'Prayer of Consecration'. The term is also used in reference to the ordination of bishops, the consecration of churches, and the setting apart of land for Christian burial.

Consecration Cross   At the consecration of a church, its interior walls are marked by the bishop with the sign of the cross, usually with chrism. In some usages four crosses are made, one on each of the four walls (traditionally in honour of the four evangelists). In other customs 12 crosses are made (in honour of the apostles); and in yet others, just a single cross of dedication is made. In some medieval churches these crosses are still visible, carved into the wall. Consecration crosses sometimes have a candle in front of them which are lit on the anniversary of the church's consecration.

Cope   An ornamental cloak worn by clergy and others, and especially bishops, on ceremonial occasions. Like the chasuble, the cope derived from civilian dress worn in the late Graeco-Roman world, and was worn in cold or wet weather. Copes originally had hoods, but this feature became vestigial and survives as a rounded or triangular piece of material, often beautifully embroidered, attached at the back below the neck-line.

Corporal   From the medieval Latin *corporalis*, meaning a body cloth. This is a piece of square linen, placed on the centre of the altar cloth on which are placed the communion vessels at the beginning of the Eucharistic Prayer. When not in use, it is carefully folded away and usually kept flat in a burse.

Cotta   From the Italian meaning 'shortened'. It is in origin a cut-down version of the surplice, which probably evolved in southern Europe where the climate was warmer. Typically it has a square yoke (as opposed to the rounded yoke of the surplice), with square cut-off sleeves and pleats. It may reach down to the waist or knee. It is worn by clergy and servers. ***See also Surplice.***

Credence table   A small, but tall, table placed near the altar, usually on the south side of the sanctuary, on which are placed the communion vessels, purificators, and cruets of wine and water, in preparation for the celebration of Holy Communion. Ablutions may also take place at the credence table, in preference to the altar itself. The table is usually covered with a simple white linen cloth when in use.

Creed   There are three so-called 'Catholic Creeds'. The Nicene Creed is said during the Eucharist. The Apostles' Creed (an ancient Western baptismal Creed) is said at Matins and Evensong, and (sometimes responsively) in the rites of Baptism and Confirmation. The so-called Athanasian Creed is no longer recited publicly. *Common Worship* stipulates that the Creed or an authorized Affirmation of Faith shall be said at every principal service on a Sunday or festival.

Crib   A representation of the crib or manger in which the baby Jesus was laid at his birth, normally assembled during the Christmas season in churches, complete with various *dramatis personae*. This popular visual devotion is reputed to have been invented by St Francis of Assisi in 1223.

Crozier   *See Pastoral staff.*

Crucifer   The person who carries a processional cross when entering or leaving church.

Crucifix   A cross displaying the suffering Christ. ***See also Christus Rex.***

Cruets   Glass or earthenware vessels containing wine and water to be used in the celebration of Holy Communion. They may be placed on the credence table in advance of the service, or at the back of the church and brought up to the sanctuary as part of an offertory procession.

Daily Office   *See Office.*

Dalmatic   The distinctive vestment of the deacon. It is worn over an alb and stole (which in deacon-custom is worn over the left shoulder, not around the neck). The dalmatic looks like a chasuble but has square cut sleeves, reaches down to the knees, and is often embroidered with two distinctive vertical stripes, running from front to back over the shoulders, with two orphreys (ornamental bands) on front and back. The name *tunica dalmatica* would seem to indicate an origin in the region of Dalmatia.

Deacon   From the Greek *diakonos*, meaning servant. One of the ancient orders of ordained ministry. By custom, the deacon reads the Gospel at the Eucharist, invites the people to confess their sins and to share the peace, prepares the bread and wine at the offertory, and says the words of dismissal at the end of the service. A deacon wears his or her stole across the left shoulder, and may wear a distinctive vestment called a dalmatic.

Dismissal   From the Latin *dismissus*, meaning 'sent away'. The title designates the end of a gathering for worship when the congregation is 'dismissed', sent out in the peace of Christ to love and serve others. It is from these closing words in Latin that the word 'mass' derived.

Dorsal (dossal)   A long, heavy curtain hung behind an altar as a backcloth.

Doxology   From the Greek *doxologia*, meaning 'glory words'. A prayer of praise said or sung at the end of a hymn, psalm or canticle, usually addressed to the Holy Trinity.

Easter Candle   The great Easter (Paschal) Candle is scored symbolically, usually at the Easter Vigil, with the sign of the cross, the symbols Alpha and Omega, the year, and five nails or large grains of incense that are gilded representing the wounds of Christ. The candle burns throughout Eastertide until and including the Day of Pentecost. It is placed on a large candlestick in a prominent place in church. Outside Eastertide, it is usually placed in the baptistery near the font and is lit at baptisms to underline the link between baptism and dying and rising with Christ. It may also be placed next to the coffin at funerals.

Easter Garden   A representation of the garden in which the body of Jesus was laid after the crucifixion. Like the crib at Christmas, the Easter Garden can be a powerful visual symbol. Customarily it has a Calvary with three empty crosses, with a path leading to an empty tomb. Its origins are uncertain. In medieval England, Easter Gardens or Sepulchres were often built into stone recesses on the north side of the high altar in churches.

Easter Vigil The church's oldest liturgical observance celebrating the resurrection of Christ, held either on Easter Eve night or very early on Easter Sunday morning. *See also Paschal Vigil.*

Elements The bread and wine of the Eucharist.

Elevation The term used to describe the action when a priest lifts the host or chalice during or at the end of the Eucharistic Prayer for people to see. In some traditions this action is accompanied by the ringing of a bell or gong.

Ember Day A day of prayer for those preparing to be ordained or exploring a vocation to Christian ministry.

English Usage *See Sarum Usage.*

Epiclesis From the Greek *epi* meaning 'upon', and *kaleo* meaning 'call'. The term designates the prayer of invocation to the Holy Spirit in the Eucharistic Prayer to sanctify the elements and those participating in the Eucharist, that together they may be transformed into the body of Christ. Priests may extend their hands over the bread and wine at this point and make the sign of the cross.

Episcopal Ring The symbol of the bishop's authority, worn usually on the third finger of the right hand.

Epistle From the Greek *epistole* and Latin *epistola*, meaning 'letter'. The passage of scripture, usually from one of the New Testament letters, read at the Eucharist, though the term in the *Book of Common Prayer* is used flexibly to include readings from the Acts of the Apostles and the Book of Revelation.

Epistle-side In the *Book of Common Prayer* the reader of the Epistle may stand at the south side (right-hand side from the congregation) of the holy table when reading at a celebration of Holy Communion.

Epistoler The person reading the Epistle at the Eucharist.

Eucharist Probably the oldest Christian title, deriving from the Greek *eukaristia* meaning 'thanksgiving', for the sacrament of the Lord's Supper. In Anglican usage, 'Holy Communion' remains the commonest title for the service. Some churches in the Catholic tradition may refer to the service as 'Mass'.

Eucharistic Prayer The great Prayer of Thanksgiving in which the President gives thanks to God for his graciousness and recalls the institution of the Lord's Supper. *Common Worship* provides a number of alternative Eucharistic Prayers, together with suitable seasonal material known as 'Prefaces'.

Eucharistic vestments Traditional robes worn by a priest when presiding at the Eucharist.

Evensong The traditional name given to Evening Prayer in the Anglican Church, corresponding to Vespers in the Roman Catholic Church.

Ewer A large pitcher with a handle, normally made of brass or pewter, used to carry water to the font in Baptism.

Exposition A term with two contrasting usages. On the lips of evangelicals, it usually refers to the careful expounding of a passage of scripture. On the lips of Catholics, the term is more likely to refer to the exposure or showing of the host (consecrated bread) for devotion.

Exsultet From the first word of the text in Latin of the great Easter proclamation sung by the deacon at the Easter Vigil, announcing the resurrection of Christ.

Faculty The formal permission granted by the Chancellor of a diocese to authorize changes to or the repair of the fabric of a church.

Fair linen The *Book of Common Prayer* states that the holy table shall be covered with 'fair linen' at the time of a celebration of Holy Communion. The term designates the long cloth that covers the table and hangs down on both sides. The term may be used more generally by sacristans to refer to all types of altar linen.

Faldstools Small, upholstered prie-dieux at which a bride and groom may kneel during their wedding.

Fall The technical term for the cloth covering that hangs down ('falls') from a lectern or pulpit. It is often embroidered and its colour may vary with the liturgical season.

Fast A day of abstinence (e.g. Ash Wednesday).

Feria   From the Latin *feria*, meaning 'holiday'. Bizarrely, the use of this term is completely different from its derivation. The term now appears in service registers indicating an 'ordinary' day, as opposed to a saint's day.

Font   From the Latin *fons*, meaning a 'spring' or 'well'. The font is usually a large bowl, often supported on stone columns, situated at the west end of a church. In medieval churches fonts often had elaborate covers, sometimes so large that they were suspended on pulleys. Many parishes, particularly where the font is inconveniently situated, also have a portable font which permits the sacrament to be celebrated in full view of the congregation.

Fraction   The ceremonial breaking of the consecrated bread during the Eucharist ready for distribution. This action may be accompanied by the singing of the anthem *Agnus dei* (Lamb of God).

Gaudete Sunday   The Third Sunday of Advent; so called because of words of St Paul to the Philippians often read on this day, 'Rejoice in the Lord; and again I say, rejoice. The Lord is at hand.' In some churches rose-coloured vestments are worn on this day.

Genuflexion   An act of reverence, originating in the Byzantine Court and imported into Christian ceremonial, in which the right knee is flexed and touches the ground echoing St Paul's words that, 'at the name of Jesus every knee shall bow'. The custom is observed by many Christians as a mark of reverence when approaching the altar to receive holy communion or when passing the place where the Blessed Sacrament is reserved. Some clergy genuflect or bow after elevating the host or chalice, or at the conclusion of the Eucharistic Prayer. **See also Bowing.**

Girdle   A rope tied round an alb or cassock at the waist.

Gloria in excelsis   The canticle based on the angels' song in St Luke's Gospel, sung (except in Advent and Lent) either at the beginning of the Eucharist (*Common Worship*), or at its conclusion in the Prayer Book rite.

Godly Play   A creative and imaginative approach to Christian nurture, geared to children, based on the Montessori tradition of religious education. It invites listeners into biblical stories as a way of preparing children to move into the worship and life of the church. Churches may advertise this as a 'Story Telling Service'.

Good Friday   The commemoration of the day of crucifixion of Jesus.

Gospeller   The person reading the Gospel at the Eucharist.

Gospel Procession   A ceremonial procession accompanying the reading of the Gospel, usually in the midst of the congregation. The procession normally consists of a crucifer, two acolytes and a server (or subdeacon) who holds the Gospel Book for the deacon or reader. Incense may be used.

Gospel-side   In the custom of the *Book of Common Prayer,* the person reading the Gospel may stand at the north side of the holy table (the left-hand side as the congregation looks at it), whereas the person reading the Epistle stands on the other side.

Gradual   From the Latin *gradus,* meaning 'step'. Historically this was a chant, but today the word usually refers to the hymn or psalm sung between the Epistle and Gospel in the Eucharist.

Great Fifty Days   The period from Easter Sunday to Pentecost during which, according to St Luke, the risen Christ appeared to his disciples.

Gregorian chant   *See Plainsong.*

Hassock   A cushion for kneeling; also known as a kneeler.

High Altar   The main altar in a church. The term is often used to differentiate it from side chapels or a nave altar.

High Mass   A celebration of the Eucharist with elaborate ceremonial, usually involving a priest, a deacon, and a subdeacon, each of whom is vested and has a distinctive liturgical role. A 'High Mass set' designates a matching set of vestments made of the same material and colour: chasuble, dalmatic and tunicle. Also known as Solemn Mass. *See also Low Mass.*

Hillsong Music   A genre of contemporary Christian music produced by Hillsong Church, a Pentecostal mega-church based in Sydney, Australia.

Holy Communion   The traditional Anglican title for the sacrament of the Lord's Supper. *See also Eucharist.*

Holy Matrimony   The traditional title in the *Book of Common Prayer* for Christian marriage.

Holy table (Communion table)   An alternative term for altar, preferred by many Evangelical clergy to dissociate the Eucharist from any sacrificial interpretation and to reinforce the communal gathering of the people of God sharing in a sacred meal. ***See also Altar.***

Holy Week   The week running up to Easter, beginning on Palm Sunday, commemorating the events leading up to the crucifixion.

Homily   A short sermon, often devotional in character.

Hood   *See Academic hood.*

Host   From the Latin *hostia*, meaning 'victim'. Medieval Catholic theology stressed the sacrificial nature of the eucharistic action, and as a consequence the term came to be applied to the consecrated bread. People's wafers may be referred to as 'people's hosts', and large wafers as 'priest's hosts'.

Houseling cloth   A rare survival from the medieval Church. At the time of communion, the communion rails have long strips of linen attached to them, in the manner of napkins or tablecloths to catch any consecrated elements that may fall during the administration of holy communion.

Humble Access   The prayer composed by Cranmer as a preparation for receiving holy communion, beginning 'We do not presume'. In the *Book of Common Prayer* it immediately precedes the Prayer of Consecration. In *Common Worship* the prayer is positioned immediately before the reception of holy communion. It provides two alternative prayers: a version of Cranmer's prayer in modern English, and a contemporary prayer beginning, 'Most merciful Lord …'

Humeral veil   From the Latin *humerale*, meaning 'of the shoulder'. A long rectangular cloth worn by the priest around the shoulders when carrying the Blessed Sacrament in ceremonial procession, particularly on Maundy Thursday, or for holding the monstrance at Benediction.

Icon   From the Greek *eikon*, meaning 'image'. Icons are the preferred objects of visual devotion in the Eastern Church, but in recent years have gained enormous popularity in the West as well. An icon is typically a flat religious picture, usually painted in egg tempera on wood. Icons may be mounted on special stands, or as in the Orthodox Church assembled into a screen known as an *iconostasis*.

IHS   The first three capital letters (IHΣ)of the Greek word for Jesus, often seen embroidered on vestments and pulpit falls.

Incense   Also known as 'frankincense' – one of the three gifts brought by the magi to the infant Jesus. It is a gum that, when specially treated, gives off a sweet odour when burnt. In churches it is burnt in a thurible, a censer suspended on chains, and represents the prayers of the people ascending to the throne of grace. *See also Thurible.*

Incense boat   A separate metal container, shaped like a small boat, containing grains of incense to be used in the liturgy. The boat comes complete with a small spoon for spooning the incense into the thurible. The boat is sometimes carried by a 'boat-boy'.

INRI   The initial letters of the Latin words which Pilate had inscribed over the cross, designating the charge against Jesus: *Iesus Nazarenus Rex Iudaeorum* (Jesus of Nazareth: the King of the Jews). The letters are often carved over crucifixes or embroidered on Passiontide vestments or Lenten Array.

Institution, Words of   The words spoken by Jesus at the Last Supper as he broke the bread and shared the cup, telling his disciples: 'Do this in remembrance of me.' The words are a composite of New Testament texts, including St Paul's words in 1 Corinthians 11. When recited by the priest presiding at the Eucharist, they constitute the solemn moment of the service. In some churches their recital may conclude with the elevation of the host/chalice by the priest for all to see, followed by a genuflexion or profound bow. In modern usage the narrative of the Eucharistic Prayer tends to be recited as a continuous whole.

Intercessions   The prayers for the church and the world, and those in need, which follow the readings and sermon in the Eucharist, or the anthem or hymn in Choral Evensong.

Interim Rite   A version of the 1928 *Book of Common Prayer* with 'additions', favoured by many Anglo-Catholic clergy, following the rejection of the revised Prayer Book by Parliament.

Intinction   The custom of dipping the consecrated bread into the wine, or placing a spot of wine on the eucharistic wafer to enable communicants to receive communion in both kinds at once. This is especially used when administering communion to sick people. The sacrament may also be reserved in this way.

Introit   The entrance hymn, psalm or chant sung at the beginning of the Eucharist.

Kiss of Peace   In the New Testament there are a number of references to a kiss of greeting, e.g. Paul speaks of a 'holy kiss' (Romans 16.16). Liturgically the term refers to the custom of embracing one another or shaking hands as a sign of the peace of Christ.

Kyrie   From the Greek *kyrie eleison*, meaning 'Lord, have mercy'. One of the oldest parts of the Eucharist, the phrase may have been derived from Jewish worship. It is still the most common response to litanies in Eastern rites. In Western liturgy it is recited or sung near the beginning of the Eucharist as part of the penitential rite. In Advent and Lent, by custom the *Kyrie* replaces the *Gloria*.

Lady Chapel   A side chapel dedicated to Mary.

Lady Day   The Feast of the Annunciation of Our Lord to the Blessed Virgin Mary, celebrated on 25 March, nine months before Christmas Day.

Lammas Day   From the Anglo-Saxon *hlaf-mas,* meaning 'loaf mass'. In many countries in northern Europe, 1 August was observed as the Festival of the Wheat and Barley Harvest. On this day it was customary to bring to church a loaf of bread baked from the new crop to be blessed. It was a 'Feast of the first fruits'.

Lauds   The traditional title of Morning Prayer in the monastic office and Roman Catholic Church.

Lavabo   From the Latin meaning 'I will wash'. The term refers to the custom of the priest ceremonially washing his or her hands at the end of the offertory before beginning the Eucharistic Prayer and handling the elements. The term derives from the opening word in Latin of a verse of Psalm 26 that is customarily said silently by the priest as he or she does this: 'I will wash my hands in innocence, O Lord, that I may go about your altar.'

Lectern   From the Latin *legere*, meaning 'to read'. A lectern is a reading desk on which the Bible or lectionary stands. Lecterns may be wooden or metal, and are often carved into the shape of an eagle with wings outstretched, or more rarely, a pelican.

Lectionary   The authorized scheme of readings from the Bible to be read during the year. The word is used in two ways: first, to refer to the scheme as adapted to suit the liturgical year ahead and published as a separate volume each Advent; or to denote the book that contains the full text of the readings selected for Feast Days and the Sunday Eucharist, the latter of which operates on a three-year cycle. The concept of the lectionary goes back to synagogue worship which also had fixed readings from the Hebrew Scriptures appointed for its feasts and Sabbaths.

Lector   Reader. The second of the traditional minor orders in the Roman Catholic Church whose function was originally to read portions of scripture at the Euchar-ist, especially from the Old Testament.

Legilium   From the Latin *legere*, meaning 'to read'. A simple, folding, wooden, portable lectern, often nicknamed the 'ironing board'.

Lent   From the Old English *lencten*, meaning 'lengthen'. The word referred to the lengthening of daylight and hence the coming of Spring. By association, the term came to designate the period of spiritual preparation for Easter.

Lenten Array   A co-ordinated collection of vestments, frontals and falls made of either sackcloth or unbleached linen used during Lent, some of which may be embroidered with symbols of the Passion. In some churches, icons, pictures and statues are covered by Lenten veils either for the whole of Lent or during Passion-tide.

Litany   From the Greek *litaneia*, meaning 'prayer': a repetitive form of interces-sory prayer, sung by a cantor with congregational responses. The first evidence for the use of litanies in Christian worship comes from Antioch in the latter part of the fourth century. In medieval England the litany was sung in procession on Rogation Days, and is still sung in some parishes during Lent when, by custom, the procession goes anti-clockwise round a church, as opposed to clockwise. The litany continues to form part of the ordination rite.

Litany of the Saints   A solemn form of the litany, particularly used in the Roman Catholic Church, invoking the prayers of the saints by name.

Liturgy   A term denoting an act of worship derived from the Greek *leitourgia*. In Hellenistic Greek the word referred to an act of public service performed by a citizen for the benefit of others. In the New Testament we find the term used in this way (e.g. Philippians 2.30). Over the centuries, however, its usage came to be confined to the service of God; and since worship was humanity's supreme service, to worship itself.

Low Mass   A celebration of the Eucharist with minimal ceremonial, sometimes with just priest and server. The title 'Said Mass' may also be used. ***See also High Mass.***

Low Sunday   The English designation for the Sunday following Easter Day, completing the Easter Octave. **Low Week** is the week following the Easter Week.

Magnificat   The Song of Mary in Luke 1.46–55, which begins, 'My soul magnifies the Lord'. Its title comes from the first word of the canticle in Latin. It is sung at Evening Prayer.

Maniple   The vestment formerly worn by ordained ministers when celebrating the Eucharist. It was a strip of cloth, in colour and decoration like a stole, but worn over the left wrist. In origin it was an ornamental towel, used by the priest or deacon for cleansing the vessels or wiping his hands at the ablutions. It was abolished by the Second Vatican Council, though old vestments will still have maniples as part of the set.

Manual acts   The term refers to the directions to a priest in the *Book of Common Prayer* at certain points during the Prayer of Consecration in the Communion service. *Common Worship* makes different provision when using modern eucharistic rites, but also permits a priest to use 'traditional manual acts'.

Mass   A title for the sacrament of Holy Communion deriving from the dismissal in the Latin rite: *Ite missa est*, meaning 'Go, be sent into the world'. The term is the normative title in Roman Catholic parishes, but unusual in Anglican parishes where Holy Communion and Eucharist are more common. ***See also Low Mass, High Mass, Midnight Mass, and Eucharist.***

Master of Ceremonies   The server who oversees ceremonial, often referred to simply as the 'MC'.

Matins   Also spelt 'Mattins'. The traditional name for Morning Prayer in Anglican usage, but in monastic circles designates the Office of Vigils or Night Office. The title varied according to what time of day or night the office was recited. Nowadays, to avoid confusion, the title Office of Readings has become more common in monasteries.

Maundy Thursday   The day before Good Friday commemorating the Last Supper and Jesus' betrayal by Judas in the Garden of Gethsemane. By custom the clergy of a diocese also attend the cathedral in the morning of Maundy Thursday at which they renew their ordination promises and the bishop blesses the holy oils; hence its common title, 'Chrism Eucharist'.

Mensa   The flat stone that forms the top of an altar.

Messy Church   An informal, non-liturgical act of worship geared to children and families, involving biblical reflection, creativity, prayer, song and a meal.

Midnight Mass   The title for a service of Holy Communion celebrated late on Christmas Eve to mark the birth of Christ.

Missal   The title (commonly used by Catholics) of the large altar book containing the Order of Service for the Eucharist, and which may also include music for the President to sing. The 'Daily Missal' contains the Collects and readings for a daily celebration of the Eucharist. The 'English Missal' was an old Anglo-Catholic version of the Roman Catholic missal, adapted for use with the *Book of Common Prayer.*

Missa Normativa   The form of Eucharistic liturgy authorized by the Roman Catholic Church since the Second Vatican Council.

Mitre   From the Greek *mitra* meaning 'a turban', designating the distinctive pointed hat worn by bishops and abbots. It is usually made of white or gold material, and may be heavily embroidered. It may be worn with a chasuble or cope, or more simply with an alb and stole. On certain occasions, such as a funeral, a bishop will wear a mitre of simple white linen. The mitre has two strips of material or 'lappets' hanging from the back, which historically may have been used to tie the mitre on when the bishop was on horseback. The mitre in the Orthodox Church has evolved into a different shape, resembling the Byzantine imperial crown.

Mixed chalice   The custom of adding a few drops of water to the wine in the chalice at the offertory can be traced back to the middle of the second century. In the 1549 *Book of Common Prayer* the custom was continued, but the direction disappeared in the 1552 Prayer Book. The revival of the custom during the nineteenth century became a matter of dispute between Anglo-Catholic clergy and their opponents, and both customs prevail today.

Monstrance   A vessel made of precious metal with a central glass panel designed to display the consecrated host to people.

Narthex   The entry area or vestibule of a church.

Nave   From the Latin *navis*, meaning 'ship', the body of the church. The term may derive from the custom of referring to the church as the ship or 'ark of God'; or from the fact that the pitched roofs of medieval churches resembled the interior of a ship.

Nave altar   An altar placed at the head of the nave in large churches or where the high altar is far away, to encourage a sense of participation in the Eucharist.

New fire   The bonfire lit at the beginning of the Easter Vigil from which the Paschal Candle is lit.

None   Pronounced with a long 'o'. The title of prayer at the 'Ninth Hour' according to the Roman clock, meaning early afternoon. ***See also Canonical Hours.***

'North end' or 'north side' celebration   The custom of presiding at the Eucharist from the 'north side of the holy table', as opposed to eastward or westward positions. This position continues to be preferred by some clergy in loyalty to the Reformation when communion tables were moved into the body of the church, usually in the chancel rather than the nave, and placed on an east–west axis. The directive that the priest should stand at the 'north side of the holy table' probably still meant that he was standing in the middle of the table, with the people gathered around him. This expressed better the renewed understanding of the Eucharist as a sacred meal. Under Archbishop Laud in the seventeenth century, the holy tables were placed back in their medieval positions against the east end wall of the church in what deemed a more seemly position. However, the rubric in the Prayer Book directing the clergy to stand at the north side of the table was never altered, with the bizarre result that the clergy ended up standing at the 'sharp end' of the table. This liturgical anomaly gradually acquired a theological justification, evangelical clergy stressing their dissociation from the elements and their rejection of any notion of 'change' in them. With the modern Liturgical Movement and the recovery of the ancient shape of the Eucharist, a growing consensus has emerged across denominations favouring the westward position for the Eucharist, with the priest facing the people.

Novena   From the Latin *novena*, meaning 'nine at a time'. A designated period of intense devotion: nine days of prayer in preparation for an important event or the celebration of a Patronal Festival.

Nunc dimittis   The Song of Simeon when he picked up the child Jesus in the temple and recognized him to be the Messiah (Luke 2.29–32). It begins, 'Now you dismiss your servant in peace'. Its title comes from its opening words in Latin. The canticle is said at Prayer Book Evensong and Compline, and may also be recited by a minister when leading a coffin out of church at the end of a funeral.

Nuptial Blessing   From the Latin *nuptialis,* meaning 'of marriage': the solemn blessing of bride and groom by the priest in the Marriage service.

Nuptial Mass   A celebration of the Eucharist either at the wedding itself or soon after.

Oblation   From the Latin *oblatio,* meaning 'offering'. The term may refer to the act of offering or to the thing offered. In worship it can refer directly to the self-offering of Jesus, or to the celebration of the Eucharist as a memorial of his sacrifice, or to the elements of bread and wine used in the Eucharist. The so-called 'Prayer of Oblation' is one of two alternative prayers separated from the Canon of the Mass in the *Book of Common Prayer* to be said by the priest after all have received communion, but originally in 1549 part of the Eucharistic Prayer.

Occasional Offices   The title for a range of pastoral services, including baptisms, marriages, funerals, and ministry to the sick.

Octave   From the Latin *octavus*, meaning 'eighth', designating a liturgical period of eight days following a major feast of the church. Following recent liturgical reforms, only two octaves are observed today after the Feasts of Christmas and Easter, though the *Book of Common Prayer* also made provision for the Feast of Pentecost (Whitsun) to be observed by an octave, culminating on Trinity Sunday.

Offertory   May designate a collection or the presentation of the elements with or without money when brought to the altar in a so-called 'offertory procession' during the Eucharist. *Common Worship* makes provision for a variety of optional prayers at this point.

Office   From the Latin *officium*, meaning 'duty'. The term designates any liturgical Service of the Word. 'Daily Office' refers specifically to the saying of Morning and Evening Prayer, which the Canons of the Church of England designate as obligatory for the clergy, part of their 'duty' to God.

Office Hymn   A short hymn sung after the opening responses but immediately before the psalms during monastic offices, and often in cathedrals in the context of Morning Prayer (Matins) or Evening Prayer (Evensong). The texts of such hymns are invariably patristic or medieval in origin. ***See Canonical Hours.***

Oils   The use of oil has a long history in Christian liturgy as a sign of God's blessing. The oil of baptism (or catechumens) is used to make the sign of the cross on a candidate for baptism. The oil of chrism is used to anoint people at their confirmation or ordination, and at the dedication of altars and churches. The oil of the sick is used to anoint sick and dying people. The oils are blessed each year by the bishop at a special Eucharist in the cathedral on Maundy Thursday, sometimes known as the 'Chrism Mass'.

Ombrellino   A ceremonial umbrella once used in processions of the Blessed Sacrament, particularly out-of-doors, but discontinued following the liturgical changes instigated by the Second Vatican Council.

Oratory   A small place set aside for prayer.

Ordinal   The rite for ordaining bishops, priests and deacons.

Ordinary of the Mass   The parts of a eucharistic rite that are invariable and do not change with the season.

Ordo   The term for the annual calendar specific to a church, cathedral or monastery, designating which saints' days will be observed etc.

Orphrey   Embroidered or ornamental strips of material sewn on vestments and altar frontals.

Pall   From the Latin *pallium*, meaning 'cloak', and thus used for any cloth that envelops or covers an object. The term is used of the large, heavy hanging that is sometimes used to cover a coffin at funerals; or the small piece of stiffened material used to cover a chalice in order to prevent insects from getting into the wine.

Palm Sunday   The Sunday next before Easter when Christians commemorate Jesus' triumphal entrance into Jerusalem riding on a donkey.

Paschal Candle   *See Easter Candle.*

Paschal Vigil   From the Greek *pascha,* itself a transliteration of the Hebrew *pesach*, meaning Passover. The celebration of the Christian *Pascha* refers to the Passion, death and resurrection of the Lord. The Paschal Vigil is held on Saturday night and/or early on Easter Sunday morning, and is the church's oldest liturgical observance. Today it is more usually called the Easter Vigil.

Passion   The consensus among biblical commentators is that the Passion Narratives, the accounts of Jesus' last supper with his disciples, his betrayal, trial and subsequent execution, were the first parts of the Gospels to be written down. They are called 'Passion Narratives' because they record God's love for the world revealed in and through the crucifixion of Jesus, the Latin root of the word, *passio,* meaning 'suffering'. By custom, the Passions of Mark, Matthew and Luke are read in rotation on Palm Sunday, and that of John on Good Friday.

Passiontide   Designates the final two weeks of Lent. It is the most solemn season in the church's year, rehearsing the events leading up to Jesus' arrest and crucifixion.

Pastoral staff   The staff of office of a bishop, abbot or abbess, customarily shaped as a shepherd's crook in symbolic remembrance of Christ the Good Shepherd. Also known as a crozier.

Paten   A shallow dish, plate or bowl on which the bread to be consecrated is placed at the Eucharist.

Pectoral cross   A large cross, normally of precious metal, worn around the neck and upon the chest by a bishop or abbot.

Pentecost   From the Greek, *pentekoste,* meaning 'fiftieth'. Originally a Jewish festival celebrated on the fiftieth day after Passover, it was the occasion when, according to Luke, the Holy Spirit descended upon the apostles. In England it has been traditionally known as 'Whitsunday' and is the final day of Eastertide.

Petition   A request to God to act.

Piscina   From the Latin *piscina,* literally meaning a 'fishpond' or 'swimming pool'. Initially the word was often used of the baptismal font, not least because the fish was one of the symbols of Christ in the primitive church. However, during the Middle Ages the term began to be applied to the niche set in the wall of the sanctuary, normally on the south side of the altar, used to carry away water used by the priest during the lavabo and at the ablutions. The drain goes straight to the earth. ***See also Lavabo.***

Plainsong   The usual English term for Gregorian chant: 'plain' because it is without harmony and sung in unison. Gregorian chant (sometimes known simply as 'the chant') evolved as a way of singing psalms in Latin. When English is sung, the rules of the chant have to be modified to account for the differing speech rhythms of English.

Pointing   A way of marking psalms or canticles for chanting. The points indicate when the note changes.

Pontifical High Mass   From the Latin *pontifex,* meaning 'bridge-builder'. The adjective refers to a celebration of the Eucharist over which a bishop presides.

Posada   From the Spanish, meaning 'lodging'. A South American tradition celebrating the journey of Mary and Joseph to Bethlehem, observed during Advent.

Post-Communion Prayer   *Common Worship* provides a variable Collect to be said after the reception of holy communion, as well as a set prayer of thanksgiving to be said by the congregation.

Preaching scarf   *See Scarf.*

Preces   From the Latin *preces,* meaning 'prayers'. Short petitions that are said or sung as versicle and response by the officiating minister and congregation as in the opening of Morning and Evening Prayer.

Preface   The passage in the Eucharistic Prayer that comes after the opening dialogue but before the Sanctus (Holy, holy, holy …) which summarizes God's gracious dealings with his people. The *Book of Common Prayer* makes provision for this to be supplemented by 'Proper Prefaces' at certain seasons, notably at Christmas and Easter. *Common Worship* provides a greater variety of material. At certain seasons or on certain Holy Days this section may be wholly replaced by an 'Extended Preface' or supplemented by a 'Short Preface' inserted towards its end, usually introduced with the words, 'And now we give you thanks'.

President   The bishop or priest presiding at the liturgy. This is the oldest title known for this function. ***See also Celebrant.***

Pricket   A prayer stand containing a number of spikes or holders into which can be fixed votive candles.

Prie-dieu   From the French, meaning 'pray God': a kneeling desk which in some designs can alternate as a chair. Some churches have a pair of such desks for use by the bride and groom at weddings. ***See also Faldstool***.

Primatial Cross   The special cross carried before an Archbishop (Primate) akin to a processional cross.

Prime   The title of the offering of prayer at the beginning of the working day in a monastery, now no longer observed. ***See also Canonical Hours.***

Propers   Those parts of the Eucharist which are variable ('appropriate') and change with the Feast Day or season. The term can also be used of those variable parts of the service which are sung chorally, such as the introit, gradual or responsorial psalm, and alleluia before the Gospel.

Psalter   The 150 psalms of the Bible. The title can also refer to special editions of the psalms which have been 'pointed' – i.e. set to music, such as Anglican chant.

Pulpit   From the Latin *pulpitum*, meaning 'platform'. Raised pulpits made out of wood (and occasionally stone) came into general use during the medieval period to assist the clergy in delivering sermons. In the early church it is likely that the bishop preached from his *cathedra* behind the altar. In England, where daylight was at a premium, the pulpit tended to be positioned on the north side. During the bulk of the day, sunlight came through the clerestory windows on the south side, thus illuminating the pulpit on the north side of the church.

Purificator   A small white cloth or napkin specially folded into a long strip, used to wipe clean the chalice between communicants.

Pyx   A small box, usually of precious metal, in which the consecrated bread is kept or carried to the sick and housebound. A pyx sometimes has a chain in order that it can be worn around the neck. A 'hanging pyx' refers to a larger vessel, suspended on a pulley over or behind an altar, in which the Blessed Sacrament is reserved. In the medieval era such pyxes were often made in the shape of a dove.

Quinquagesima   From the Latin meaning 'fiftieth'. The title in the *Book of Common Prayer* for the Sunday approximately fifty days before Easter, now known as the 'Sunday Next before Lent'.

Reader   When spelt with a capital 'R' this designates a person who has received theological training and is licensed by the bishop to assist the clergy in the leading of public worship and in preaching. Readers (formerly known as 'Lay Readers') are invested with a blue preaching scarf as a sign of their office.

Reliquary   A receptacle for the relics or remains of a saint.

Requiem   From the Latin *requiem*, meaning 'rest', it is more properly termed 'Requiem Mass'. It denotes a Eucharist celebrated in memory of a dead person either at their funeral or soon after, or on the annual commemoration of the faithful departed on 2 November (All Souls' Day). In popular usage the word refers to a number of musical settings which may be performed independently of liturgical commemoration. The term comes from the old Latin introit of the service, 'Grant unto them eternal rest'. ***See also Agnus dei.***

Reredos   A decorated screen in wood, stone or alabaster, set above and behind an altar. ***See also Retable.***

Reserved Sacrament   From the Latin *resevere*, meaning 'to keep'. The custom of setting aside some of the consecrated elements (either both the bread and the wine, or just the consecrated bread) for the communion of the sick and house-bound was discontinued at the Reformation in England, but was reintroduced in the nineteenth century and has since become commonplace in many parts of the Church of England. Communion of the housebound is also known as 'communion by extension'. *See also Aumbry, Pyx, Tabernacle.*

Responses   Frequent shorthand for the musical setting of the responsorial prayers sung at Morning and Evening Prayer. *See also Versicles and Responses.*

Responsorial Psalm   A psalm sung responsively by cantor or choir and congregation, often between the Old Testament reading and the Epistle at the Eucharist.

Retable   A framed altarpiece, raised slightly above the back of an altar, on which may be placed a cross and candlesticks. *See also Reredos.*

Reverencing the altar   In most Anglican churches it is customary for the minister at the beginning and end of a service to turn and bow to the altar. *See also Bowing.*

Riddel Posts   From the French *rideau*, meaning 'curtain'. In medieval England, and again in the nineteenth-century revival, altars were often enclosed on three sides by curtains suspended between four posts or pillars. This ecclesiastical style is sometimes known as an 'English altar'.

Robes   A general term for special clothes worn during worship by clergy and others.

Rochet   A long, white garment worn by bishops over the cassock under the chimere: a cross between a surplice and an alb. It has a rounded neck, but full sleeves gathered at the wrist often in a ruff made fast with scarlet or black bands.

Rogation Days   Days of intercession or prayer, usually in Eastertide, seeking God's blessing on a community and its land. In many rural districts this may be accompanied by the ceremonial 'beating of the bounds' of a parish.

Rood   From the Old English for the cross. The rood was a great focus of medieval devotion. It consisted of a large crucifix, supported by figures of the Blessed Virgin

Mary and the Beloved Disciple on either side. It was set up either above a rood screen or independently high up on a beam at the front of the nave. **Rood screens** were usually wooden, though sometimes stone, and separated the chancel from the nave. They were often painted with representations of saints. Most were dismantled at the Reformation. Few original medieval screens have survived intact.

Rosary   A method of rhythmical prayer using prayer-beads popularized during the Counter-Reformation in which different episodes in the life of Our Lord or Mary are meditated upon. The prayers include the 'Hail Mary', the 'Our Father' and the *Gloria patri*.

Rubrics   From the Latin *ruber*, meaning 'red': the ceremonial directives for liturgy, customarily printed in medieval prayer books using red ink to distinguish them from the text of prayers. *Common Worship* has returned to this convention, though not all modern prayer books do. Regardless of colour, the term 'rubric' is still used to mean ceremonial directions.

Sacristan   The person appointed to look after the communion vessels and vestments of a church, and make all the practical arrangements for services of Holy Communion.

Sacristy   From the Latin *sacer*, meaning 'holy': a designated room for keeping and preparing the communion vessels used in the Eucharist, vestments and other supplies.

Sanctuary   The part of the church in which the altar is located.

Sanctuary bells (Sacring bells)   From the Latin *sacer*, meaning 'holy': a small hand-held bell or bells, or sometimes gong, rung to focus people's attention, particularly at the elevation of the host and chalice during the Eucharistic Prayer.

Sanctuary lights   Ornamental lamps of oil or candles suspended from brackets or the ceiling in the sanctuary or side chapels of a church. By custom, a red or more usually white light denotes that the Blessed Sacrament is reserved; a red light may be placed adjacent to an icon or saint's statue; and a blue light may be hung in a Lady Chapel or beside a statue of Mary.

Sanctus   The anthem in most Eucharistic Prayers beginning, 'Holy, holy, holy Lord'.

Sarum Usage   Sarum is the old name for Salisbury, and the term refers to the distinctive liturgical customs associated with its medieval cathedral which became dominant in southern England prior to the Reformation. In the late-nineteenth century the term was reinvented by Anglo-Catholic clergy as a way of promoting good liturgical practice and displaying their catholic credentials in a distinctively Anglican, as opposed to Roman Catholic, way. Also known as 'English Usage'.

Scarf   A long broad strip of black material (silk or woollen), resembling a stole, worn by the clergy round their neck over the surplice, often with their academic hood hung down their back. The ends of the scarf may be cut straight or pinked. Also known as a preaching scarf or tippet. Readers' scarves are blue. **See also Tippet and Choir Dress.**

Sedilia   From the Latin *sedile*, meaning 'a seat' or 'bench'. The word refers to the seats for the celebrant, deacon and subdeacon at the Eucharist. These were often stone benches set into the side of the south wall of the sanctuary, and often had ornate carved canopies.

Selah   A recurrent instruction in the Hebrew psalms to pause and to reflect. Originally it may have indicated a musical interlude.

Sentences   Short passages of scripture read out in services. In the Prayer Book these are used as introductions to the Prayers of Penitence. Funerals usually begin with the minister leading the coffin into church, reciting sentences of scripture that declare both the finality of death and belief in the resurrection.

Septuagesima   From the Latin meaning 'seventieth'. The title in the *Book of Common Prayer* for the Sunday approximately seventy days before Easter, now known as the 'Third Sunday before Lent'.

Sequence   A special musical interlude or hymn written for the major feasts of the church to be sung in plainsong before the Gospel. In the medieval liturgy there were a number of these, the most famous of which are still sung in translation as hymns.

Server   A lay person, usually robed, who assists in the performance of the liturgy. The modern server has inherited many of the functions performed by the parish clerk in earlier centuries. **See also Acolyte and Master of Ceremonies.**

Service of the Word   An authorized service in the Church of England which in many parishes is replacing Morning Prayer on Sundays. *Common Worship* supplies a structure of Preparation, Liturgy of the Word, Prayers and Dismissal, for such a service, together with a variety of resources. Its flexibility is designed to 'allow for considerable local variation and choice within a common structure'.

Setting   A shorthand for the musical setting of the canticles sung at Matins or Evensong. ***See also Versicles and Responses.***

Sexagesima   From the Latin meaning 'sixtieth'. The title in the *Book of Common Prayer* for the Sunday approximately sixty days before Easter, now known as the 'Second Sunday before Lent'.

Sext   The title of the offering of prayer at the 'Sixth Hour' in a monastery according to the Roman clock, meaning midday. ***See also Canonical Hours.***

Sexton   The person with oversight of a churchyard.

Solemnity   From the medieval Latin *solemnitas*, designating (in Roman Catholic custom) the most important feasts of the church, such as Christmas, Easter and Pentecost. In Anglican usage, they are usually called 'Principal Feasts'.

Stall   A fixed seat for the clergy or choir, usually in the chancel of the church.

Stations of the Cross   From the Latin *stare*, meaning 'to stand'. Following the victory of the Emperor Constantine, Christians began to go on pilgrimage to the Holy Land where they liked to trace the route Jesus took to his execution, the so-called *Via Dolorosa*. This led to the emergence of a similar devotion in parish churches across Europe. A series of 14 tableaux or 'stations' depicting various incidents in the final journey of Christ to his crucifixion began to be arranged around the walls of churches. People move slowly from one scene to the next, meditating on the Passion. At each picture or 'station' a short Bible reading may be said, followed by prayers and meditation. The devotion (also known as The Way of the Cross) continues to be popular in many parishes during Lent and Holy Week. *Common Worship* also provides for 'Stations of the Resurrection' in Eastertide.

Stock   A small container made of precious metal for the keeping of holy oil.

Stole   A long narrow strip of coloured and often highly embroidered material, worn by clergy. The origin of the stole is obscure, but its use by Christian clergy seems to have come from the custom of Roman officials who wore a distinctive scarf as a mark of their rank. A priest's stole is worn around the neck and hangs down to the knees. A deacon's stole is worn across the left shoulder and is tied under the right arm at the waist. The stole may be worn either over an alb but under the chasuble, or over an alb without a chasuble or cope. It can equally be worn over a surplice or cotta, particularly at christenings. As with other vestments its colour varies with the liturgical season.

Stoup   A basin, often set in a carved recess in the entrance porch of a church, containing holy water with which people may cross themselves upon entering the church in remembrance of their baptism.

Subdeacon   An order of ministry below that of deacon in the medieval church which was abolished by the Roman Catholic Church in 1970, but which still exists liturgically in some cathedrals and parish churches. The subdeacon assists the deacon and priest at the Eucharist and normally reads the Epistle. The tunicle is the vestment of the subdeacon. ***See also Tunicle.***

Superfrontal   A panel that hangs over the edge of some altar frontals. It is usually sumptuously embroidered, while matching the main frontal in design and colour.

Surplice   An ampler version of the alb, but with much fuller sleeves, worn by clergy, servers and choirs over their cassocks. It was adopted in northern Europe for wear over fur-lined cassocks, but not in southern Europe where the climate was warmer; hence the name, *superpelliceum,* meaning over a fur garment. Clergy may wear it with a preaching scarf and academic hood at choir offices, or with a stole for sacramental services. The medieval priest's surplice was customarily very full, of ankle length, with long pointed sleeves. This is sometimes referred to as an 'Old English surplice'.

Surrogate   A member of the clergy appointed by the bishop to grant common licences for marriage without the legal preliminary of banns.

Sursum corda   From the Latin, meaning 'Lift up your hearts': the traditional name for the opening dialogue of the Eucharistic Prayer.

Tabernacle A metal safe for the exclusive reservation of the Blessed Sacrament usually placed on the High Altar or on a dedicated side altar. The term is used to distinguish this method of reservation from an aumbry, where the sacrament is reserved in a cupboard set in the wall. *See also Aumbry and Pyx.*

Taperers Servers who bear lighted candles. *See also Acolyte and Server.*

Terce The title of the offering of prayer at the 'Third Hour' in a monastery according to the Roman clock, meaning around 9 o'clock. *See also Canonical Hours.*

Tester The roof of a canopy built over an altar or saint's tomb indicating its importance. *See also Baldacchino.*

Three-decker pulpit A rare survival from the eighteenth-century ordering of many parish churches. It had the Parish Clerk's stall at the bottom; the incumbent's stall in the middle; and the pulpit at the top from which the clergyman preached.

Three Hours Devotion A service consisting of hymns, readings, sermons and meditations held on Good Friday between noon and 3 o'clock marking the time Jesus hung on the cross. Designed by the Jesuits in the sixteenth century as a devotional exercise, it traditionally focused on the 'Seven Last Words' spoken by Our Lord from the cross, but its content nowadays is more variable.

Thurible From the Latin *thus,* meaning incense, a thurible is the metal vessel in which it is burnt. It is also known as a censer. It is usually suspended on three chains, with a central chain to raise and lower the lid. This allows it to be swung freely during censing and processions. The **thurifer**, the server who bears the thurible, is often accompanied by a younger server known as a 'boat-boy' whose job is to hold the incense.

Tippet Originally a broad black scarf in silk or wool, now more commonly worn by some clergy round the shoulders, either over the cassock as a short shoulder cape, or with a surplice and hood. *See also Scarf.*

Triduum The three solemn days of Holy Week: Maundy Thursday, Good Friday and Holy Saturday.

Triptych A religious picture painted on three folding hinged panels to permit closure during Lent, usually set behind an altar as a focus of devotion.

Trisagion   The name of the ancient hymn originating in the Byzantine rite where it corresponds to the *Gloria in excelsis* in Western liturgy. It consists of a three-fold invocation of God: 'Holy God, Holy and Strong, Holy and Immortal, have mercy on us.'

Tunicle   From the Latin *tunicula*, meaning 'small tunic'. The outermost garment worn by a subdeacon, crucifer or leading server. In appearance it is almost identical to the dalmatic worn by a deacon, except that it has only one instead of two horizontal orphreys.

Unction   The rite of anointing. **See also Oils.**

Veil   The term is used in two principal ways. It may refer either to a square cloth of linen used to cover the consecrated elements after communion if the ablutions are to be delayed until the end of the service; or to a coloured, often embroidered cover for the chalice and paten when these are not in use. In the latter case, it often has a matching burse, and corresponds to the liturgical colour. **See also Burse, Humeral veil and Lenten Array.**

Venite   The Latin title of Psalm 95, 'O come, let us sing to the Lord'. This psalm has formed the opening of Morning Prayer for centuries and was retained by Cranmer for the beginning of Matins in the Prayer Book.

Verger (Virger)   From the Latin *virga*, meaning 'rod'. The name given to someone who looks after the interior of a church and who, in processions, customarily carries a 'virge', a wand of office. Like churchwardens' staves, these wands often have a decorated head. **See also Sacristan and Sexton.**

Versicles and Responses   The technical terms for the opening of Morning and Evening Prayer. The versicle is said or sung by the officiant and answered with a said or sung response by the congregation or choir.

Vespers   The traditional title of Evening Prayer in the monastic office and Roman Catholic Church.

Vestry   From the Latin *vestarium*, meaning 'wardrobe': the room attached to a church in which clergy, servers and choir robe in preparation for leading worship. **See also Sacristy.**

Via Dolorosa The route in Jerusalem along which by tradition Jesus was taken to his crucifixion on Calvary.

Wafer box A box of wood or metal containing a store of communion wafers, normally arranged in compartments of five or ten for convenience, for use at the Eucharist. Also known as a 'bread box'.

Year's mind The custom of remembering publicly a deceased person in prayer on the anniversary of their death. This may be done in the context of the regular intercessions on a Sunday, or at a special Requiem Mass, particularly on the first anniversary of death. Names may be inscribed in a Book of Remembrance and kept in a prominent place in a church.

Resources

I am grateful to George Lane, Chair of Praxis NW, for drawing my attention to various liturgical resources, and for his comments and observations on the Guide.

1 WORSHIP MATTERS

Andrew Atherstone, *Charles Simeon on 'The Excellency of the Liturgy'*, Norwich: Alcuin Club, Joint Liturgical Studies 72, 2011.

Dilly Baker, *A Place at the Table: Liturgies and resources for Christ-centred hospitality*, Norwich: Canterbury Press, 2008.

Paul Bradshaw and Peter Moger, eds, *Worship Changes Lives: How it works, why it matters*, London: Church House Publishing, 2008.

Doug Chaplin, *Leading Common Worship Intercessions: A Simple Guide*, London: Church House Publishing, 2009.

Church House Publishing, *New Patterns for Worship (Common Worship: Services and Prayers for the Church of England)*, London: Church House Publishing, 2012.

Mark Earey, *Liturgical Worship: A fresh look, how it works, why it matters*, London: Church House Publishing, 2002.

Richard Giles, *At Heaven's Gate: Reflections on Leading Worship*, Norwich: Canterbury Press, 2010.

Liturgical Commission of the Church of England, *Words for Worship: Prayers from the heart of the Church of England*, London, Church House Publishing, 2012.

Michael Perham, *A New Handbook of Pastoral Liturgy*, London: SPCK, 2000.

Steven Shakespeare, *Prayers for an Inclusive Church: Resources for Sundays and holy days*, Norwich: Canterbury Press, 2008.

Bryan D. Spinks, *The Worship Mall: Contemporary responses to contemporary culture*, London: SPCK, 2010.

Ian Tarrant, *Worship and Freedom in the Church of England*, Cambridge: Grove Worship Series 210, 2012.

2 THE CONTEXT WE SET

In enabling parishes to improve their ministry of welcome, there are few better courses than *Everybody Welcome* by Bob Jackson and George Fisher, London: Church House Publishing, 2010. The course evolved out of research which revealed that 'improving its welcome' is the single most significant strategic action a church can take towards growth. The course has an optional fifth section on how to set up a welcome team, but the welcome principle is one that needs to be embraced and implemented by every member of every church.

Richard Giles has produced an excellent guide to liturgical re-ordering, *Re-Pitching the Tent*, Norwich: Canterbury Press, 3rd edn, 2004.

Worship Audits

A number of dioceses have produced worship review materials. In addition, Mark Earey has produced a helpful guide: *Worship Audit: Making Good Worship Better*, Cambridge: Grove Worship Series 133, 1995.

3 BRINGING TEXTS TO LIFE

The full text of *Common Worship,* together with all authorized services, is available on the Church of England website and is able to be downloaded.

Copyright conditions are also set out: www.churchofengland.org

Church House Publishing, *Visual Liturgy Live*, downloadable version with upgrades available every year.

Brendan Clover, *Good Liturgy Guide to Festivals: The festivals of the Christian year*, Norwich: Canterbury Press, 2012.

Mark Earey, *Finding Your Way Round Common Worship*, London: Church House Publishing, 2011.

Anne Harrison, *Recovering the Lord's Song: Getting sung scripture back into worship*, Cambridge: Grove Worship Series 198, 2009.

Christopher Irvine (ed.), *The Use of Symbols in Worship*, London: SPCK, 2007.

John Leach, *How to Use Symbol and Action in Worship*, Cambridge: Grove Worship Series 184, 2005.

Jean Lebon, *How to Understand the Liturgy*, ET by Margaret Lydamore and John Bowden, London: SCM Press, 1987.

Dorothea McEwan, Pat Pinsent, Ianthe Pratt, *Making Liturgy: Creating rituals for life*, Norwich: Canterbury Press, 2008.

Peter Moger, *Crafting Common Worship: A practical, creative guide to what's possible*, London: Church House Publishing, 2009.

Sue Pickering, *Creative Ideas for Quiet Days: Resources and Liturgies for Retreats and Reflection*, with CD Rom, Norwich: Canterbury Press, 2008.

Sue Pickering, *Creative Retreat Ideas: Resources for short, day and weekend retreats*, with CD Rom, Norwich: Canterbury Press, 2010.

Philip Tovey, *Mapping Common Worship*, Cambridge: Grove Worship Series 195, 2008.

Holy Communion: *Book of Common Prayer*

Paul Thomas has produced a guide to the conduct of Prayer Book services: *The Book of Common Prayer: Finding your way around*, London, Church House Publishing, 2012.

Holy Communion: *Common Worship*

Mark Beach, *Using Common Worship: Holy Communion*, London: Church House Publishing, 2000.

Richard Giles has produced a companion volume to *Re-Pitching the Tent*, entitled *Creating Uncommon Worship: Transforming the Liturgy of the Eucharist*, Norwich: Canterbury Press, 2004.

John Waller, *How to Prepare and Preach a Sermon*, Cambridge: Grove Worship Series 182, 2005.

The Royal School of Church Music (RSCM) has produced several volumes of music resources designed specifically for use with *Common Worship*. These are available direct from the RSCM. See their website: www.rscm.com

All-Age Services

Jan Brind and Tessa Wilkinson, *Creative Ideas for Evening Prayer: For Seasons, Feasts and Special Occasions throughout the Year*, with CD Rom, Norwich: Canterbury Press, 2008.

Jan Brind and Tessa Wilkinson, *Creative Ideas for Whole Church Family Worship*, with CD Rom, Norwich: Canterbury Press, 2011.

Common Worship: Additional Eucharistic Prayers, with Guidance on Celebrating the Eucharist with children, 2012.

Common Worship: Collects and Post-Communions, 2004. This volume includes both the original *CW* Collects, and additional Collects in contemporary English which may be used alongside them.

Barbara Mary Hopper, Michael Walsh, Kathy Walsh, *A Handbook for Children's Liturgy*, Norwich: Canterbury Press, 2003.

Sarah Lenton, *Creative Ideas for Children's Worship – Year A*, with CD Rom, Norwich: Canterbury Press, 2011.

Sarah Lenton, *Creative Ideas for Children's Worship – Year B*, with CD Rom, Norwich: Canterbury Press, 2012.

Sarah Lenton, *Creative Ideas for Children's Worship – Year C*, with CD Rom, Norwich: Canterbury Press, 2012.

Trevor Lloyd, *A Service of the Word,* Cambridge: Grove Worship Series 151, 2000.

Tim Stratford, *Using Common Worship: A Service of the Word,* London: Church House Publishing, 2002.

Ian Tarrant has produced a guide for the use of overheads in worship, including the use of PowerPoint: *How to Worship with Data Projection,* Cambridge: Grove Worship Series 192, 2007.

Evensong

For a general guide to the Prayer Book service, see Paul Thomas (see p. 277).

By far the most comprehensive guide on taking Evensong is Gilly Myers, *How to Lead Evensong,* Cambridge: Grove Worship Series 183, 2005.

The music of the responses, typically sung at Evensong in parish churches, is published by The Royal School of Church Music (RSCM): *Ferial Versicles and Responses,* and may be purchased cheaply from them. See their online shop at www.rscm.com

Various collections of traditional prayers are in print. These are wonderful resources when preparing the intercessions at Evensong. One of the most comprehensive, though no longer in print and somewhat dated, is that compiled by Frank Colquhoun, *Parish Prayers,* London: Hodder & Stoughton, 1967 & 1980. There is also *The Oxford Book of Prayer,* compiled by George Appleton, Oxford: Oxford University Press, 1985.

Baptisms

Jan Brind and Tessa Wilkinson, *Creative Ideas for Pastoral Liturgy: Baptism, Confirmation and Liturgies for the Journey,* with CD Rom, Norwich: Canterbury Press, 2010.

Gift: 100 Readings in Celebration of Birth and Baptism, compiled by Robert Atwell, Norwich: Canterbury Press, 2005, is a selection of poems, readings and short biblical passages celebrating birth and baptism. It can be a helpful resource for readings at a service of Thanksgiving for the Birth of a Child, or Baptism.

Weddings

Jan Brind and Tessa Wilkinson, *Creative Ideas for Pastoral Liturgy: Marriage Services, Wedding Blessings and Anniversary Thanksgivings*, with CD Rom, Norwich: Canterbury Press, 2009.

The Church of England's 'The Wedding Project' has garnered a huge amount of information and good practice. The Weddings Project Resource Centre is online, and is a major resource for clergy and couples preparing for marriage.

Greg Forster, *Taking a Wedding: A Step-by-Step Guide for Church of England Ministers,* Cambridge: Grove Pastoral Series 121, 2010. It includes a helpful 'dealing with awkward questions' section.

Love: 100 Readings in Celebration of Marriage and Love, compiled by Robert Atwell, Norwich: Canterbury Press, 2005, is a selection of poems, readings and short biblical passages suitable for use at weddings.

Funerals

I am grateful to the University of Chester for permission to share the (as yet) unpublished findings from its Funeral Project in and around Warrington: J. Brookman, B. Davies, L. Gittins, S. Kimmance, C. Watkins and S. Wright (2012). Church of England: Deanery of Great Budworth Funeral Project, Department of Media, University of Chester.

Jan Brind and Tessa Wilkinson, Creative Ideas for Pastoral Liturgy: Funerals, Memorials and Thanksgiving Services, with CD Rom, Norwich: Canterbury Press, 2008.

R. Anne Horton, *Using Common Worship: Funerals,* London: Church House Publishing, 2000.

Remember: 100 Readings for Those in Grief and Bereavement, compiled by Robert Atwell, Norwich: Canterbury Press, 2005, is a selection of poems, readings and short biblical passages suitable for Funeral and memorial services, or as a devotional resource for those in bereavement.

Funerals: A guide to prayers, hymns and readings, ed. James Bentley, Andrew Best and Jackie Hunt, London: Hodder & Stoughton, 1994.

In Sure and Certain Hope: Liturgies, Prayers and Readings for Funerals and Memorials, compiled by Paul Sheppy, Norwich: Canterbury Press, 2003.

Leading Public Worship: A beginner's guide

I am grateful to Dr Christopher Burkett and colleagues in the Diocese of Chester for permission to use material from the Diocesan course, 'The Beginner's Guide to Leading Public Worship'.

Processions and Protocols

The Church of England Guild of Vergers has a range of information available on its website.

4 ENRICHING THE CHRISTIAN YEAR

The largest and best liturgical resource in this area is *Common Worship: Times and Seasons,* London: Church House Publishing, 2006. General studies and commentaries include:

Tom Ambrose, *Together for a Season: Feasts and Festivals*, London: Church House Publishing, 2009.

Benjamin Gordon-Taylor and Simon Jones, *Celebrating Christ's Victory: Ash Wednesday to Trinity,* London: Alcuin Club, 2009.

David Kennedy, *Using Common Worship: All Saints to Candlemas,* London: Church House Publishing, 2006.

Two anthologies of readings from the Fathers and other spiritual writers by Robert Atwell can enrich the celebration of the Christian Year, as well as feed personal devotion: *Celebrating the Saints,* Norwich: Canterbury Press, 3rd edn, 2004; *Celebrating the Seasons,* Norwich: Canterbury Press, 1999.

Advent

Gillian Ambrose, Peter Craig-Wild, Diane Craven and Mary Hawes, *Together for a Season: All-Age Seasonal Material for Advent, Christmas and Epiphany*, London: Church House Publishing, 2006.

Candles and Conifers, ed. Ruth Burgess, Glasgow: Wild Goose Publications, 2005.

Posada

The Church Army no longer actively promotes Posada, but it offers a variety of resources for Posada worship and activities: 'Making Room for Jesus this Christmas' which can be downloaded free from its website: www.churcharmy.org.uk

Christmas and Christingle

Gillian Ambrose, Peter Craig-Wild, Diane Craven and Mary Hawes, *Together for a Season: All-Age Seasonal Material for Advent, Christmas and Epiphany*, London: Church House Publishing, 2006.

Hay and Stardust, ed. Ruth Burgess, Glasgow: Wild Goose Publications, 2010.

Christingle resources, including free downloads, details of how to make them, where to get materials from, worship resources and ideas for sermons may be found on the Children's Society website: www.childrenssociety.org.uk

Lent and Holy Week

Gillian Ambrose, Peter Craig-Wild, Diane Craven and Peter Moger, *Together for a Season: Lent, Holy Week and Easter*, London: Church House Publishing, 2007.

Eggs and Ashes, ed. Ruth Burgess and Chris Polhill, Glasgow: Wild Goose Publications, 2001.

Stages on the Way, ed. John Bell and the Wild Goose Worship Group, Glasgow: Wild Goose Publications, 2000.

Easter

Gillian Ambrose, Peter Craig-Wild, Diane Craven and Peter Moger, *Together for a Season: Lent, Holy Week and Easter*, London: Church House Publishing, 2007.

Common Worship: Times and Seasons, London: Church House Publishing, 2006, provides a comprehensive set of readings, prayers and instructions for the celebration of the Easter Liturgy. See also:

Fire and Bread, ed. Ruth Burgess, Glasgow: Wild Goose Publications, 2006.

Rogationtide

Common Worship: Times and Seasons, London: Church House Publishing, 2006, provides sets of readings and prayers for the agricultural year (pp.594–633). Additional Rogationtide material is available on the Arthur Rank Centre website and from the Farm Crisis Network (FCN) which, courtesy of Glyn Evans, has produced an imaginative liturgy for a Rogationtide procession.

Lammastide

I am grateful to Anne Lawson for information about the celebration of Lammastide at Haslington, and to Verena Breed, Stephen Southgate and other rural ministers for their insights. The Arthur Rank Centre maintains a website with various worship resources: www.ruralchurch.org.uk/worship-resources.

Another useful compendium of resources for the agricultural cycle of Plough Sunday, Rogationtide, Lammas, and Harvest, is compiled by The Staffordshire Seven, *Seasonal Worship from the Countryside,* London: SPCK, 2003.

5 BEHIND THE SCENES

Brendan Clover and Chris Verity, *Being a Server Today,* Norwich: Canterbury Press, 2005.

Thomas J. D. Robertson, *The Sacristan in the Church of England: A practical guide,* London: Kevin Mayhew, 1992.

Visual Liturgy Live

Visual Liturgy Live is the latest version of the highly successful and user-friendly software package used by thousands of churches to plan and prepare services.

This powerful program helps users look up lectionary readings, make hymn selections and chose prayers and liturgy from a wide range of material. It is an invaluable tool for preparing or presenting acts of worship.

Visual Liturgy Live includes:

- The Common Worship Main Volume
- The President's Edition
- Pastoral Services
- Christian Initiation
- Daily Prayer
- New Patterns for Worship
- Times and Seasons

Additionally, in 2010, the entire text of The Book of Common Prayer and the Remembrance Services in *They Shall Grow Not Old* (Canterbury Press) were made available to those with a live subscription.

With *Visual Liturgy Live* you can:

- View and edit a complete service as you create it
- Browse easily through options for hymns, liturgy and readings
- Save multiple services for forward planning and return to them later
- Print your service booklets in a range of layouts
- Export saved services to Microsoft Word and other programs whilst retaining all formatting and layout
- Put together monthly rotas and calendars for church events
- Create and print a list of readings
- Install the official Common Worship fonts on your computer
- Find out which liturgical colours are to be worn on any given date
- Look up important additional guidance notes on service style and structure
- Listen to extracts from hymns

This is the first version of *Visual Liturgy* to include online content and software updates. These will be provided via download on a regular basis for one year from the date of registration, together with access to technical support. Further updates and support after the first year will be available by purchasing an annual subscription.

Acknowledgements

Every effort has been made to trace copyright ownership of material included in this Guide. The Author and Publishers apologize to those who have not been traced at the time of going to press or whose rights have inadvertently not been acknowledged. They would be grateful to be informed of any omissions or inaccuracies in this respect. The Author and Publisher are grateful for permission to reproduce material under copyright, and are grateful to the following copyright holders:

Frank Kacmarcik, OblSB, St John's Abbey, for illustrations on pp. xvi, 36, 56, 123 and 186. Used with permission.

Canterbury Press, for the quotations from Richard Giles, *Re-Pitching the Tent*, 3rd edn, 2004; and *Creating Uncommon Worship*, 2004, Norwich.

Penguin, for the quotation from Peter Brook, *The Empty Space*, London: Pelican, 1968, p. 152.

Dr Christopher Burkett and other colleagues of the Committee for Ministry of the Diocese of Chester for permission to use material from the Diocesan course, 'The Beginner's Guide to Leading Public Worship'.

The Church of England for the following:

- *Common Worship: Additional Eucharistic Prayers, with Guidance on Celebrating the Eucharist with children,* London: Church House Publishing, 2012.

- *Common Worship: Collects and Post-Communions*, London: Church House Publishing, 2004. This volume includes both the original *CW* Collects, and additional Collects in contemporary English which may be used alongside them.

John Murray (Publishers) for the quotation from John Betjeman's poem, 'Blame the Vicar', *Collected Poems* © The Estate of John Betjeman 1955, 1958, 1962, 1964, 1968, 1970, 1979, 1981, 1982, 2001.

Annie Dillard, *Teaching a Stone to Talk: Expeditions and Encounters*, London: Harper Perennial, 1988.

Mark Earey for his hymn, 'Advent Candles tell their story' © Mark Earey. The words of the hymn may be reproduced for use in worship by churches which have a CCLI copyright licence. The use of the song should be recorded in the annual report to CCLI.

Roger Ferlo, *Sensing God: Reading Scripture with All Our Senses*, New York: Cowley Publications, 2001.

Trevor Lloyd, *A Service of the Word*, Cambridge: Grove Worship Series 151, 2000.

Ronald Knox, *Stimuli*, London: Sheed and Ward, 1951.

Bloodaxe Books, for David Scott's poem, 'A long way from bread', first published in *The Franciscan,* for the Hilfield Families Camp.

Stephen Southgate, for his carol, 'In the fullness of the summer time' © Stephen Southgate, 2012.

The Sayings of the Desert Fathers: The Alphabetical Collection, tr. Benedicta Ward, Collegeville MN: Cistercian Publications Inc., 2005.

The Staffordshire Seven, *Seasonal Worship from the Countryside*, London: SPCK, 2003, for liturgical material for Lammastide.

Tim Stratford, *Using Common Worship: A Service of the Word*, London: Church House Publishing, 2002.